CURRICULUM ESSENTIALS

SECOND EDITION

CURRICULUM ESSENTIALS

A Resource for Educators

Jon Wiles
University of North Florida

PEARSON

Boston   New York   San Francisco
Mexico City   Montreal   Toronto   London   Madrid   Munich   Paris
Hong Kong   Singapore   Tokyo   Cape Town   Sydney

Series Editor: Traci Mueller
Editorial Assistant: Janice Hackenberg
Senior Marketing Manager: Elizabeth Fogarty
Editorial-Production Service: Omegatype Typography, Inc.
Composition Buyer: Linda Cox
Manufacturing Buyer: Andrew Turso
Cover Administrator: Kristina Mose-Libon
Electronic Composition: Omegatype Typography, Inc.

For related titles and support materials,
visit our online catalog at www.ablongman.com.

Between the time Website information is gathered and then published, it is not
unusual for some sites to have closed. Also, the transcription of URLs can result
in typographical errors. The publishers would appreciate notification where
these errors occur so that they may be corrected in subsequent editions.

Library of Congress Cataloging-in-Publication Data

Wiles, Jon.
    Curriculum essentials : a resource for educators / Jon Wiles.—2nd ed.
      p.   cm.
    Includes bibliographical references and index.
    ISBN 0-205-41824-4 (alk. paper)
     1. Curriculum planning—United States—Handbooks, manuals, etc. 2. Education—
United States—Curricula—Handbooks, manuals, etc. I. Title.

LB2806.15.W557   2005
375'.001—dc22

                2004040036

CONTENTS

LIST OF FIGURES

PREFACE

In its initial edition, *Curriculum Essentials* attempted to provide an inexpensive resource that covered all of the really important information about the field of curriculum. Although the first goal was achieved, the second proved more difficult. Curriculum is complex and truly difficult to conceptualize. The literature, dating back nearly a century, is voluminous. The boundaries that define what is and what is not curriculum are vague. This author's attempt to identify the essentials to be mastered might not be the same as others teaching and writing in this area of study. Still, the comments of reviewers and users were encouraging. The first edition was a valued resource for theoreticians and practitioners alike. It "hit" most of the bases.

The second edition is modified to meet many of the suggestions of those kind enough to offer opinions about the book. In addition to the usual updating of references, users wanted a better referencing mechanism. The observation that they did not really understand how to use this guide in the classroom has led to a number of changes including an early illustration and chapter outlines. Following this theme, many of the applications from the first edition are carried over into the chapters in the second edition to show more clearly how curriculum work progresses.

Areas of emphasis added since the first edition include standards and testing, Internet-assisted curriculum, and futurism. It is obvious to the author that curriculum, as a field of inquiry, is experiencing a major paradigm shift. This edition directs users to the best available resources for understanding these most recent changes.

In developing this edition, I have searched for consensus among curriculum leaders of the past and present concerning major areas, such as the literature, models, research, tools, and processes. The goal of such a collection is to synthesize past achievements with current practice. The author believes that there is a cohesive collection of information and exhibits that will allow anyone unfamiliar with this field to quickly understand the role of curriculum as a major subspecialty in professional education. Professors using this book will, of course, add their own emphasis and exhibits. *Curriculum Essentials* is, simply, the beginning of a collection of important resources for professional practice rather than a conclusive work in this area.

ACKNOWLEDGMENTS

Many thanks to this edition's reviewers—Sandra Lee Jones, Troy State University, Dothan and Virginia Voinovich, Northern Arizona University—for their helpful suggestions.

J. W. W.

USING THIS BOOK

Curriculum development is a dynamic process carried out under the influence of many variables. The convergence of these many factors helps educators make wise decisions with the most relevant information possible. Borrowing from the social sciences, educational leaders in curriculum use a broad knowledge base in their everyday work, as seen in the figure on page xvi. In this resource book for educators, the author has included the following categories of information: history, best readings, models, practice applications, research, and legal decisions. Although not all curriculum developers will use information from each of these sources, the process of curriculum development involves collecting and assessing information, making value-laden decisions, and designing responses to persistent problems.

For example, many schools and districts today engage in building inclusion models to service children with exceptional learning needs. This is not a new concern, and the curriculum worker will want to be familiar with historic efforts to service such learners. There are, of course, widely recognized books that conceptualize this effort as well as laws that define the requirements. Models of human development and exceptionality, research that studies these efforts, and practice applications in real school districts complete the information needed to make a wise decision about inclusion.

In Chapter Five, readers are encouraged to collect resources from previous chapters and try their hands at making wise and informed decisions about a number of programs for learners. It is a fact that such collecting, assessing, deciding, and designing is no more than a practiced habit. Such informed decision making, however, delineates the professional educator from others with only opinion.

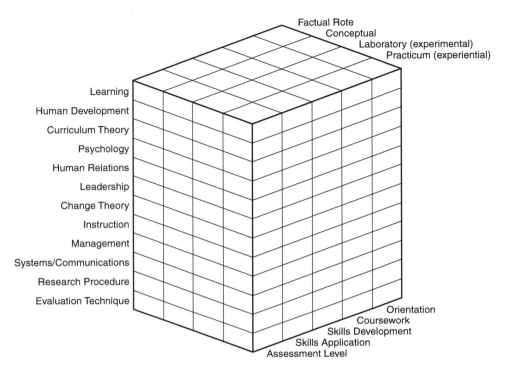

Curriculum Study Model

CURRICULUM ESSENTIALS

1

IDEAS ABOUT CURRICULUM

OVERVIEW

American education has developed over several centuries according to forces that have shaped beliefs, practices, and operating procedures. For the reader, an important organizer involves using a historical lens to understand practices. For example, it has been observed that about 90 percent of all secondary school teachers use lecture as their primary method. Why? Or, are many schools not in session in the summer? These questions, and their answers, have a historical rationale.

Reviewing history provides a common set of references and understandings for professionals. Persons in curriculum may speak of the Committee of Ten or the Seven Cardinal Principles as a sort of shorthand for a concept or position in planning. For the same reason, names of famous curriculum persons represent a set of ideas that are generally understood by persons in the field. Without such a collection of reference points, there could be little professional communication.

This first chapter maps out the names, dates, works, and ideas that form the field of study in curriculum. These core items define or form the intellectual concerns, inquiries, and values that curriculum leaders believe are important. These commonalities also define the professional responsibilities of workers in this field. Once addressed, the reader will find these items referenced in later sections of this book.

DATES OF HISTORICAL SIGNIFICANCE

Study of curriculum almost always begins with the origins of our schooling system. In a nutshell, many of the practices in today's modern school date from the early years of Western civilization. In our schools today, for example, exists the influence of both a highly elite Greek system of education and the more common form of citizenship education found in the Roman Empire. The separation of church and state, the early legality of schooling in America, and our continuing efforts to fully educate all of the future citizens in our democracy all stem from the past.

Certain events represent the turning points in defining American education, such as the work of the Committee of Ten in the 1890s and the more popular definition of education at the secondary level provided by the Committee on the Reorganization of Secondary Education in 1918. Sometimes, social or economic events "steered" the redefining of our largest social institution, the school.

The accompanying time line identifies many of the major events that serve as reference points for curriculum developers. The time line begins in ancient Greece with a tutorial model of education and ends in 1995 with public access to the Internet established by Congress.

Time Line

400 B.C.	Height of Greek influence when ideas of tutorial learning and elite leadership training were first formalized
400 A.D.	Height of the Roman Empire that modeled a far more popular "citizenship model" education system
800	Beginning of "Dark Ages" during which civilization declined and knowledge was preserved by individual scholarship and early monastic libraries
1200	Beginning of the Enlightenment during which civilization reemerged. Early universities founded in France, Italy, Spain, and England
1456	First books printed by printing presses—dispersion of knowledge to masses begins
1492	Columbus finds the Americas
1500	First Latin grammar schools in England
1536	First classical secondary school (Gymnasium) established in Germany
1620	Plymouth Colony, Massachusetts, established
1635	Boston Latin grammar schools founded
1636	Harvard University founded
1647	In Massachusetts the Old Deluder Satan Act compels establishment of schools when fifty households are present in a community
1650	First tax support for schools in Massachusetts
1751	Benjamin Franklin establishes the first academy (secondary school)

1779	Thomas Jefferson proposes a "free school" for Virginian men and women for up to three years
1787	Northwest Ordinance passed, which established provisions for territories to becomes states, including mandatory school sites in townships
1789	Constitution of the United States adopted
1805	New York Free School society established to educate 500,000 pupils without expense
1821	Boston English Classical School established. First tax-supported secondary school
1852	First compulsory school laws passed in Massachusetts by Horace Mann
1862	Morrill Land Grant Act establishes land for public universities in all states (engineering, military science, and agriculture)
1874	State Supreme Court in Michigan upholds tax support for secondary schools
1883	Francis Parker establishes the first subject matter groupings as an early form of curriculum
1892	First comprehensive study of American education by Joseph M. Rice
1892	Charles Eliot, president of Harvard University, forms the Committee of Ten
1896	John Dewey opens the University of Chicago Laboratory School to demonstrate alternative teaching methods
1904	First comprehensive physiological studies of schoolchildren in New York by G. Stanley Hall
1905	First mental measurement scales on intelligence published by Alfred Binet
1909	First junior high school established
1918	Franklin Bobbitt publishes the first text in curriculum
1918	Commission on the Reorganization of Secondary Education publishes The Seven Cardinal Principles
1919	Progressive Education Association founded
1932	The Eight Year Study begins (1932–1940)
1938	The Educational Policies Commission publishes its four-point objectives for education—The Purposes of Education in American Democracy
1946	Congress passes the G.I. Bill to further the education of veterans
1954	U.S. Supreme Court rules in *Brown v. Topeka* that public schools must racially integrate previously "separate but equal" schools

1957	Russia launches Sputnik satellite, beginning both a space and an education race
1958	U.S. Congress passes the National Defense Education Act, initiating serious federal funding of public education
1964	Civil Rights Act passed by Congress
1965	The Elementary and Secondary Education Act (ESEA) passes, bringing "titled" programs to public schools
1972	Title IX amendment to the ESEA outlaws discrimination on the basis of sex
1975	Public Law 94-142 provides federally guaranteed rights for all children with disabilities in public schools
1979	U.S. Department of Education established
1985	Commercial availability of personal computers in United States
1990	Congress passes the Individuals with Disabilities Education Act (IDEA); concept of inclusion
1995	Public access to the Internet is established by Congress

DEFINITIONS OF CURRICULUM

Persons studying the area of Curriculum soon notice that there are many existing definitions and that the literature on Curriculum seems to place great importance on the exact words used to define the area. Initially, one might think that such specificity is irrelevant given the many concerns of curriculum planners; after all, what difference does it make if the programs are "experienced" or "intended"? But in curriculum work, there is good reason for such detailed definitions because the definition of the task serves to define the scope of responsibilities. Programs are also defined by the definition of the work to be done.

Traditionally, Curriculum was perceived as information passed from one generation to another in the form of organized knowledge. Under such a definition, Curriculum would be comprised of essential subjects or even the mastery of a collection of books.

Later, during the massive social changes of the early twentieth century, the definition of Curriculum broadened as the basic curriculum was delivered to a general (not elite) population. Frustration in delivering such a curriculum caused planners to define curricula as an intention rather than a subject.

During the middle years of the twentieth century, this definition of Curriculum broadened even further as the diversity of learners and our understanding of differences in students broadened. The focus was now on what was experienced by the student.

Finally, in the last third of the twentieth century, and driven largely by financial concerns, curriculum planners refocused their efforts and defined Curriculum according to the product or outcomes. By identifying the outcomes in advance, curriculum planners could work backward to set the conditions necessary to achieve their goals.

The reader will see in the section on educational philosophies (pages 00–00) that when these assumptions about purpose (the definition) are formalized, the collected values (a philosophy) become the basis for curriculum development. The four common definitions of curriculum by well-known curriculum leaders from each group are as follows.

Curriculum as Subject Matter

The Curriculum should consist of permanent studies—the rules of grammar, reading, rhetoric and logic, mathematics and, at the secondary level, the greatest books of the Western world. (Robert Hutchins)

The Curriculum must consist essentially of disciplined study in five areas: command of the mother tongue and systematic study of grammar, literature, and writing; mathematics; the sciences; history; and foreign language. (Arthur Bestor)

The Curriculum should consist entirely of knowledge that comes from the disciplines. (Philip Phenix)

A Curriculum is a written document. (George Beauchamp)

Curriculum as a Plan

The Curriculum is a planned program of learning opportunities to achieve broad educational goals and related objectives. (William Alexander)

The Curriculum is all of the learning of students that is planned by and directed by the school to attain its educational goals. (Ralph Tyler)

The Curriculum is (a set of) planned and guided learning experiences for the learners' continuous and willful growth. . . . (Daniel and Laura Tanner)

A Curriculum is a plan for learning. (Hilda Taba)

A Curriculum is a plan for what is to be taught and is composed of what is to be taught, to whom, when, and how. (John McNeil)

The Curriculum is planned actions for instruction. (James Macdonald)

The Curriculum of a school can be conceived of as a series of planned events that are intended to have educational consequences for one or more students. (Elliot Eisner)

Curriculum as an Experience

A Curriculum is those experiences set up by the school for the purpose of disciplining students and youth in group ways of thinking and acting. (B. O. Smith, William Stanley, and Harlan Shores)

The Curriculum is generally considered to be all of the experiences that learners have under the auspices of the school. (Ronald Doll)

The Curriculum is that series of things that children and youth must do and experience. (Franklin Bobbitt)

The Curriculum is the life and program of the school . . . an enterprise in guided living. (Harold Rugg)

The Curriculum is composed of all the experiences children have under the guidance of teachers. (Hollis Caswell and Doak Campbell)

The curriculum is now seen as the total experience with which the school deals in educating young people. (Eight Year Study Report)

The curriculum is a goal or set of values that is activated through a development process and culminates in classroom experiences for students. (Jon Wiles)

Curriculum as an Outcome

The Curriculum is a planned learning outcome for which the school is responsible. (James Popham and Henry Baker)

The Curriculum is a structured set of learning outcomes (objectives) resulting from instruction. (K. Howell, S. Fox, and K. Morehead)

Curriculum is concerned not with what students will do in the learning situation, but with what they will learn as a consequence of what they do. Curriculum is concerned with results. (Maurice Johnson)

The Curriculum is all of the experiences that individual learners have in a program of education whose purpose is to achieve broad goals and related specific objectives. (Glen Hass)

NAMES TO KNOW IN CURRICULUM STUDY

To select forty names of persons who have had major influence on the area of Curriculum from the hundreds of individuals who are obviously important in the field of education is a qualitative decision. Although others might be added or deleted from such a list, it is probable that most of these persons would be on any list, and all of these persons are known to educators working in Curriculum.

Each of these persons has made a lasting contribution to our knowledge base, but often in different ways. Some are historical figures, such as Franklin, Froebels, Jefferson, Mann, and McGuffy, who helped establish belief and practices. A second kind of contributor may be an outsider, such as Piaget, Bloom, or Maslow, who have given us powerful ideas or models. A third kind of contributor has been distinguished by developing an idea so that we might understand it more fully. Dewey and Taba are such persons. Finally, there are some contributors who have had an idea so profound or compelling that it has changed our way of thinking. McLuhan, Illich, and Toffler are examples of such a type.

The reader can certainly feel free to amend such a list, but to become familiar with the work of these educators and contributors would certainly ensure a firm grasp of most of the basic concerns of the area of Curriculum.

Harold Benjamin (1893–1969). Wrote the widely read book *The Saber-Tooth Curriculum* (1939) under the pseudonym J. Abner Peddiwell.

Benjamin Bloom (1913–   ). Professor at the University of Chicago. Known for the development of a taxonomy of cognitive processing, thereby allowing the targeting of curriculum outcomes.

John Franklin Bobbitt (1876–1956). Long-term professor at the University of Chicago. Wrote the first text in the field, *The Curriculum* (1918).

Jerome Bruner (1915–   ). Professor at Harvard University. Headed the Woods Hole conference and advocated "Structures of the Disciplines" organization of subject matter. Best known work: *The Process of Education* (1960).

Hollis Caswell (1901–1988). With Doak Campbell wrote *Curriculum Development* (1935) defining Curriculum as a set of guided experiences rather than subjects.

Werrett (W. W.) Charters (1875–1952). Early proponent of audiovisual learning, especially instruction by radio.

James Coleman (1926–1995). Johns Hopkins researcher whose study, "Equality of Educational Opportunity" (1964), structured the Elementary and Secondary Education Act (ESEA) of 1965.

James B. Conant (1893–1978). Served as president of Harvard and publicly advocated changes in the American high school. Best known works: *The American High School Today* (1959) and *The Comprehensive High School* (1967).

George Counts (1889–1974). Professor at Columbia from 1927 to 1950. Active in politics. Best known for *Dare the Schools Create a New Social Order?* (1932).

John Dewey (1859–1952). America's best known educator-philosopher. Advocated "connectionism" between subjects and pupils through applied learnings. Directed a laboratory school at the University of Chicago. Best known work: *Democracy and Education* (1916).

Charles Eliot (1834–1926). President of Harvard University for forty years. Called together the Committee of Ten (1892) to establish new college entrance requirements and curricula.

Benjamin Franklin (1706–1790). Founder of the Academy of Philadelphia (early high school form). Also presided over the U.S. Constitutional Convention in 1787. Wrote *Proposals Relating to the Education of Youth in Pennsylvania* (1749).

Friedrich Froebels (1782–1852). Established the first kindergarten (Klein-kinderbeschaftig) in Germany. Froebels emphasized natural development in children and the need for readiness materials.

A. L. Gessell (1880–1961). Directed Yale Clinic for Child Development and there conducted early studies of the norms and characteristics of mental and physical growth. Best known works: *The Child from Five to Ten* (1946) and *The Years from Ten to Sixteen* (1956).

John Goodlad (1920–   ). Well-known curriculum theorist advocating change in his best known books: *Behind the Classroom Door* (1967) and *A Place Called School* (1984).

Robert Havighurst (1900–1991). Served as professor at the University of Chicago 1941–1965. Early sociologist studying education. Best known works: *Growing Up in River City* (1962) and *Developmental Tasks in Education* (1972).

Robert Hutchins (1889–1977). President of Chicago University from 1929–1945. Educational conservative. Best known work: *The Learning Society* (1968).

Ivan Illich (1926–2002). Ordained priest and college professor. Believed schooling interfered with real learning. Early revolutionary in education. Best known work: *Deschooling Society* (1970).

Thomas Jefferson (1743–1826). Author of Declaration of Independence. Strong advocate for free education for impoverished students. Developed an early plan for a comprehensive education system in the Virginia colony.

William Heard Kilpatrick (1878–1965). Professor at Columbia from 1909–1938. Proposed the "project method" of study to implement Dewey's ideas. Best known work: *Education for a Changing Civilization* (1926).

Leonard Koos (1881–1974). Advocate of the junior high movement during the period 1910–1925. Wrote *The Junior High School* (1920).

Horace Mann (1796–1859). Referred to as the Father of American Education. Instrumental in drafting and passing legislation in Massachusetts that established public schooling precedent.

Abraham Maslow (1908–1970). Psychologist who developed a widely referenced hierarchy of need satisfaction, Maslow's Hierarchy.

William McGuffy (1800–1873). Developed early texts, the *McGuffy Readers,* for grades 1–6 and high school. Over 122 million books sold.

Marshall McLuhan (1911–1973). Canadian educator who first addressed the effects of technological mediums in curriculum delivery. Best known work: *The Medium Is the Message* (1967).

Charles McMurry (1857–1929). Founded the National Herbert Society. Wrote numerous texts on teaching methods.

Marie Montessori (1870–1952). European educator advocating a personal and progressive curriculum for children. Today, many of her ideas exist in the Montessori schools of America.

A. S. Neill (1883–1973). English educator who advocated freedom for children. For years Neill operated an "existential" program at his school, chronicled in his best known work: *Summerhill* (1960).

Francis Parker (1837–1902). Called the Father of Modern Education by Dewey, Parker was an early founder of the Progressive Movement. As superintendent of Quincy, Massachusetts, schools, Parker is credited with forming up the first "subject" areas.

Johann Pestalozzi (1746–1827). Humanistic European educator and child advocate who believed in learning by doing. His phrase, "the head, the heart, and the hand," are often quoted as a comprehensive view of child development. Best known work: *Leonard and Gertrude* (1781).

Jean Piaget (1896–1980). Swiss child development specialist emphasizing cognitive growth. Piaget developed a model of stages of cognitive development that was used widely in early childhood programs in the 1960s and 1970s.

Joseph Mayer Rice (1857–1934). A medical doctor who studied child development and disease. He left medicine to conduct an eight-year study of one hundred American schools and systems. The findings, reported in *The Public School System of the United States* (1893), contributed to reform efforts of the era.

Carl Rogers (1902–1987). Rogers advocated a nondirective and client-centered approach to teaching. Best known work: *On Becoming a Person* (1961).

Jean Jacques Rousseau (1712–1778). European educator who saw children "unfolding" through natural development. In his book, *Emile,* Rousseau stated that children were innately good, rather than evil.

Harold Rugg (1886–1960). Professor at Columbia University from 1920–1951. A leading progressive educator. Best known works: *The Child-Centered School* (1930) and *Foundations of American Education* (1947).

Charles Silberman (1925–   ). Journalist who, like J. M. Rice in the previous century, conducted a study of American schools reported in his best-selling book, *Crisis in the Classroom* (1970).

B. F. Skinner (1904–1990). Advocate for operant conditioning in learning and programmed instruction. Best known works: *The Technology of Teaching* (1968) and *Beyond Freedom and Dignity* (1971).

Hilda Taba (1902–1967). Known as a practical curriculum developer and instructional design specialist. Best known work: *Curriculum Development: Theory into Practice* (1962).

Edward Thorndike (1874–1949). Contributed over 450 writings on measurement and evaluation in education. Best known work: *The Measurement of Intelligence* (1926).

Alvin Toffler (1928–   ). A futurist whose impact on educational thinking in the second half of the twentieth century has been very strong. Best known work: *Future Shock* (1970).

Ralph Tyler (1902–1994). Director of the Eight Year Study (1932–1940). Advocated outcome assessment and the Tyler "curriculum cycle." Best known work: *Basic Principles of Curriculum and Instruction* (1949).

ESSENTIAL BOOKS FOR CURRICULUM STUDY

In the past, the central ideas of curriculum theory and practice were captured in the print media. Although this is changing rapidly, to recapture the past achievements of this field certain print sources must be reviewed. A critical collection of the books, reports, and monographs in this section are listed according to criteria previously mentioned in the preface.

Although some of these works may be more important than others, each presents a thought or idea that structures curriculum theory. For the self-taught reader, there are categories of things that curriculum persons know and use regularly, such as the following:

Philosophy	Leadership
Curriculum theory	Change theory
Education history	Management and systems theory
Uses of knowledge	Research and evaluation
Human development	Technology
Learning theory	Politics
Human relations	

A tailored set of readings for each of these areas is presented for the reader in Appendix A of this book to aid in self-study. Further, through the remainder of this text, books from this essential list may be referenced as appropriate to indicate enlargement of ideas presented (for example, see Bloom, 1956).

ANNOTATED BIBLIOGRAPHY

Adler, Mortimer. *The Paideia Proposal: An Education Manifesto* **(1982).**   The democratic process is not served by a system of education that divides students into sheep and goats. A democratic society must provide equal educational opportunity, and does this best by providing one track for all. The best education for the best is the best education for all.

This single track system should meet three goals: (1) to prepare all students to take advantage of every opportunity for personal development, (2) to provide an adequate preparation for the responsibility of citizenship, and (3) to give students the basic skills common to all work in our society.

Electives are not appropriate except in the case of specialization and only a second language is recommended by the author. The author prescribes three areas of the curriculum to discuss: subjects, skills, and books.

Aiken, M. *The Story of the Eight Year Study* **(1942).**   In this historical review, the author chronicles the classic contest between traditionalists and progressives from 1932 to 1940. By agreement, students from thirty innovative high schools were matched with students in traditional high schools and then studied during the eight years of high school and college. Three hundred universities provided "open admission" for this experiment.

Results of this study, recorded in five volumes of evaluative data, showed that students who attended an array of progressive schools outperformed those attending traditional high schools in all college subjects except foreign language. Students from progressive schools also were more active in college extracurricular activities. The researchers concluded that (1) graduates of progressive schools were not handicapped in their college work, (2) departures from the prescribed curriculum did not lessen the students' readiness for higher education, and (3) the most fundamental changes in the progressive curriculum resulted in the greatest achievement differences in comparison to students of like ability in traditional programs.

Apple, Michael. *Ideology and Curriculum* **(1990).** Schools instill beliefs necessary for the functioning of a culture's primary institutions. Learning in schools tends to be apolitical and ahistorical, thus hiding power sources and true meanings. The study of knowledge is always a study of ideology. Schools not only control people but they also control meaning.

One of the primary legacies of the field of curriculum is a commitment to maintaining continuity and to promoting cultural homogeneity and values consensus.

Apple, Michael. *Official Knowledge: Democratic Education in a Conservative Age* **(1993).** Conservatives are restructuring the schools to their liking. The agenda is increasingly effective attacks on the curriculum with the needs of business and industry being seen as more and more the primary goals of education.

Using fear tactics when raising issues of violence, falling test scores, and declining values, the right wing is trying to disenfranchise groups considered outside of the mainstream. Such groups advocate a textbook curriculum because it is safe and allows the control of knowledge.

Curriculum is not neutral knowledge, and a common culture can never be an extension of the Western tradition. A common culture requires conditions that are needed for all persons to create meanings and values.

Aronowitz, S. and Giroux, H. *Postmodern Education* **(1991).** The disruptions of the twentieth century have freed us from the modernist images of progress and history. We are experiencing radical changes in the ways in which the culture is produced, and a new hyper-reality has been established.

The purpose of the old curriculum, never value-free, was to name and privilege particular histories and experiences. Such a curriculum linked knowledge and power in highly specific ways; doing so in a manner to marginalize or silence the voices of subordinate groups.

Elements of discontinuity, rupture, and differences provide a different set of referents, freeing educators of the modernist images of progress and history. New leaders should help expand oppositional space and allow "practical" knowledge to command the schools of the future.

Bagley, W. C. *The Educative Process* **(1905).** Representing the essentialist position (traditional), the author argues that there are things all students should know. The author attacks the child-centered curriculum of the early progressives as "enfeebling."

This book advocates a return to the nineteenth-century methodology of "mental discipline" by which students master and recite.

Banks, James. *Teaching Strategies for Ethnic Studies* **(1975).** This book highlights the purposes and needs of multicultural education and provides incremental models of multicultural curricula. The concept of personal understandings of ethnicity is delineated as well.

A second section of this book furnishes a chapter on each of America's primary ethnic groups including a chronology of significant events, an annotated bibliography for teachers, and a list of teaching resources.

Beauchamp, G. *Curriculum Theory* **(1968).** The book contains a discussion of the elements of a theory, defined in this work as a set of statements so arranged to give functional meaning to a series of events. The author advocates making curriculum theory subordinate to general educational theory.

Benne, Kenneth. *The Task of Post-Contemporary Education* **(1990).** America has changed dramatically since World War II and the author reviews those changes in power and authority, capitalism, nationalism, bureaucracy, and access to information. The author then focuses on the relationship between education and democracy.

The old view of democracy held that it was a form of government, but a new understanding of the term is emerging: a way of living, degrees of freedom, civil guarantees, and intellectual freedoms. A curriculum that incorporates the most desirable values from different cultures into an emerging outlook toward a human future is advocated.

The author describes a process of experimental and participative learning that will allow for three ends: socialization, enculturation, and learning. Individuals, says the author, must become participants in new and radically different groupings.

Bennis, Warren. *The Planning of Change* **(1961).** In this widely read set of readings about the process of change, numerous models and theories are discussed and illustrated. Various change strategies, including rational, normative, and coercive strategies, are analyzed and discussed.

Bennis, Warren. *Why Leaders Can't Lead* **(1989).** In this discussion of university-level administration, the author identifies conditions that hinder true leadership. He calls for caring leaders who can refocus on things that are really important to program development.

Of interest are a set of "laws of leading" including the Law of Academic Pseudodynamics that states that "routine work drives out nonroutine work and smothers to death all creative planning." The author also distinguishes between leaders (people who do the right things) and managers (people who do things right).

The author calls for leaders to focus on managing four things: institutional attention, vision, trust, and self.

Bestor, Arthur. *The Restoration of Learning* **(1955).** The purpose of public education is to raise the intellectual level of the American people as a whole. Certain intellectual disciplines are fundamental in the public school curriculum because they are fundamental in life: science, history, mathematics, English, and foreign languages.

Schools are in trouble because curriculum-making has fallen into the hands of self-serving professors of education who are trading in the production of intelligent citizens for a host of social services of no consequence.

Renewal of the curriculum should focus on teacher training that would provide all teachers with a strong liberal arts preparation. To not address teacher training is to leave a vacuum in the historic curriculum development process.

Bloom, Benjamin. *Taxonomy I: The Cognitive Domain* **(1956).**   In this widely used education resource, the author defines cognition as a six-step hierarchy that includes knowing, comprehending, applying, analyzing, synthesizing, and evaluating. The development of learning objectives is discussed in terms of this model.

The targeting of student outcomes (behavioral objectives) has been heavily dependent on the cognitive taxonomy, as well as Krathwohl's affective taxonomy and Harrow's psychomotor taxonomies.

Bobbitt, Franklin. *The Curriculum* **(1918).**   Credited as the first formal textbook in Curriculum, this book addresses the changing knowledge of learning; reviews of the child-centered and the project methods are included.

The author perceived life as becoming increasingly specialized and advocated a skill-based approach to learning through real experiences. These skill sequences, likened to behavioral objectives, allowed the learner to gain functional knowledge in a rapidly changing world.

Boulding, Kenneth. *The Meaning of the Twentieth Century* **(1964).**   It is the author's thesis that the world is undergoing major changes, similar in scope to the pre-civilization to civilization change. This revolution, and these "systems breaks," are worldwide in their impact.

Knowledge and the impact of scientific change are providing an economic takeoff that requires serious educational study.

Bowles, Samual and Gintis, Herbert. *Schooling in Capitalist America* **(1976).** The educational system is the laboratory in which competing solutions to the problems of personal liberation and social equity are tested. Patterns of social relationships fostered in schools are not an accident, but rather are admirably suited to nurturing attitudes and behaviors consonant with participating in the labor force. The school reproduces inequalities and perpetuates class structures.

Educational reform in the United States has failed time and again. Educators have failed to understand that the U.S. economy is a totalitarian system embedded in a democratic political system. It is the overriding objectives of the capital class, not the ideals of the reformers, that have shaped education and blocked schools from pursuing equality and human development. Schools reproduce the capitalist social division of labor.

Bruner, Jerome. *The Process of Education* **(1960).**   Faced with an ever-growing body of critical knowledge, this author called a conference of scholars at Woods

Hole, Massachusetts, to discuss how education in science might be improved in the nation's schools.

After deliberation, it was recommended that the curricula focus on the "broader fundamental structures of a field of study," rather than on content per se. The structures of the discipline will accelerate readiness: "Any subject can be taught effectively in some honest intellectual form to any child at any stage of development."

The book addresses intuitive thinking, as opposed to deductive logic, and calls for greater instructional inquiry into this methodology.

Bruner, Jerome. *Toward a Theory of Instruction* **(1966).**   Exploring the question of how cognitive growth and development occurs, the author offers four principles for a theory of instruction: (1) It should specify how to predispose the learner, (2) it should specify the structure of the knowledge, (3) it should identify the sequencing of the knowledge, and (4) it should specify the nature of the pacing and rewards.

Using the social studies curriculum, Man A Course of Study (MACOS) as a model, the author portrays learning as a natural act that should be guided without undue pressure by the teacher. Learning and curiosity are human qualities, natural qualities. They are nearly involuntary acts. But because there is so much to know, it is up to the teacher to guide the student in general understandings.

Callahan, Raymond. *Education and the Cult of Efficiency* **(1962).**   Looking backward to the early 1900s, the author reviews the "efficiency movement" in American business and how it influenced schools. Employing a factory model, educators stressed objectives, standards, and testing to promote a uniform and efficient product.

The by-products of this approach, says the author, are the dominance of business concerns over educational concerns, school leaders who are managers more than educators, and the strengthening of an already-present anti-intellectual climate in the nation.

Caswell, Hollis and Campbell, Doak. *Curriculum Development* **(1935).**   Early proponents of defining curriculum as "an experience," these authors focus on the planning efforts needed to structure a planned experience in schools.

The authors hold that the definition of social ideals is a responsibility of the school and that Curriculum should address these ends.

Charters, W. W. *Curriculum Construction* **(1923).**   A classic statement of curriculum development methodology from an efficiency perspective. The author reviews the procedural steps needed to ensure desired outcomes.

Combs, Arthur and Snygg, Donald. *Individual Behavior* **(1949).**   The authors postulate that all behavior, without exception, is the product of the perceptual field of the person. To produce change in behavior (learning), there must be a change in perception.

The authors explore self-concept theory, personality, learning, teaching, and the atmosphere needed for maximum growth of the learner. They conclude that "to understand the behavior of another person it is necessary to understand how things seem to him, to have some grasp of the nature of his phenomenal field."

Conant, James. *The Comprehensive High School* **(1967).** In this book a former president of Harvard University advocates that the American public school must serve all youth at the secondary level, combining the general education functions with those of the college-bound.

This so-called comprehensive school would avoid the dangerous separation of students into classes with predetermined destinations.

Counts, George. *The American Road to Culture* **(1930).** Americans regard education as the means by which inequalities among individuals are to be erased and by which every desirable end is to be achieved. The most magnificent product of American democracy is the single education system.

The American society is not planned; it grows in response to the drive of internal forces. Likewise, the schools grow because of the spontaneous and uncoordinated efforts of individuals and groups. Schools hold a principle of philosophic uncertainty—based on a mistrust of government, the championing of private initiative, the opposition to centralization, a rejection of authoritarianism, a lack of confidence in formulas, and a strong fondness for pragmatism in American philosophy.

Counts, George. *Dare the Schools Create a New Social Order?* **(1932).** Educators are faced with the question of how much influence they should have over a child's development. This author believes that professional educators, particularly the nation's teachers, should become leaders and use their influence to create a better nation. Schools must shape attitudes, develop tastes, and even impose ideas.

The author sees America as possessing an irreconcilable conflict between the freedoms of our democratic tradition and the fierce competition of our economic system. Teachers should not bow down before the gods of chance and should not reflect the drift of the social order. Rather, they should "reach for the power and make the most of their conquest."

Cremin, Lawrence. *The Transformation of the School* **(1961).** In this historical account of ideas that have shaped the form of American education, the author reviews the ideas of Mann, Dewey, Parker, Kilpatrick, Bobbitt, Rugg, and others whose thinking was "progressive" and influential.

A description of the findings of the Eight Year Study under the direction of Ralph Tyler is offered as proof of the success of these "progressive ideas" that were introduced in this country.

Cremin, Lawrence. *The Genius of American Education* **(1965).** Citing Plato, Thomas Jefferson, Horace Mann, and John Dewey, the author reviews contributions to the unique form of education in America. Our academic freedoms in schools and the right to criticize the society must be encouraged because they allow ideas to grow and flourish.

The author identifies the unique relationship of the education profession and the lay public as one of inherent strain and tension, one in which the public possesses the legal and financial authority to keep educators in check.

Dewey, John. *School and Society* **(1900).**   In this early work, the author observes that the child represents a society's only chance for new possibilities. Society can serve itself by being true to its children.

Since the industrial revolution, the household has been removed from the training of the child. The school must seek to provide learnings that are meaningful, not occupational and filled with worthless facts.

To be effective, schools must relate to the experiences of the child and to capitalize on the imagination of children; this is where they live. The author calls on educators to know their clients better.

Dewey, John. *The Child and the Curriculum* **(1902).**   There are two schools of thought for curriculum: One school concentrates on the importance of subject matter, the other on the contents of the child's own experience. It is the growth of the child that is important, not the studies. The child-centered school is personal, unitary, and practical.

"Children cannot be expected to develop truth or facts out of their own minds because 'nothing can be developed out of nothing.' " Developing experiences for children, and activities that will guide them, are the tasks at hand.

Dewey, John. *Democracy and Education* **(1916).**   Development of social skills takes place by interaction in the society, not by instruction. A democratic society must have a type of education that gives individuals a personal interest in social relationships; this is the key to social order.

Methods cannot be separate subjects. Experience and reason need to be balanced in the curriculum. Moral education is an intrinsic component of all education-based activity.

The author observes that by placing knowledge in the hands of children, the barriers between knowledge and human affairs might be overcome.

Dewey, John. *Experience and Education* **(1938).**   The ideal aim of education is to develop the power of self-control in each individual student. The primary source of social control does not rest in the teacher, but rather in the nature of the work done and the social setting to which everyone both contributes and feels responsible.

Everything depends on the quality of the child's experience. The main point of education is to select the kind of experiences that will have value in confronting future experiences.

It is a cardinal precept of the newer school of education that the beginning of instruction shall be made with the experiences learners have already had.

Dow, Peter. *Schoolhouse Politics: Lessons from the Sputnik Era* **(1991).**   In this work the author reviews the origins of postwar school reform in America. Tracing the failings of the progressive movement, and the arguments of critics of public education, the author reviews curriculum renewal with a special focus on the MACOS project.

Various perils of innovation in education following the launch of Sputnik are identified and analyzed.

Education Policy Committee. *Education for ALL Youth* **(1944).**   Following World War II, the Education Policy Commission of the National Education Association sought to develop goals of schooling applicable to all students. This broad statement endorses a comprehensive program.

Eisner, Elliot. *Cognition and the Curriculum* **(1982).**   Curriculum has become eviscerated; tight prescriptive curriculum structures, sequential skill development, and the frequent use of testing and rewards are classic examples of form becoming content.

Educators can and ought to exercise leadership roles in curriculum work by stating their reasons for favoring one over another choice. Efforts to renew curriculum need to be grounded in a view of how humans construct meaning from their experiences.

Elkind, David. *A Sympathetic Understanding of the Child* **(1978).**   Focusing on the stages of development, infancy, childhood, and adolescence, the author describes growth activities and advocates a child-centered approach to rearing children.

The author explains that children think differently from adults, but this does not indicate inferiority. Educators and parents should understand both the stages and the growth periods in planning for cognitive development. We must plan to meet the two basic needs of young learners: individuality and sociality.

Elkind, David. *Images of the Young Child* **(1993).**   Using Piaget as a source of theory, the author explains in great detail how children think and learn. The author reminds educators that, when we teach young children, we need to remember that they think concretely and that often their language far exceeds their cognitive understandings.

The author introduces the idea of a "developmentally appropriate curriculum discussing this notion in terms of knowledge, learning, and learning materials."

Franklin, Benjamin. *Proposals Relating to the Education of Youth in Pennsylvania* **(1749).**   This small book addresses education concepts that are bedrock values in America. The author proposes that public schools should become compatible with democratic traditions and the government of our emerging nation.

Freire, Paolo. *Education for Critical Consciousness* **(1973).**   In closed societies the "elite" imposes its values on the people. The author calls for educators to move beyond the "helping" relationship with the poor and construct curricula in which "extended thinking" can flourish.

The author describes three levels of consciousness and suggests that an education for liberation would redefine the use of traditional knowledge delivered in traditional settings. The author explores the power human communities possess to increase dialogue to overcome traditional obstacles.

Freire, Paolo. *The Politics of Education* **(1985).**   Education represents a struggle for meaning and power. Using education, the ruling class can perpetuate a "culture of silence" among the masses. Schools can serve as a mechanism for maintaining social control.

The minds of the poor have been invaded. To study is not to consume ideas, but to create and re-create them. People in schools should work together to see their world differently, to reform it, and to improve the lot of humankind everywhere.

Gagne, Robert. *Learning and Individual Differences: A Symposium* **(1967).**   In this work twenty authors who participated in a 1965 symposium address the question of how people learn. In addition to Gagne, participants included William Glasser, Lee Cronbach, and Arthur Jensen. The authors generally focus on the rate, style, and quality of learning.

Gardner, Howard. *Frames of Mind* **(1983).**   This book reports the findings of a Harvard University team studying human potential in the late 1970s. In this report, the author identifies seven types of intelligence: linguistic, logical-mathematical, spatial, musical, bodily-kinesthetic, interpersonal, and intrapersonal. This suggests that intelligence is not a single unitary item easily measured with a numeric score.

The book calls for schools to develop these intelligences and assist learners in locating work that is appropriate to their particular spectrum of intelligence. Such schools would be based on two assumptions—that people have different abilities and interests and that not everything can be learned. People should be able to make informed choices about the alternatives.

Gardner, Howard. *The Unschooled Mind* **(1991).**   Although some schools may appear successful, their students may lack true understanding. In every student, says the author, there is a five-year-old mind waiting to get out and express itself.

The author introduces seven types of intelligence and projects "learning styles." Schools should teach to such styles, and student learning should be assessed in different ways. The author feels that progressive education in the 1930s was a step in the right direction. A school curriculum dominated by apprenticeships, projects, and technology is envisioned.

Gessell, A. L. *The Child from Five to Ten* **(1946);** *The Years from Ten to Sixteen* **(1956).**   In this review of human development, the author addresses development cycles, characteristics of each year, and special interest areas, such as emotional expression, interpersonal relations, and philosophical outlook.

Made obsolete by their age-to-development orientation, these books nevertheless provide an excellent review of what children are like at certain times in their lives and are most useful in envisioning appropriate teacher behaviors.

Giroux, Henry. *Schooling and the Struggle for Public Life* **(1988).**   Since the 1980s there has been an ideological shift in our conception of citizenship. Schools and curriculums have been linked to the concepts of equity and justice. Educators need to redefine schools as public spheres in which the dynamics of popular engagement and democratic politics can be cultivated.

The author calls for classroom teachers to organize citizenship training around a critical inquiry of our society.

Goodlad, John. *A Place Called School* **(1984).**   Schools provide many functions, including intellectual development, but educational functions are not exclusively emphasized. Schools teach more than they know implicitly; the way they present the curriculum teaches too.

The author calls for reform around a combination of action learning with academic work. Grades should be eliminated, many methods should be used, and students should become responsible for their own learning. Such a curriculum should also be future-focused. The author warns that such change will take considerable time.

Hall, G. Stanley. *Adolescence: Its Psychology and Its Relation to Physiology, Anthropology, Sociology, and Sex, Crime, Religion, and Education* **(1904).**   The author, credited with the first major study of adolescent youth (New York City Schools, 1904), believed that human development occurs in three stages. The methodology utilized by the teacher should be a function of the particular stage of development. Content is prescribed for adolescents and strict discipline is prescribed for preadolescents whom the author characterized as "little savages."

Harvard University. *General Education in a Free Society* **(1945).**   This report by the Harvard Committee notes the movement in our schools toward citizenship education in the years 1870–1940. Because only one-quarter of youth were college-bound, this citizenship function was evermore important.

The abilities to think effectively, to communicate thought, to make relevant judgments, and to discriminate among values were seen as important ends for public schooling. A liberal arts education is prescribed for all students to link all future citizens and the common culture of the present.

Havighurst, Robert. *Growing Up in River City* **(1962).**   This book is an account of a study of sixth graders growing up in a midwestern town, who were observed in school and in the community. Results from the study, conducted from 1951–1958, documented the effect of social class on education. Those students in the lowest socioeconomic class were predictably poorer students.

The author makes a case to aid disadvantaged students at an early age. A failure to read is identified as the first sign of the student giving up.

Hirsch, E. D. *Cultural Literacy* **(1988).**   The author holds that there is a certain background knowledge necessary for functional literacy in America. Such literacy is essential to national communication and tranquility. Because some citizens do not understand issues, they do not trust the system.

The author calls for curriculum reform to narrow the focus of what is learned by all children. Underprivileged children need the same mainstream literacy as the middle class.

Hutchins, Robert. *The Learning Society* **(1968).**   This author believes that the task of education is not practical but rather to help people become intelligent. Culture and the education system must be synchronized. The author advocates a liberal arts education for all.

The same curriculum does not mean that everyone must be educated at the same rate or in the same way. In a learning society everybody is continuing liberal learnings either inside of or outside of institutions.

Illich, Ivan. *Deschooling Society* **(1971).**   Illich believes that learning is curtailed by formal schooling because educators package instruction like any other product. Students are sorted and selected according to allegiance to these marketed values. The author calls for breaking the monopoly of schools by forming "learning communities" that allow free access to knowledge.

Deschooling means an end to the obligatory curriculum. It means an end to the age-specific, instructor-related, defined curriculum process that is mandatory for all. A new educational format, based on learning webs (based on interests), are constructed.

Katz, Michael. *Reconstructing American Education* **(1987).**   According to Katz, five forces have influenced the emergence of the American education model: democracy, industrialization, urbanization, class structures, and the welfare state. Capitalism and industrialization led to the formation of institutions such as the public schools, the purpose being to lower poverty and the crime rate by providing a superior alternative environment for children of the lower classes.

The author identifies four models that dominated the nineteenth century in American education.

Kaufman, Bel. *Up the Down Staircase* **(1965).**   An early criticism of the bureaucratic state of this nation's public schools. The author takes the reader into the workings of an urban school and identifies the many forces in schools that make life difficult for America's teaching force.

Kilpatrick, William. *Foundations of Method* **(1926).**   As a student of John Dewey, the author is a believer in progressive education. The contribution of this work is the explanation of the so-called "project method" of teaching.

The author discusses motivation as "stirring interest in the child." He sees learning as a process of remaking experience that includes planning, executing, and judging. Project work accomplishes all of these functions and is the best way for the student to internalize learning. "We cannot learn what we do not practice."

Kliebard, Herbert. *The Struggle for the American Curriculum 1893–1951* **(1995).** In this very detailed description of the progressive era, the author presents changes in a chronological narrative form. The ferment of the 1890s, the Dewey era, scientific curriculum, and the life adjustment movement are described. The Afterward section of the book analyzes the meaning of these twentieth-century events.

Different curriculum issues are discussed: the child-centered curriculum, scientific curriculum, subject alignment, experiential education, and life adjustment curriculums.

Krug, E. A. *The Shaping of the American High School* **(1964);** *The Shaping of the American High School (1920–1941)* **(1972).**   In this two-volume set, the author traces the evolution of secondary education in America. Significant details about the ideas of the men and women who have shaped this institution are presented and analyzed.

Litwin, George. *Motivation and Organizational Climate* **(1968).**   This author believes that climates can activate human motivation when there is a match between organizational tasks and individual needs. The author reviews research in a number of organizational settings and the effects of nine variables on the activation of individual motivation.

Mager, Robert. *Goal Analysis* **(1972).**   In this small and simple book, the author stresses the need for clear and concise goals as the prerequisite for planning. The reader is directed through a series of steps to produce clear goal statements.

A goal is a statement describing a broad or abstract intent, state, or condition. The test of a clear goal, observes the author, is that someone can show, demonstrate, or convince that this condition exists.

Maslow, Abraham. *Motivation and Personality* **(1954).**   In this work, the author introduces his now-classic theory of human motivation based on higher and lower levels of needs. The author advocates a self-actualizing person and identifies conditions for this desired state of existence.

A five-step model is provided as a means of thinking about a hierarchy: physiological needs, safety needs, belonging or love needs, esteem, and self-actualization. According to the author, the more members of society who achieve self-actualization, the closer we shall come to the "good society."

McLuhan, Marshall. *The Medium Is the Message* **(1967).**   As an early observer of the effects of technology on learning, the author uses multiple examples to demonstrate how the learning medium can influence meaning.

McLuhan referred to the "global village" in which all persons experience a common culture through the media (television in this case). He projected that social issues would become global and that new technology might even change our character.

Graphics by co-author Fiore are intriguing and demonstrate that, indeed, the medium is the message.

Mead, Margaret. *The School in American Culture* **(1959).**   Americans have an image of the school as a little red schoolhouse, but this is hardly the case. Today's schools are filled with resistant learners who are disoriented because of the speed of change occurring around them.

The author discusses a wide variety of concerns, such as teacher training, control of American schools, and bureaucracy, from an anthropological vantage point. This work projects an increasingly political future for our schools.

Mead, Margaret. *Culture and Commitment: The Generation Gap* **(1970).**   The author addresses squarely the problem of relevance in teaching by investigating how time-focus differs between the young and the adult. Students who value only the present and future meet awkwardly with teachers who dwell on the past.

In this work the author divides people and cultures by their time orientation: The postfiguratives rely on the past as a guide to the future. Cofiguratives accept that change will occur but still embrace the knowledge of the past. In prefigurative cultures (youth) the complex immediacy of the moment defines reality. Communication between these three groups of time travelers is poor at best, resulting in a true "generation gap."

Mungazi, Dickson. *Educational Policy and National Character* **(1993).**   Education is critical to national development and must be consistent with national purpose. Designing the curriculum, formulating objectives, and implementing the curriculum determine the character of society. National values constitute a set of essential elements needed to build national character.

National Education Association. *Report on the Committee of Fifteen* **(1895).** Committee report summaries from the most famous committee of elementary school educators who discuss teacher training and the correlation of studies prior to the twentieth century.

National Education Association. *Cardinal Principles of Secondary Education* **(1918).**   Report of a committee of secondary educators who met for five years to discuss the secondary school needed by the American society. A prescription for a broad and practical curriculum is offered.

Neill, A. S. *Summerhill* **(1960).**   For many years the only example of the application of existential philosophy, Summerhill has become one of the best known schools in the world. The author, who directed the school for many years, addresses its establishment and rules.

Parker, Francis. *Talks on Pedagogics* **(1894).**   A figure credited with drawing together subjects for schools discusses the various acts of teaching and curriculum designs.

Peddiwell, J. *The Sabre-Toothed Curriculum* **(1939).**   In this work the author speaks of a mythical school in which animal teachings have become dysfunctional because of evolving conditions. Eventually, radicals (called progressives) force revisions in the curriculum.

The author points out that although a society successfully hones its skills through a school curriculum, they fail to take into account changes that dramatically affect the livelihood of society.

Phenix, P. *Realms of Meaning* **(1964).**   The author describes six realms of meaning in humans: (1) symbolic, (2) empirics, (3) esthetics, (4) synnoetics (personal knowledge), (5) ethics, and (6) synoptics.

The author advocates for all six areas in any curriculum. The author also provides five basic principles to help answer philosophical questions about curriculum decisions. Further discussions are held on the nature of literacy, the teacher's role in defining meaning, and changes needed in educational theory.

Rice, Joseph M. *The Public School System of the United States* **(1893).**   A non-educator interviews 1200 teachers in thirty-three school districts and finds the public school system wanting. The author divides all schools and curriculum into those that are scientific and those that are not.

This book had heavy influence on the deliberations of the Committee of Ten and makes interesting parallel observations to a 1970 book by Charles Silberman, *Crisis in the Classroom.*

Rickover, Hyman. *Education and Freedom* **(1959).**   The head of America's nuclear submarine program denounces public education and calls for a science and mathematics orientation in the secondary schools.

Rogers, Carl. *Freedom to Learn* **(1969).**   This author believes that all individuals have within themselves the ability to guide their own lives. It is proposed that schools must be changed to allow students to be freed to find inner wisdom and confidence. According to the author, there are two types of learning: from the neck up (passive) and self-initiated (active).

Examples of "freeing" students to learn are taken from a sixth-grade classroom and from the author's college classes. A client-centered approach to teaching is advocated, and the author provides ten principles to assess your approach to learning.

Rugg, Harold. *Foundation for American Education* **(1947).**   Written in the latter stages of his long career, this progressive educator prescribes a rich and applied curriculum for American public school students.

As a strong progressive, Rugg endorses activity learning and the full involvement of the student in the learning process.

Sarason, Seymour. *The Predictable Failure of Educational Reform* **(1990).**   Educational reform in America fails because those outside do not understand the system and those inside are preoccupied with their own particular locus of control. The author calls for a reallocation of power within the system in favor of teachers.

Silberman, Charles. *Crisis in the Classroom,* **(1970).**   This widely read survey of educational practices in the late 1960s by a non-educator indicts American education for "mindlessness" in its everyday pursuits. The author addresses the new "open" schools found in Britain as a possible alternative model for America.

Descriptions of promising schools and practices are drawn from various school visits.

Skinner, B. F. *The Technology of Teaching* **(1968).**   A behaviorist's view of curriculum development and instruction advocating control of the field of learning. In terms of stimulus, response, and conditioning the author describes teaching machines and programmed instruction as well as classroom variables such as student motivation and discipline.

The author observes that schools are in desperate need of being overhauled. The placement of technology in the classroom can contribute mightily to this end.

Smith, B. O. and colleagues. *Fundamentals of Curriculum Development* **(1950).** Along with William Stanley and Harlan Shores, Smith discusses the fundamental properties of sound curriculum development in this widely used text.

The authors define the four aspects of curriculum development as the following: determining direction, choosing procedures, selecting experiences, and determining evaluation methods.

Spring, Joel. *American Education: An Introduction to Social and Political Aspects* **(1989).** The efforts of the public schools to serve public purposes, for example, teaching values such as patriotism, tie it to nonpermanent conditions in society. Changing conditions of an ethnic, religious, or political nature will therefore cause the purpose of curriculum in our schools to change constantly. The search for common republican principles should be left to other agencies.

According to this author, the most important goals of education are educating citizens, selecting future political leaders, creating a political consensus, and socializing individuals for the political system.

Stanley, William B. *Curriculum for Utopia* **(1992).** A review of American education ideologies with special emphasis on reconstructionism, a movement holding that change is inevitable. The writings of Dewey, Rugg, and Counts are analyzed by the author.

The author presents some of the elements of reconstructionist thought: a focus on the political nature of schooling, using the school site to resist dominant order, seeing teachers as transformers, a central concern with ethical positions, and an attempt to combine pragmatism and radicalism.

Taba, Hilda. *Curriculum Development: Theory into Practice* **(1962).** In this general curriculum text the author provides detailed steps for the implementation of curriculum plans. A problem-solving procedure is projected following the traditional curriculum development cycle.

Toffler, Alvin. *Future Shock* **(1970).** The future is arriving at a bewildering speed, disrupting traditional ways of living. The author uses numerous technological examples to orient the reader to this now permanent state of living in the last third of the twentieth century.

Toffler, Alvin. *Learning for Tomorrow* **(1974).** Technological and social change is outracing the school system. The future is not a subject, and the future is not predetermined. Student motivation is directly tied to perceptions of the future, and schools may be betraying our youth. A new orientation is needed featuring action learning and the understanding of trends.

Toffler, Alvin. *Powershift: Knowledge, Wealth, and Violence at the Edge of the 21st Century* **(1990).** This book indicates three important sources of power in our society: violence, wealth, and knowledge. Power is shifting rapidly throughout our society. Currently, the United States is shifting from historic patterns of agriculture and industrialization to a new information age. This "third wave" will have a dramatic effect on persons living in the twenty-first century.

Curriculum must focus on finding and analyzing knowledge and then processing and organizing it to meet the requisite tasks. Knowledge is the central resource of an advanced society and the source of the highest-quality power.

Tyler, Ralph. *Basic Principles of Curriculum and Instruction* **(1949).** Tyler believes that concepts of goals are essential to good curriculum planning. Educational objectives serve as criteria for all further planning. The author organizes inquiry into this topic around four basic questions.

The integral components in answering questions about curriculum are the learner and the learner's life outside the school.

Whipple, G. (Ed). *The Foundations of Curriculum Making* **(1926).** In this National Society for the Study of Education (NSSE) Yearbook (two parts), the contributors review innovative schools and the processes by which they developed their programs. A strong historic orientation of early curriculum development is presented.

Wildavsky, Aaron. *The Politics of the Budgetary Process* **(1979).** Conventional wisdom, says this author, has budget development as a logical process, but this is rarely true. Human nature is never more evident than when individuals are struggling to gain a larger share of the funds.

The author advocates a Planning, Programming, Budgeting System (PPBS) and a Zero-Based Budgeting (ZBB) process. Budgets, says the author, reveal who wins and who loses the contest.

Wiles, Jon and Lundt, John. *Leaving School: Finding Education* **(2004).** The authors detail the decline of schools as we enter the New Information Age and Internet connectivity. Individual learning portals are projected for the twenty-first century. The transition to the new education format is discussed in terms of vouchers and alternate funding sources.

IDEAS AND THEORIES ABOUT CURRICULUM

The curriculum of only one century ago was a form of mental discipline by which learned men committed knowledge to memory. In the ensuing one hundred years, any number of forces have splintered that conception of schooling. The revolutions in technology, communication, and formatting of knowledge have given us unlimited options in learning. The massive social transformation of American society has demanded new uses and applications from the school. Our growing understanding of the uniqueness of humans has impacted our attempts to deliver the curriculum.

Some things have not changed much in this same period. The basis of our American curriculum remain the resources of Western civilization. The delivery of the curriculum continues to occur in a school building that is remarkably unchanging, often resulting in function following form. Finally, the value base of all teachings in a school setting continues to be recognized for what it is—a programming of the next generation. For this reason, Curriculum remains a political process with high stakes.

The period from 1892 (the Committee of Ten) to 1918 (the Committee on the Reorganization of Secondary Education) remains a fascinating one in terms of the development of educational philosophy. As the voices of this era spoke of purposes, procedures, the nature of the student, and the way in which learning occurs, differences in beliefs became apparent. Various spokespersons attempted to identify their primary beliefs and the field of curriculum emerged as a sort of intellectual referee. Focus in the fray centered on two very different concerns: (1) defining the curriculum and (2) developing the curriculum.

The Experts on Curriculum Theory

Most educators resist using the word *theory* because it suggests an unusable blue-sky conception of reality. In fact, theory is necessary as an organizer for action in curriculum planning. Theory can (1) explain facts, as opposed to describing facts; (2) provide a few high-level generalizations; (3) help to distinguish between trivial and more crucial events; and (4) communicate by accounting for any series of events without proof. In this section, the reader is provided with a "range" of ideas about theory that reflect twentieth-century thought in curriculum.

According to one group of educators: "Theory evolves from or crystallizes the verbalization of basic assumptions, principles, observations, and notions that are held about a particular phenomenon or area of activity. When these are collated in an orderly manner so that they constitute a constellation of supporting ideas and evidence, the theory is identified. On the basis of theory, a model can be developed which will illustrate the theoretical concepts. This allows the practitioner not only to verbalize organization of ideas, but also a design for his plan of action."[1]

In an applied sense, such theory also is prerequisite for the successful application of curriculum through the development process. As Katz observes: "The ability to see the organization as a whole; it includes recognizing how . . . the various functions of the organization depend on one another, and how change in one part affects all the others. Recognizing these relationships and perceiving the significant elements in any situation, the administrator should then be able to act in a way which advances the overall welfare of the organization."[2]

Curriculum theory as it appeared in the first curriculum text, *The Curriculum* (1918) by Franklin Bobbitt, was quite simple:

> *The central theory [of curriculum] is simple. Human life, however varied, consists in the performance of specific activities. Education that prepares for life is one that prepares definitively and adequately for these specific activities. However numerous and diverse they may be for any social class they can be discovered. This*

requires only that one go out into the world of affairs and discover the particulars of which these affairs consist. These will show the abilities, attitudes, habits, appreciations, and forms of knowledge that men need. These will be the objectives of the curriculum. They will be numerous, definite and particularized. The curriculum will then be that series of experiences which children must have by way of attaining these objectives.[3]

Unfortunately, the worldly assumptions of Bobbitt turned out to be simplistic. Human life was not always reducible to specific activities, and the affairs of the world were increasingly bewildering. Most of all, the world was changing too fast to allow the simple programming of skills in children based on the present.

The philosophy, psychology, and pedagogy of the moment was wrapped up in the person of John Dewey who, recognizing the choices ahead, observed that "the history of educational theory is marked opposition between the idea that education is developed from within and that it is formation from without."[4]

Ralph Tyler is credited with reducing this understanding to a series of four short questions that would differentiate all curriculum theorists:

1. What educational purposes should the school seek to attain?
2. What educational experiences can be provided that are likely to attain these purposes?
3. How can these educational experiences be effectively organized?
4. How can we determine whether these purposes are being attained?[5]

According to McNeil, curriculum inquiry has multiple purposes: to advance conceptualization and understanding of the field, to conceive new visions of what and how to teach, to influence curriculum policy, to question normative premises about curriculum, and to improve programs for learning. He divides all such into two camps: the quantitative inquiry that seeks to identify relationships and the qualitative inquiry that seeks to understand meanings of interactions.[6]

The importance of such inquiry is identified by Hilda Taba, who said when speaking of definitions of curriculum: "these variations in the conception of the function of education are not idle or theoretical arguments. They have concrete implications for the shape of educational programs. If one believes that the chief function of education is to transmit perennial truths, one cannot but strive toward a uniform curriculum. . . . as such, differences in these concepts naturally determine what are considered to be the 'essentials' and what are the dispensable frills in education."[7]

Finally, Joyce and Weil connect the conception to the program by stating, "educational procedures are generated from general views about human nature and about the goals and environments that enhance human beings. Because of their frame of reference—their view of man and what he should become—educators are likely to focus on specific kinds of learning outcomes and to favor certain ways of creating educational environments. . . ."[8]

McNeil and Wiles reduce the variance in beliefs to what can be seen in the school setting. According to these authors, schools and classrooms are either high in structure or flexible. In the structured environments (ordered) there is a desire to eliminate distortion and distraction and to implement a fixed and predetermined curriculum to the student. By contrast, in the flexible learning environment, educators encourage diversity and seek the individual growth of the student.[9]

Efforts to develop models in curriculum have been largely unsuccessful, with the notable exception being "Dewey's rationale for education in a Democracy." Again, Hilda Taba describes the problems involved:

> *Decisions leading to change in curriculum organizations have been made largely by pressure, by hunches, or even in terms of expediency instead of being based on clear cut theoretical considerations or tested knowledge. The scope of curriculum has been extended vastly without an adequate consideration of the consequences of this extension on sequential or cumulative learning. The fact that these perplexities underlying curriculum change have not been studied may account for the proliferation of approaches to curriculum making.*[10]

In reviewing practice in the field, Alexander suggests that the traditional subject matter is at the center of curriculum theory in America:

> *Certainly, a review of the plans made and implemented today and yesterday leaves no doubt that the dominant assumption of past curriculum planning has been the goal of subject matter mastery through a subject curriculum, almost inextricably tied to a closed school and graded school ladder, to a marking system that rewards successful achievement of fixed content and penalizes unsuccessful achievement, to an instructional organization based on fixed classes in the subjects and a time table for them.*[11]

Eisner distinguishes between normative theory and descriptive theory in curriculum. In the former, there is a concern with the articulation and justification of a set of values. Because education is value laden, curriculum theorists should be aware of the outcomes of their activities. The descriptive wing, by contrast, seeks to explain and predict the events in curriculum without concern for the values. Working as a scientist or social scientist, the descriptive theorists remain objective in their study.[12]

Over time, the principles of curriculum have evolved as core procedures rather than theoretical guidelines. Maccia has called this the "proxiological approach" to theorizing, as opposed to a more philosophical or theoretical approach.[13]

Daniel and Laura Tanner have noted "In the absence of a holistic conception of curriculum, the focus is on the piecemeal and mechanical functions . . . the main thrust in curriculum development and reform over the years has been directed at the micro curricular problems to the neglect of the macro curricular problems."[14]

Finally, Bruce Joyce presents the state of the art in curriculum theory in this manner: "In the past, educational planners have been technically weak (unable often to clarify ends or engineer means) . . . curriculum workers have defined themselves as helpers, not leaders, letting the community and teachers make decisions and then assisting in the implementation of those decisions. By focusing on schools and teachers in schools, curriculum is being forced to operate within the parameters of the institution . . . by far the most paralyzing effect of the assumptive world in which the curriculum specialist lives is that it tends to filter out all ideas which might improve education but which fit awkwardly into the school pattern."[15]

And so, curriculum theory has been largely unsuccessful in utilizing the value dimensions of school planning. Although many philosophies of education exist that might serve as lenses for inquiry, or to guide program development, American curriculum theorists have chosen most often to focus on the mechanics of the development process in the literature.

SUMMARY

Curriculum, as a subset of professional education, is a relatively new area of inquiry dealing with the who, what, why, and when questions posed by philosophy. Curriculum links ideas with practices, and in the time since the first book in curriculum (1918) a significant literature has developed.

Up to the period around 1995, most of what was known in curriculum was captured in the print media. This book introduces those new to curriculum to this collection of books and documents and ideas. Most of these resources are tied to visible leaders who are known to all workers in the field. The author has presented leads to the sources, attempting to identify what seems "essential" from a historical perspective. These works are important to understand and a prerequisite to understanding the thoughts and issues in this area of inquiry.

In the period 1995 to the present, events have occurred that make print media a less reliable source of information about what is happening in curriculum development. Many events are taking place beyond education, for non-educational reasons, and they are transpiring at the speed of technology. Future curriculum specialists will need supplemental means to monitor such changes.

SUGGESTED READINGS

Eisner Elliot, *The Educational Imagination,* 4th ed., (New York: Macmillan, 2002).

Marzano, Robert, *What Americans Believe Students Should Know* (Mid-West Regional Educational Laboratory [McREL], U.S. Department of Education, 1998).

Pratt, David, *Curriculum Planning: A Handbook for Professionals* (Fort Worth, TX: Harcourt, Brace, 1994).

Slattery, Patrick, *Ethics and the Foundations of Education: Convictions in a Postmodern World* (Boston: Allyn & Bacon, 2003).

ENDNOTES

1. Glen Eye, Lanore Netzer, and Robert Key, *Supervision of Instruction* (New York: Harper & Row, 1964), p. 48.

2. Robert Katz, "Skills of an Effective Administrator," *Harvard Business Review,* (Jan./Feb. 1955), 35–36.

3. Franklin Bobbitt, *The Curriculum* (Boston: Houghton-Mifflin, 1918), p. 14.

4. John Dewey, *The Child and the Curriculum* (Chicago: University of Chicago Press, 1902), p. 4.

5. Ralph Tyler, *Basic Principles of Curriculum and Instruction* (Chicago: University of Chicago Press, 1949), p. 18.

6. John McNeil, *Curriculum,* 5th ed. (New York: Macmillan, 1996), p. 443.

7. Hilda Taba, *Curriculum Development: Theory into Practice* (New York: Harcourt, Brace, Jovanovich, 1962), p. 30.

8. Bruce Joyce and Marsha Weil, *Models of Teaching,* 5th ed. (Boston: Allyn & Bacon, 1996), p. 5.

9. John McNeil and Jon Wiles, *Essentials of Teaching* (New York: Macmillan, 1990), p. 91.

10. H. Taba op. cit. p. 9.

11. William Alexander, "Curriculum Planning as It Should Be," Address to ASCD, Chicago, October 29, 1971.

12. Elliot Eisner, *The Educational Imagination* (New York: Macmillan, 1994), pp. 35–38.

13. Elizabeth Maccia, "Curriculum Theory and Policy," paper presented at American Educational Research Associates, Chicago, 1965.

14. Daniel and Laura Tanner, Preface to *Curriculum Development: Theory into Practice,* 3rd ed. (New York: Macmillan, 1975).

15. Bruce Joyce, "The Curriculum Worker of the Future," *The Curriculum: Retrospect and Prospect,* Seventy-First Yearbook of the National Society for the Study of Education, University of Chicago Press, 1971, p. 307.

2

MODELS, DOCUMENTS, LAWS, AND RESEARCH

OVERVIEW

In curriculum work, practitioners reference a body of knowledge that helps structure school programming and planning. Usually, such references are known to others in the field and serve as a kind of shorthand in communication. Such nomenclature is characteristic of all professions. In this chapter, widely known school models, documents, paradigms, legal decisions, and significant classroom research is featured as we begin to define curriculum as an area of study.

Schools featured in this chapter are historically significant because of practices or curriculum innovations. For example, the Lancaster Plan is synonymous with the monitorial system in which a teacher instructs a few students who then teach other students. The Winnetka Plan is the primary model for all extracurricular programs in schools. Parkway schools refer to the use of nontraditional buildings to house school programs. Unfamiliarity with such historic schools when engaged in curriculum design may lead to "reinventing the wheel" unnecessarily.

In the documents section, twenty important works that have defined American education are presented chronologically. Each of these documents explains why we do certain things in schools and, as such, provides common denominators for communication about school design. The Seven Cardinal Principles, for example, is the document that led to a comprehensive school curriculum. The SCANS Report is the basis for most state standards and testing.

Most important legal cases affecting American education have been resolved in the U.S. Supreme Court. Once "law," these cases determine the form of many kinds of curriculum. A notable exception to this generalization is the *Kalamazoo* case, a Michigan Supreme Court decision, that to this day allows taxation for schools at the secondary level.

Many of the conceptual models that curriculum planners use come from areas in the social sciences. Maslow's hierarchy of needs, for example, is a theoretical model of motivation that is often used in classrooms to explain behavior and establish disciplinary programs.

Finally, there is an emerging resource base in education that can guide curriculum planners on a daily basis. Although these studies are not prescriptive, they do indicate general strategies that can be replicated with a high degree of confidence.

In summary, the items in this chapter are "should know" references that allow persons in curriculum to communicate and work with efficiency. Persons entering leadership in the area of curriculum can quickly master these items and add them to their own collection of knowledge as needed.

SCHOOL MODELS

Curriculum leaders have more than 200 years of experience to draw on in designing schools and educational programs. In this section, the best known schools are identified and their contributions highlighted.

Baltimore Plan (1900).   Featuring a flexible schedule and differentiated grading, this plan for gifted students provided six years of lateral enrichment and then six years of acceleration through subjects.

Batavia Plan (1875).   Flexible grading and promotion plans that assisted teachers in bringing slower learners up to grade level so that they could be promoted.

Cambridge Plan (1910).   Designed to meet the needs of gifted students, featuring two parallel curriculums. The normal track took eight years but gifted students could complete the same material in six years.

Dalton Plan (1919).   Individualized paths through the curriculum provided by jobs. Students would select a job, each divided into twenty units, and "contract" with the teacher. At the end of each month the teacher would check the progress of the students in completing these tasks.

Dewey School (1896).   This University of Chicago Laboratory School focused on training students for cooperative and mutually helpful living as preparation for life in a democracy. Focusing on occupations, the curriculum simulated a community and its interdependencies.

Foxfire School (1985).   A late 1980s school located in the rural mountains of Georgia, this school was known for its progressive learning procedures and student-oriented culture.

Gary Plan (1908).   Innovative in many ways, this school had four quarters (year round), elementary and secondary school under one roof (educational park), and academic acceleration as early as the fifth grade. The schools were open on Saturdays for community participation.

John Adams High (1970).   In the early 1970s this Portland, Oregon, high school gained exposure as a model of "democratic processes." Students and faculty used the New England town meeting procedure to solve problems and plan change.

Lancaster School (1815).   Also known as a "monitorial" model, this school used students to teach other students as a response to overcrowding. The master teacher would instruct one to one hundred pupils who would then each teach ten additional students.

Lincoln School (1920).   Operated as an experimental program at Teachers College that focused on ends such as creativity and insights. Synthesizing the subjects and focus on the utility of knowledge was a goal of this program. Units of work were featured.

Nova High School (1970).   A Fort Lauderdale, Florida, school that featured early technical applications to the instructional process. Funded by a Ford Foundation grant, Nova featured early computer applications as well as advanced video technology.

Parkway Schools (1975).   Created in a time of financial crisis, this Philadelphia school network demonstrated that schools could be created "without walls," using the resources of the city as the learning environment. This program, still in existence, was widely studied in the 1970s.

Skyline High School (1970).   A Dallas, Texas, school offering a comprehensive program under one roof. Students in this school could study almost any curriculum and prepare for many occupations based on the nature of the curriculum.

Summerhill School (1965).   An English school run by A. S. Neil, Summerhill is often used as an example to describe existential or highly flexible school environments.

Winnetka School (1919).   Featured a two-part curriculum: (1) basic skills and knowledge and (2) activities for self-expression. Students progressed through a fixed curriculum in their own way without attempts to standardize outcomes.

IMPORTANT DOCUMENTS

In this section, the reader is presented with those documents that are most often referenced by curriculum planners as benchmarks. The documents are listed chronologically as they influenced school programming.

Old Deluder Satan Act (1647).   An early regulatory act passed by the colonists to promote literacy. The act followed the belief of Martin Luther that it was necessary for people to read God's word in order to "secure their eternity." The act called for the establishment of schools in Massachusetts towns where fifty families were present.

Thomas Jefferson's Free School Proposal (1779).   Proposed that the Virginia legislature establish school districts and provide three free years of education for all children and longer for the best students. Although the proposal failed, Jefferson continued to see education as vital. In 1816 he wrote, "If a nation expects to be ignorant and free in a state of civilization, it expects what never was and never will be. . . ."

Northwest Ordinance (1787).   The law included provisions for territories desiring statehood and included National Land Grants to promote schooling. States entering the Union after Ohio (1802) were to receive the sixteenth section for the support of schools and two townships of land for the endowment of a state university.

The Morrill Act (1862).   Also known as the Land Grant College Act. This legislation served to promote colleges with a practical curriculum in areas such as mechanics and agriculture. Most major state universities date from this act.

Committee of Ten Prescription (1893).   This committee of college presidents began the process of structuring secondary education by calling for an identified subject matter, credits for graduation, and a six-year high school. Further committees filled in these goals in the 1890s. (See Figure 2.1.)

Committee on the Reorganization of Secondary Education (1918).   A call for universal and comprehensive education for all youth. Meeting for five years, the committee advocated the "Seven Cardinal Principles" or directions for the secondary curriculum in America. (See Figure 2.2.)

Eight Year Study (1932).   A comparative study of thirty schools selected by the Progressive Education Association similar to traditional schools. This study followed 1475 matched pairs of students through high school and college. In twenty areas the students in the "progressive" excelled over their traditional counterparts. A five-volume report was published in 1942.

Education Policy Commission Statement (1938).   In 1935 the National Education Association (NEA) created the Education Policy Commission to study the effect of the Great Depression. Their report stressed four aims of education: self-realization, human relations, economic efficiency, and civic responsibility.

Education for ALL American Youth (1944).   In this document the Educational Policies Commission rejects an "academic only" curriculum and identifies ten imperative needs of youth that must be served by the school curriculum. (See Figure 2.3.)

Brown v. Topeka **(1954).**   In this historic Supreme Court decision, the concept of "separate but equal" (*Plessy v. Ferguson,* 1896) was overturned. The integration of public schools by race followed and continues today in all fifty states.

National Defense Education Act of 1958.   In response to Sputnik, Congress passed a $1 billion NDEA bill (1958) with most emphasis given to science and

FIGURE 2.1   Curricular Offerings (High School) as Proposed by the Committee of Ten on Secondary School Studies, 1893. The Committee of Ten was a prestigious body of university presidents meeting in 1892 to address the problem of quality control in a decentralized education system. Under the direction of Charles Eliot of Harvard, they prescribed a fixed curriculum of a classical nature. Other committees in this period established credit requirements and extended the high school to a six-year program.

1st Secondary School Year	2nd Secondary School Year
Latin .... 5 p.	Latin .... 4 p.
English Literature, 2 p. ⎫ " Composition, 2 p. ⎬ .... 4 p.	Greek .... 5 p.
German [or French] .... 5 p.	English Literature, 2 p. ⎫ " Composition, 2 p. ⎬ .... 4 p.
Algebra .... 4 p.	German, continued .... 4 p.
History of Italy, Spain, and France .... 3 p.	French, begun .... 5 p.
Applied Geography (European political—continental and oceanic flora and fauna) .... 4 p. 25 p.	Algebra,* 2 p. ⎫ Geometry, 2 p. ⎬ .... 4 p. Botany or Zoology .... 4 p. English History to 1688 .... 3 p. 33 p. *Option of bookkeeping and commercial arithmetic.

3rd Secondary School Year	4th Secondary School Year
Latin .... 4 p.	Latin .... 4 p.
Greek .... 4 p.	Greek .... 4 p.
English Literature, 2 p. ⎫ " Composition, 1 p. ⎬ ...... 4 p. Rhetoric 1 p. ⎭	English Literature, 2 p. ⎫ " Composition, 1 p. ⎬ ...... 4 p. " Grammar, 1 p. ⎭
German .... 4 p.	German .... 4 p.
French .... 4 p.	French .... 4 p.
Algebra,* 2 p. ⎫ Geometry, 2 p. ⎬ .... 4 p.	Trigonometry, ⎫ Higher Algebra, ⎬ .... 2 p.
Physics .... 4 p.	Chemistry .... 4 p.
History, English and American .... 3 p.	History (intensive) and Civil Government .... 3 p.
Astronomy, 3 p. 1st ½ yr. ⎫ Meteorology, 3 p. 2nd ½ yr. ⎬ .... 3 p. 34 p. *Option of bookkeeping and commercial arithmetic.	Geology or Physiography, 4 p. 1st ½ yr. ⎫ Anatomy, Physiology, and Hygiene, 4 p. 2nd ½ yr. ⎬ .... 4 p. 33 p.

Source: Committee of Ten, *Report of the Committee of Ten on Secondary School Studies* (Washington, DC: National Education Association, 1893), p. 4.

FIGURE 2.2   The Seven Cardinal Principles of Secondary Education: Committee on the Reorganization of Secondary Education, 1918. This document, issued by the Commission on the Reorganization of Secondary Education after five years of deliberation (1913–1918), represents the origin of a distinct American curriculum at the secondary level. Abandoning the pure classical model, this NEA-sponsored group called for a broad and comprehensive education for American school students. This new curriculum would take into account the differences of the many students in attendance.

1. Health

   A secondary school should encourage good health habits, give health instruction, and provide physical activities. Good health should be taken into account when schools and communities are planning activities for youth. The general public should be educated on the importance of good health. Teachers should be examples for good health, and schools should furnish good equipment and safe buildings.

2. Command of Fundamental Processes

   Fundamental Processes are writing, reading, oral and written expression, and math. It was decided that these basics should be applied to newer material instead of using the older ways of doing things.

3. Worthy Home Membership

   This principle "calls for the development of those qualities that make the individual a worthy member of a family, both contributing to and deriving benefit from that membership." This principle should be taught through literature, music, social studies, and art. Co-ed schools should show good relationships between males and females. When trying to instill this principle in children, the future as well as the present should be taken into account.

4. Vocation

   The objective of this principle is that the student gets to know himself or herself and a variety of careers so that the student can choose the most suitable career. The student should then develop an understanding of the relationship between the vocation and the community in which one lives and works. Those who are successful in a vocation should be the ones to teach the students in either the school or workplace.

5. Civic Education

   The goal of civic education is to develop an awareness and concern for one's own community. A student should gain knowledge of social organizations and a commitment to civic morality. Diversity and cooperation should be paramount. Democratic organization of the school and classroom as well as group problem solving are the methods that should be used to teach this principle.

6. Worthy Use of Leisure

   The idea behind this principle is that education should give the student the skills to enrich his or her body, mind, spirit, and personality in his or her leisure. The school should also provide appropriate recreation. This principle should be taught in all subjects but primarily in music, art, literature, drama, social issues, and science.

7. Ethical Character

   This principle involves instilling in the student the notion of personal responsibility and initiative. Appropriate teaching methods and school organization are the primary examples that should be used.

FIGURE 2.3   Educational Policies Commission on Education for ALL American Youth, 1944. Following World War II, the Educational Policies Commission issued a call for a highly practical curriculum that included ten imperative educational needs of youth in America. This prescription is both broad and comprehensive.

1. All youth need to develop salable skills and those understandings and attitudes that make the worker an intelligent and productive participant in economic life. To this end, most youth need supervised work experience as well as education in the skills and knowledge of their occupations.

2. All youth need to develop and maintain good health and physical fitness.

3. All youth need to understand the rights and duties of the citizen of a democratic society, and to be diligent and competent in the performance of their obligations as members of the community and citizens of the state and nation.

4. All youth need to understand the significance of the family for the individual and society and the conditions conducive to successful family life.

5. All youth need to know how to purchase and use goods and services intelligently, understanding both the values received by the consumer and the economic consequences of their acts.

6. All youth need to understand the methods of science, the influence of science on human life, and the main scientific facts concerning the nature of the world and of [people].

7. All youth need opportunities to develop their capacities to appreciate beauty in literature, art, music, and nature.

8. All youth need to be able to use their leisure time well and to budget it wisely, balancing activities that yield satisfactions to the individual with those that are socially useful.

9. All youth need to develop respect for other persons, to grow in their insight into ethical values and principles, and to be able to live and work cooperatively with others.

10. All youth need to grow in their ability to think rationally, to express their thoughts clearly, and to read and listen with understanding.

Source: Educational Policies Commission on Education for ALL American Youth, National Education Association, 1944, pp. 225–226.

mathematics. Various sections of the bill were called "Titles," a funding term that remains with us today (sometimes called chapters).

***The Conant Report* (1959).**   The president of Harvard argues in three books written between 1959 and 1961 (*The American High School Today, Education in the Junior High School,* and *Slums and Suburbs*) for a return to a more traditional curriculum. Conant also calls for the removal of small secondary schools and the development of the comprehensive high school.

Education of All Handicapped Children Act (1975).   Known as Public Law 94-142 (Ninety-Fourth Congress, bill 142), this federal law guarantees the rights of all handicapped students by extensive and detailed procedural prescriptions. (See Figure 2.4.)

ASCD Goals for Education (1982).   In this wide survey of curriculum leaders, ten goals were identified as targets for curriculum development efforts:

FIGURE 2.4   Education of All Handicapped Children Act, 1975 (P.L. 94-142).
The Ninety-Fourth Congress, in passing Public Law 142, created
federal protection for the rights of all handicapped children attending school from ages three to twenty-one. This legislation was
based on six principles. This baseline legislation has been revised
several times since 1975. Most recently, P.L. 94-142 has been replaced by IDEA (Individuals with Disabilities in Education Act).

P.L. 94-142 was enacted by Congress in November, 1975. Its major purpose, as stated in the act, is
as follows:

It is the purpose of this Act to assure that all handicapped children have available to them . . . a
free, appropriate public education which emphasizes special education and related services
designed to meet their unique needs, to assure that the rights of handicapped children and
their parents or guardians are protected, to assist States and localities to provide for the education of all handicapped children, and to assess and assure the effectiveness of efforts to educate
handicapped children. (Sec. 601 [c])

There are six major principles of P.L. 94-142:

1. *Principle of Zero Reject*

   This principle, simply stated, requires that all handicapped children be provided with a free,
   appropriate public education. States are required to provide full educational opportunities
   to all handicapped children in the age range of 3–18 by September 1, 1978, and to all handicapped children in the age range of 3–21 by September 1, 1980. The principle is implemented
   by conducting a child fund program on an annual basis to locate, identify, and evaluate all
   handicapped children who reside in the jurisdiction of each public agency. If local agencies
   comply with this principle, they become eligible to receive federal funds based on the number of handicapped children being served, not to exceed 12 percent of the school population.

   In addition to providing an educational program to all handicapped children, the public
   agency must ensure that handicapped children have equal opportunities with nonhandi-
   capped children to participate in nonacademic and extracurricular services. In addition,
   physical education must be provided to every handicapped child.

2. *Principle of Nondiscriminatory Evaluation*

   A handicapped child must receive a full individual evaluation prior to placement in a special education program. A placement decision should be made by a group of persons knowledgeable about the child, the meaning of the evaluation data, and the placement options.
   The placement recommendation may be suggested by the evaluation team and finalized by
   a committee who has the responsibility for writing the individual educational plan (IEP). All
   handicapped children must be completely reevaluated every three years.

3. *Individualized Educational Programs*

   The legislative approach for ensuring that educational programs are tailored on an individual
   basis to the needs of handicapped students is through the requirement of providing individual
   educational plans for all handicapped students. The IEP must contain the following essentials:

   a. Current level of student's educational performance.
   b. Annual goals.
   c. Short-term objectives.
   d. Documentation of the special education services to be provided.
   e. Time the student will spend in special education and related services.
   f. Time student will spend in regular education.

FIGURE 2.4 *Continued*

g. Dates for initiating service and anticipated duration.

h. Evaluation procedures and schedules for determining mastery of the objectives.

Members required to be in attendance at the IEP meeting must include the following:

a. Representative of the public agency.

b. The child's teacher.

c. Child's parents.

d. The child, when appropriate.

e. Other individuals at the request of the parents.

f. Individuals who provided the evaluation.

4. *Least Restrictive Environment*

To the maximum extent appropriate, handicapped children should be educated with children who are not handicapped. The removal of handicapped children to special classes and
separate facilities should occur only when the nature of severity of their handicap prevents
them from successfully being educated in regular classes with the use of supplementary
aids and services.

5. *Due Process*

Due process is a procedure which seeks to ensure the fairness of educational decisions and
the accountability of both the professionals and parents making these decisions. It can be
viewed as a system of checks and balances concerning the identification, evaluation, and
provision of services regarding handicapped students. It may be initiated by the parent or
public agency as an impartial forum for presenting complaints regarding the child's identification, evaluation, and placement or for challenging decisions made by another party.

6. *Parent Participation*

Each of the principles has either the direct or indirect implications for parental participation.
At the local level, parents should be permitted to review any educational records on their
child which are used by the agency before the meeting to develop the IEP and within a forty-
five-day period after receipt of the request.

These six principles of P.L. 94-142 provide the basis for the legislative definition of free,
appropriate public education.

---

self-concept, understanding others, basic skills, capability for continuous learning, responsible member of society, mental and physical health, creativity,
informed economic participation, use of accumulated knowledge, and coping
with change.

The Paideia Proposal (1982).   A call for a uniform, required twelve-year curriculum for all schoolchildren. The author, Mortimer Adler, advocates a return
to basic schooling with no elective choices except a second foreign language.
(See Figure 2.5.)

A Nation at Risk **(1983).**   A report by the probusiness Commission on Excellence claiming that public schools are causing decline in America. Traditional
education and work skills are advocated.

FIGURE 2.5   **The Paideia Proposal.** The conservative, traditional, or classical wing of American education has consistently held as a basic premise that certain knowledge, skills, and values are embedded in the American culture and should be preserved. Mortimer Adler, in his 1982 proposal, calls for a single curriculum for all U.S. students. To provide multiple tracks, he observes, would be to discriminate against those students not receiving the "best" learning.

	Column One	**Column Two**	**Column Three**
Goals	Acquisition of Organized Knowledge	Development of Intellectual Skills and Skills of Learning	Improved Understanding of Ideas and Values
	by means of	*by means of*	*by means of*
Means	Didactic Instruction, Lecturing, and Textbooks	Coaching, Exercises, and Supervised Practice	Maieutic or Socratic Questioning and Active Participation
	in these three subject areas	*in these operations*	*in these activities*
Subject Areas, Operations, and Activities	Language, Literature, and Fine Arts; Mathematics and Natural Science; History, Geography, and Social Studies	Reading, Writing, Speaking, Listening, Calculating, Problem Solving, Observing, Measuring, Estimating, Exercising Critical Judgment	Discussion of Books (Not Textbooks) and Other Works of Art; Involvement in Music, Drama, and Visual Arts

The three columns do not correspond to separate courses, nor is one kind of teaching and learning necessarily confined to any one class.

Source: Adapted from Mortimer Adler, *The Paideia Proposal: An Education Manifesto* (New York: Macmillan, 1982).

Turning Points **(1989).**   In this Carnegie Council report the middle school is identified as "potentially society's most powerful force to recapture millions of youth adrift. . . ." Calls for a decentralized and general curriculum connected to home and the family.

Goals 2000 (1990).   In February 1990, the president of the United States and all fifty governors met in an educational summit to establish expectations for education. Five critical goals were identified: (1) All children will start school ready to learn; (2) high school graduation will increase to at least 90 percent; (3) students will demonstrate competence over challenging subject matter; (4) every American will be literate; and (5) every school will be free of violence and drugs. These goals then served as organizers for reform at the state level. (See Figure 2.6.)

IDEA (1990).   The Individuals with Disabilities Education Act mandates automatic "inclusion" of all children in regular classrooms except under "direst circumstances" (20 U.S. Code 1412[5][b]).

FIGURE 2.6 **National Education Goals—Goals 2000.** In February 1990, then-president George Bush met with all fifty governors (under the leadership of then-governor Bill Clinton) to formulate a set of national goal targets for the year 2000. Although the U.S. Constitution does not provide for a national system of education, the assembly of persons from all fifty states represented a first-ever national policy effort in education in the United States.

- *School Readiness*

  By the year 2000, all children in America will start school ready to learn.

- *School Completion*

  By the year 2000, the high school graduation rate will increase to at least 90 percent.

- *Student Achievement and Citizenship*

  By the year 2000, all students will leave grades four, eight, and twelve having demonstrated competency over challenging subject matter including English, mathematics, science, foreign languages, civics and government, economics, arts, history, and geography, and every school in America will ensure that all students learn to use their minds well, so they may be prepared for responsible citizenship, further learning, and productive employment in our nation's modern economy.

- *Mathematics and Science*

  By the year 2000, U.S. students will be first in the world in mathematics and science achievement.

- *Adult Literacy and Lifelong Learning*

  By the year 2000, every adult American will be literate and will possess the knowledge and skills necessary to compete in a global economy and exercise the rights and responsibilities of citizenship.

- *Safe, Disciplined, and Alcohol- and Drug-Free Schools*

  By the year 2000, every school in the United States will be free of drugs, violence, and the unauthorized presence of firearms and alcohol, and will offer a disciplined environment conducive to learning.

- *Teacher Education and Professional Development*

  By the year 2000, the nation's teaching force will have access to programs for the continued improvement of their professional skills and the opportunity to acquire the knowledge and skills needed to instruct and prepare all U.S. students for the future.

- *Parental Participation*

  By the year 2000, every school will promote partnerships that will increase parental involvement and participation in promoting the social, emotional, and academic growth of children.

SCANS (1992). This set of recommendations by the U.S. Secretary of Labor proposes that the schools prepare workers for the world beyond school. The reorganization of the K–12 curriculum is suggested with workplace skills serving as frameworks. (See Figure 2.7.)

FIGURE 2.7 Five Competencies of SCANS. In the 1990s, the school-to-work interface has become a concern of the business community in the United States. To compete in the new world market, business leaders argue, business must have highly educated and motivated workers. The U.S. Department of Labor created a list of competencies that business leaders believe should be achieved by students in our public schools.

Resources: Identifies, organizes, plans, and allocates resources
  A. *Time*—Selects goal-relevant activities, ranks them, allocates time, and prepares and follows schedules
  B. *Money*—Uses or prepares budgets, makes forecasts, keeps records, and makes adjustments to meet objectives
  C. *Material and facilities*—Acquires, stores, allocates, and uses materials or space efficiently
  D. *Human resources*—Assesses skills and distributes work accordingly, evaluates performance and provides feedback

Interpersonal: Works with others
  A. *Participates as member of a team*—Contributes to group effort
  B. *Teaches others new skills*
  C. *Serves clients/customers*—Works to satisfy customers' expectations
  D. *Exercises leadership*—Communicates ideas to justify position, persuades and convinces others, responsibly challenges existing procedures and policies
  E. *Negotiates*—Works toward agreements involving exchange of resources, resolves divergent interests
  F. *Works with diversity*—Works well with men and women from diverse backgrounds

Information: Acquires and uses information
  A. *Acquires and evaluates information*
  B. *Organizes and maintains information*
  C. *Interprets and communicates information*
  D. *Uses computers to process information*

Systems: Understands complex interrelationships
  A. *Understands systems*—Knows how social, organizational, and technological systems work and operates effectively with them
  B. *Monitors and corrects performance*—Distinguishes trends, predicts impacts on system operations, diagnoses deviations in system's performance, and corrects malfunctions
  C. *Improves or designs systems*—Suggests modifications to existing systems and develops new or alternative systems to improve performance

Technology: Works with a variety of technologies
  A. *Selects technology*—Chooses procedures, tools, or equipment, including computers and related technologies
  B. *Applies technology to task*—Understands overall intent and proper procedures for setup and operation of equipment
  C. *Maintains and troubleshoots equipment*—Prevents, identifies, or solves problems with equipment, including computers and other technologies

Source: "What Work Requires of Schools: A SCANS Report for America 2000," U.S. Department of Labor, June 1991.

CRITICAL LEGAL RULINGS

Legal rulings have influenced the development of school curriculum. The following cases are often referenced in discussions of school planning:

Equality and Opportunity: *Brown v. Topeka* **(1954).** Struck down the concept of "separate but equal" and ushered in school integration efforts.

Taxation: *Kalamazoo v. State of Michigan* **(1874).** Extended taxation upward from the elementary to include taxation for secondary education.

Per Pupil Expenditure: *San Antonio v. Rodriguez* **(1973).** Guaranteed a minimum educational finance platform through equalization formula.

Freedom of Expression: *Tinker v. Des Moines* **(1969).** Guarantees students the constitutional right of freedom of speech in schools.

Flag Salute: *West Virginia v. Barnett* **(1943).** Students (and teachers) may not be forced to salute the U.S. flag.

Prayer in School: *Lee v. Weisman* **(1992)** and *Santa Fe v. Doe* **(2000).** Prayer at school events violates the First Amendment rights of students.

Language in School: *Lau v. Nichols* **(1974).** School districts must take affirmative steps to rectify language deficiencies in students.

AIDS: *School Board v. Arline* **(1987).** Prohibits discrimination based on disability. In this case, the court ordered the accommodation rather than segregation of a student with AIDS.

IDEA: *Board of Education v. Rowley* **(1982).** Schools must follow the mandated procedural requirements of the Individuals with Disabilities Education Act.

Disruptive Students: *Honig v. Doe* **(1988).** Supports the notion that a ten-day suspension of an exceptional student violated the rights of placement under IDEA.

Expulsions: *Goss v. Lopez* **(1975).** Guarantees due process under the Fourteenth Amendment for students facing disciplinary actions, such as suspensions.

Corporal Punishment: *Ingraham v. Wright* **(1977).** Students may sue schools for obvious cruel and unusual punishment during disciplinary applications.

Student Searches: *New Jersey v. Tico* **(1985).** School officials may search a student if reasonable suspicion exists (lower than "probable cause" as defined by the Fourth Amendment).

Sexual Harassment: *Franklin v. Gwinett* **(1992)** and *Davis v. Monroe* **(1999).** Students are protected by Title IX of the educational amendments and students may sue if there is employee-to-student or peer-to-peer harassment that is allowed to go uncorrected.

PARADIGMS AND CONCEPTUAL MODELS

Curriculum leaders tend to use various paradigms and models to represent an understanding or set of assumptions of how things work. Although they are usually not supported by research, such models, nonetheless, are valuable in explaining and preparing curricula. Piaget's model of cognitive development, for example, is inferred from the observation of children but is not a research-based construct. Nonetheless, it has guided educators for a quarter of a century in thinking about how children learn. Such models can be thought of as a working hypothesis. Following are the paradigms and models most often referenced by curriculum persons.

The Managerial Grid (Blake and Mouton, 1964)

Robert Blake and Jane Mouton suggest that leadership is a function of four complex variables that can be graphed as a "style." This model has utility to curriculum planners because it provides a "cause-and-effect" hypothesis about why curriculum change does or does not happen in a school setting. Leaders who hold a particular style, when matched with an organization that has a set of needs, seem to be more successful in bringing about changes. Using this construct, the relationships between leaders and organizations can be studied. (See Figure 2.8.)

Taxonomy of Educational Objectives: Cognitive Domain (Bloom, 1956)

In 1956 Benjamin Bloom developed the first of three taxonomies or hierarchies dealing with educational objectives. The other two, the Affective Domain by David Krathwohl (1964) and the Psychomotor Domain by Harrow (1972), are also presented for the reader's review. These taxonomies help curriculum planners "target" the meaning of experiences and the measuring of educational outcomes.

When teachers deliver a curriculum, there are many possible outcomes. As the reader has seen in the definitions section in Chapter One, the teacher could be delivering a planned curriculum, an experience, or a curriculum based on specific outcomes. The taxonomies differentiate the cognitive level (or affective/psychomotor) that is expected of the student because of what the teacher taught. (See Figures 2.9 through 2.11.)

Stages of Growth in Adults (Erikson, 1963)

Erik Erikson has developed a four-tier conception of adult development useful to curriculum planners in formulating staff development and learning strategies. (See Figure 2.12.)

Characteristics of Multiple Intelligences (Gardner, 1990)

Howard Gardner has provided ideas about seven unique kinds of intelligence that might be found in schools. Most recently (1998) he has suggested that even more

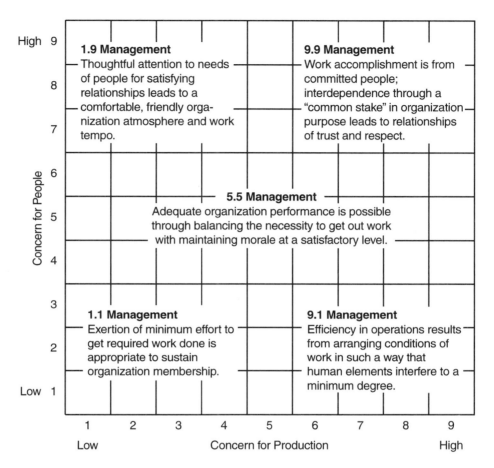

FIGURE 2.8   The Leadership Grid

kinds of intelligence may be present (eight and even nine types). This model is useful to curriculum developers because for years the basic assumption in American education was that intelligence was a mental capacity. If, as Gardner suggests, there are many kinds of intelligence, then learning programs and their evaluation can be diversified to meet the individual differences of students. The impact on an area such as school testing would be profound. This model definitely stretches professional thinking about teaching and learning. (See Figure 2.13.)

Dimensions of Individualized Instruction (Gibbons, 1971)

Thirteen dimensions of individualizing instruction are provided in this early 1970s model by Maurice Gibbons. The classification suggests ways in which the

FIGURE 2.9   Bloom's Taxonomy—Cognitive Domain

Knowledge (ability to recall; to bring to mind the appropriate material)	Comprehension (ability to comprehend what is being communicated and make use of the idea without relating it to other ideas or material or seeing fullest meaning)	Application (ability to use ideas, principles, theories in new particular and concentrated situations)	Analysis (ability to break down a communication into constituent parts in order to make organization of the whole clear)	Synthesis (ability to put together parts and elements into a unified organization or whole)	Evaluation (ability to judge the value of ideas, procedures, methods, using appropriate criteria)
					Requires synthesis
				Requires analysis	Requires analysis
			Requires application	Requires application	Requires application
		Requires comprehension	Requires comprehension	Requires comprehension	Requires comprehension
	Requires knowledge	Requires knowledge	Requires knowledge	Requires knowledge	Requires knowledge

Source: From *Taxonomy of Educational Objectives, Book 2: Affective Domain* by David R. Krathwohl, Benjamin S. Bloom, and Bertram B. Masia. Published by Allyn and Bacon, Boston, MA. Copyright © 1984 by Pearson Education. Reprinted by permission of the publisher.

curriculum can be adjusted to accomodate learner differences. For more than a third of a century the Gibbons model has suggested different variables that make up individualization. Developed in a time when educators were seeking to adjust a set curriculum to a diverse student population, the model structured "categories" such as "pace" and "method" for design work. (See Figure 2.14.)

Developmental Tasks (Havighurst, 1972)

For curriculum designers, the task of "targeting" the curriculum to meet the developmental needs of learners has been aided by this global depiction of human development tasks. Havighurst has provided a conception of the order and scope of tasks required to grow and develop into a healthy adult. Applying this model to the various stages of growth has led educators to think of the organization of a school as a four-tier model (early childhood, late childhood, preadolescence, and adolescence) as opposed to the old three-tier model (elementary school, junior high school, and high school). (See Figure 2.15.)

FIGURE 2.10   Taxonomy of the Affective Domain

		Valuing (accepts worth of a thing, an idea, or a behavior; prefers it; consistent in responding; develops a commitment to it)	**Organization** (organizes values; determines interrelationships; adapts behavior to value system)	**Characterization** (generalizes certain values into controlling tendencies; emphasis on internal consistency; later integrates these into a total philosophy of life or world view)
	Responding (makes response at first with compliance, later willingly and with satisfaction)		Requires organization of values	
			Requires development of values	Requires development of values
Receiving (attending; becomes aware of an idea, process, or thing; is willing to notice a particular phenomenon)		Requires a response	Requires a response	Requires a response
	Begins with attending	Begins with attending	Begins with attending	Begins with attending

Source: From *Taxonomy of Educational Objectives, Book 2: Affective Domain* by David R. Krathwohl, Benjamin S. Bloom, and Bertram B. Masia. Published by Allyn and Bacon, Boston, MA. Copyright © 1984 by Pearson Education. Reprinted by permission of the publisher.

Motivation–Hygiene Model (Herzberg, 1967)

Frederick Herzberg, a management theorist, has provided educators with a model of motivation that seeks to explain how rewards activate behavior. His model of lower and higher motivational factors seems perfectly suited to the world of the classroom teacher who receives more intrinsic benefits than extrinsic rewards. According to this model, extrinsic rewards (such as salary) do not really satisfy individuals but merely cleanse (hygiene) the dissatisfaction. What truly motivates individuals, says Herzberg, are factors such as interesting work, responsibility, and the possibility of achievement. (See Figure 2.16.)

FIGURE 2.11   Taxonomy of the Psychomotor Domain

Observing	Imitating	Practicing	Adapting
			Adapting (makes individual modifications and adaptations in the process to suit the worker and/or the situation)
		Practicing (repeats steps until some or all aspects of process become habitual, requiring little conscious effort, performs smoothly)	
	Imitating (follows directions; carries out steps with conscious awareness of efforts, performs hesitantly)		Requires practice
Observing (watches process; pays attention to steps or techniques and to finished product or behavior; may read directions)		Requires imitation	Requires imitation
	Requires observation, or reading of directions	Requires observation, or reading of directions	Requires observation, or reading of directions

Source: From *Taxonomy of Educational Objectives, Book 2: Affective Domain* by David R. Krathwohl, Benjamin S. Bloom, and Bertram B. Masia. Published by Allyn and Bacon, Boston, MA. Copyright © 1984 by Pearson Education. Reprinted by permission of the publisher.

FIGURE 2.12   Stages of Growth in Adults

Stage 1	Role Identity—seeking to emerge from the role confusion of adolescence by projecting ideas and roles found acceptable by other adults.
Stage 2	Intimacy—sharing oneself by commiting to ongoing relationships rather than remaining isolated. Self-absorbtion declines.
Stage 3	Generativity—a period of creativity and assistance to the next generation. A need for personal renewal (not stagnation) drives the individual forward.
Stage 4	Ego Integrity—self-acceptance and a commitment to lifestyle as an adult. A period of personal dignity.

Source: Adapted from *Childhood and Society* by Erik H. Erikson. Copyright 1950, © 1963 by W. W. Norton & Company, Inc., renewed © 1978, 1991 by Erik Erikson.

Developmentally Appropriate Practice (Elkind, 1995)

David Elkind has contrasted developmental and psychometric learning as two points of origin in planning school programs. Psychometric designs see the child's abilities as measurable. The goal of education is to produce children who score high on achievement tests. The developmental approach sees the learner as having developmental abilities and different rates of intellectual growth. For the developmental psychologist, learning is a process.

FIGURE 2.13   Gardner's Multiple Intelligences

Type of Intelligence	Learns Best By
Linguistic	Saying, hearing, and seeing words
Logical/Math	Categorize, classify, reason
Spatial	Visualize, sense, imagine, build
Musical	Use of rhythm, musical memory
Kinesthetic (body)	Touch, movement, use of senses
Interpersonal	Communicating, sharing, cooperating
Intrapersonal	Work alone, follow instincts

Source: Adapted from Howard Gardner, *Frames of Mind,* 2nd ed. (New York: Basic Books, 1994).

FIGURE 2.14   Gibbons's Dimensions of Individualized Instruction

1. *Attendance*	Optional	School not class	Class not subgroup	Mandatory
2. *Materials for study*	Individual choice	Individual prescribed	Subgroup prescribed or discussed	Class/grade prescribed
3. *Method of studying materials*	Individual choice	Individual prescribed	Subgroup prescribed or discussed	Class/grade prescribed
4. *Pace of study*	Individual choice	Individual prescribed	Subgroup prescribed or discussed	Class/grade prescribed
5. *Activity*	Individual choice	Individual prescribed	Subgroup prescribed or discussed	Class/grade prescribed
6. *Decision making*	Student (permissive)	Student and teacher (responsive)	Teacher (active)	Administrative authority
7. *Teaching focus*	Values	Processes	Skill concepts	Content
8. *Teaching function*	Teacher available	Teacher guides	Teacher presents	Teacher directs
9. *Teaching method*	Unspecified discovery (permissive)	Guided discovery (problem solving)	Explanation and discussion	Drill exercise repetition
10. *Environment*	Community	School	Classroom or resource area	Desk
11. *Time structure*	Nonstructured	Fluid	Structured nonstructured	Structured
12. *Evaluation*	Student self-evaluation	Broad assessment	Quantity of work	Exam-class rank
13. *Purposes of program*	Continuous development to maturity	Adjustment	Understanding	Efficient mastery

Source: Reprinted by permission of the publisher from M. Gibbons, *Individualized Instruction: A Descriptive Analysis* (New York: Teachers College Press, © 1971 by Teachers College, Columbia University. All rights reserved.), p. 32.

FIGURE 2.15   Havighurst's Developmental Tasks

Early Childhood
Developing motor control
Emerging self-awareness
Mapping out surroundings
Assigning meaning to events
Exploring relationships with others
Developing language and thought patterns

Middle Childhood
Structuring the physical world
Refining language and thought patterns
Establishing relationships with others
Understanding sex roles

Late Childhood
Mastering communication skills
Building meaningful peer relations
Thinking independently
Acceptance of self
Finding constructive expression outlets
Role projection

Preadolescence
Handling major body changes
Asserting independence from family
Establishing sex-role identity
Dealing with peer group relationships
Controlling emotions
Constructing a values foundation
Pursuing interest expression
Utilizing new reasoning capacities
Developing acceptable self-concept

Adolescence
Emancipation from parent dependency
Occupational projection selection
Completion of value structure
Acceptance of self

Source: Adapted from Robert J. Havighurst, *Developmental Tasks and Education,* 3rd ed. (New York: McKay, 1972).

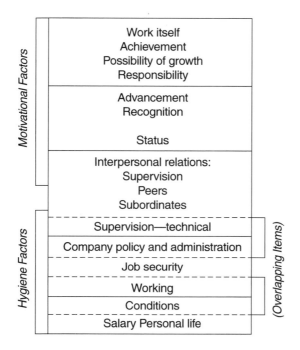

**FIGURE 2.16   Herzberg's Motivation–
Hygiene Model**

Source: From Keith Davis, *Human Relations at Work,* 3rd
ed., p. 37. Copyright © 1967 by the McGraw-Hill Companies, New York. Used by permission of the McGraw-Hill
Companies.

FIGURE 2.17   Jung's Learning Styles Model

Typology	Learning Problems If
Thinker (logical)	Must learn concept before knowing the parts
	Has to operate in disorderly environment
Intuitor (conceptual)	Not given time to process
Feeler (interactive)	Not allowed to talk
	Impersonal delivery system
Sensor (concrete)	Asked to memorize
	Asked to extend attention span

Source: Adapted from Carl Jung, *Psychological Types* (New York: Harcourt, Brace, 1921).

Developmentally Appropriate Practice refers to curriculum that is tailored to meet the students' needs at their own particular stage and rate of development. Children, not assessments, are the basic material of education.

Personality and Learning Style Typology (Jung, 1921)

Carl Jung (pronounced Young) hypothesized about learning preferences and learning styles more than seventy-five years ago. His model, shown in adapted form in Figure 2.17, is the basis for many of the well-known learning style instruments, such as the Dunn and Dunn, Hansen and Silver, and Myers-Briggs inventories.

In the twenty-first century, with the aid of computers, it is probable that educators will deliver highly individualized educational programs to students after assessing their learning preferences. This model by Jung structures the way we currently think about this relationship. (See Figure 2.17.)

Stages of Moral Development (Kohlberg, 1970)

Lawrence Kohlberg has provided a model of how he believes morality is developed in children, starting with the lowest level (obedience and punishment) and ascending to an all-time ethical orientation. Educators can use such a model in thinking about school discipline and the purpose of social instruction in school. (See Figure 2.18.)

Ice Cube Change Model (Lewin [Levin], 1951)

One of the difficult questions for curriculum planners concerns the nature of change in organizations. Although many models show how this occurs, one of the simplest and most compelling was provided by Kurt Lewin (Levin, a persecuted Jew, changed his name after coming to America following World War II). Lewin saw change as an alteration in the form of the organization. Without reformation,

FIGURE 2.18 Kohlberg's Moral Development Model

1. Obedience and punishment orientation—avoids punishment and "bad" label

2. Naive instrumental hedonism—orientation to egalitarianism and exchange

3. Interpersonal concordance—"good boy" orientation, seeking approval

4. Authority and social order orientation—social order maintenance

5. Contractual legalistic orientation—avoidance of violation of majority will

6. Universal ethical orientation—respect for all human rights

Source: Adapted from Moshe M. Blatt and Lawrence Kohlberg, "The Effects of Classroom Moral Discussion upon Children's Level of Moral Judgment," in Bill Puka (ed.), *Fundamental Research in Moral Development* (New York: Garland Publishing, 1994), pp. 129–130.

he said, the new ways of working will not fit the old structure. He used the analogy of the ice cube to explain how this change happens. (See Figure 2.19.)

Organizational Climate (Litwin and Stringer, 1968)

For George Litwin and Robert Stringer, the motivation of any person in an organization results from the interaction of that person with certain factors common to all organizations. Based on research in a variety of organizations (schools, businesses, hospitals), they hypothesized that nine critical variables could be studied and, more importantly, manipulated by leaders. These nine variables, defined in Figure 2.20, construct a climate that they define as a subjective and group "feeling."

Litwin and Stringer hypothesized that various combinations of these nine things, in varying degrees, would create different "climates." Further, they felt that each climate (achievement, affiliation, and power) would activate the "needs" of some persons within that organization. For example, people with power needs (to control) would be drawn to "power tasks" within the organization. If that pattern of variables were emphasized by leadership, an "organizational climate" could be developed (an achieving organization, a friendly or affiliative organization, an aggressive and competitive organization). An example of their research findings is summarized in Figure 2.20 and more fully discussed in Chapter 4. This work is of special value to curriculum designers in thinking about the mix of variables in schools. (See Figure 2.20.)

Motivation—Needs Hierarchy Model (Maslow, 1955)

If there is one model that all those working in curriculum know, it is Maslow's hierarchy. Abraham Maslow was the first to suggest that the needs of an individual are "ordered" according to a prepotency: physiological needs (lowest), safety needs, social needs, ego or status needs, and self-fulfillment needs (highest). Maslow believed that the individual will do whatever is necessary to achieve or "satisfy" a need, and when that need is met the individual will seek to satisfy a higher need.

School planners use the hierarchy to develop student motivation as well as to speak of things that satisfy or engage teacher motivation. (See Figure 2.21.)

FIGURE 2.19   Lewin's "Ice Cube" Change Model

Stage One	Unfreezing. The way of doing things is broken down or dismantled.
Stage Two	Reformation. The way of working is redesigned within the organization fabric to become more efficient.
Stage Three	Refreeze. The new procedure is institutionalized or given official status as policy or procedure.

FIGURE 2.20   Litwin and Stringer's Climate Variables

1. Structure—the feeling that employees have about the constraints in the group, how many rules, regulations, procedures there are; is there an emphasis on "red tape" and going through channels, or is there a loose and informal atmosphere?

2. Responsibility—the feeling of being your own boss; not having to double-check all your decisions; when you have a job to do, knowing that it is your job.

3. Reward—the feeling of being rewarded for a job well done; emphasizing positive rewards rather than punishments; the perceived fairness of the pay and promotion policies.

4. Risk—the sense of riskiness and challenge in the job and in the organization; is there an emphasis on taking calculated risks, or is playing it safe the best way to operate?

5. Warmth—the feeling of general good fellowship that prevails in the work group atmosphere: the emphasis on being well-liked; the prevalence of friendly and informal social groups.

6. Support—the perceived helpfulness of the managers and employees in the group: emphasis on mutual support from above and below.

7. Standards—the perceived importance of implicit and explicit goals and performance standards; the emphasis on doing a good job; the challenge represented in personal and group goals.

8. Conflict—the feeling that managers and other workers want to hear different opinions: the emphasis placed on getting problems out in the open, rather than smoothing them over or ignoring them.

9. Identity—the feeling that you belong to a company and you are a valuable member of a working team; the importance placed on this kind of spirit.

Application Example

*Summary of Hypotheses and Preliminary Evidence Regarding
the Relationship of Climate Dimensions and Achievement Motivation*

Climate Dimension	Hypothesized Effect on Achievement Motivation	Findings	Hypothesis Support	Revised Hypothesis
Structure	reduction	mixed	moderate	—
Responsibility	arousal	consistent positive	weak-moderate	—
Warmth	no effect	some negative	moderate	—
Support	arousal	positive	moderate	—
Reward	arousal	consistent positive	strong	—
Conflict	arousal	mixed	very weak	arousal
Standards	arousal	mixed	weak	—
Identity	no effect	negative	none	
Risk	arousal	some positive	weak-moderate	

Source: Adapted and reprinted by permission of Harvard Business School Press from George H. Litwin and Robert A. Stringer, Jr., *Motivation and Organizational Climate* (Boston: Division of Research, Harvard Business School, 1968), p. 100. Copyright © 1968 by the Harvard Business School Publishing Corporation; all rights reserved.

FIGURE 2.21   Maslow's Needs Hierarchy Model

Self-realization and fulfillment

Esteem and status

Belonging and social activity

Safety and security

Physiological needs

Source: Adapted from *Motivation and Personality,* 3rd ed., by Abraham Maslow. Copyright 1954, 1987 by Harper & Row, Publishers Inc.

Theory X and Theory Y Management (McGregor, 1957)

Douglas McGregor provides educators with a contrasting set of management styles based on the assumption the leader makes about those being led. McGregor believed that these assumptions could force a self-fulfilling prophecy. (See Figure 2.22.)

Theory of Intellectual Development (Piaget, 1920)

Early in the twentieth century, the Swiss educator Jean Piaget developed a theory about how cognitive development occurs in children. His work was discovered by American educators (writings of Flavell) in the 1960s about the time when early childhood education was established. For a period, Piaget's work was almost a dogma and is still considered the best single model of how such development might occur. Based on this model, most curriculum programs see intellectual development as a "staged" rather than a less linear development. (See Figure 2.23.)

Curriculum Cycle (Tyler, 1949)

In 1949 Ralph Tyler of the University of Chicago wrote his short text, *Principles of Curriculum and Instruction,* in which he identified four fundamental questions in planning curriculum: (1) What educational purposes should the school seek to attain? (2) What educational experiences can be provided to attain these purposes? (3) How can these educational experiences be effectively organized? (4) How can we determine whether these purposes are attained?

The first three of these questions had been asked since the time of John Dewey (turn of the twentieth century), but the fourth question suggested a "feedback loop." Tyler is credited with ushering in an era of evaluation in modern education and although Tyler never used the illustration shown in Figure 2.24, curriculum designers refer to the Tyler "cycle" when speaking of the curriculum planning cycle of analyze, design, implement, and evaluate.

FIGURE 2.22   Assumptions Underlying McGregor's Theory X and Theory Y Management Styles

Traditional (X)	Potential (Y)
1. People are naturally lazy; they prefer to do nothing.	People are naturally active; they set goals and enjoy striving.
2. People work mostly for money and status rewards.	People seek many satisfactions in work: pride in achievement; enjoyment of process; sense of contribution; pleasure in association; stimulation of new challenges, etc.
3. The main force keeping people productive in their work is fear of being demoted or fired.	The main force keeping people productive in their work is desire to achieve their personal and social goals.
4. People remain children grown larger; they are naturally dependent on leaders.	People normally mature beyond childhood; they aspire to independence, self-fulfillment, responsibility.
5. People expect and depend on direction from above; they do not want to think for themselves.	People close to the situation see and feel what is needed and are capable of self-action.
6. People need to be told, shown, and trained in proper methods of work.	People who understand and care about what they are doing can devise and improve their own methods of doing work.
7. People need superiors who will watch them closely enough to be able to praise good work and reprimand errors.	People need a sense that they are respected as capable of assuming responsibility and self-correction.
8. People have little concern beyond their immediate, material interests.	People seek to give meaning to their lives by identifying with nations, communities, churches, unions, companies, causes.
9. People need specific instruction on what to do and how to do it; larger policy issues are none of their business.	People need ever-increasing understanding; they need to grasp the meaning of the activities in which they are engaged; they have cognitive hunger as extensive as the universe.
10. People appreciate being treated with courtesy.	People crave genuine respect from their fellow men.
11. People are naturally compartmentalized; work demands are entirely different from leisure activities.	People are naturally integrated; when work and play are too sharply separated both deteriorate; "The only reason a wise man can give for preferring leisure to work is the better quality of the work he can do during leisure."
12. People naturally resist change; they prefer to stay in the old ruts.	People naturally tire of monotonous routine and enjoy new experiences; in some degree everyone is creative.
13. Jobs are primary and must be done; people are selected, trained, and fitted to predefined jobs.	People are primary and seek self-realization; jobs must be designed, modified, and fitted to people.
14. People are formed by heredity, childhood, and youth; as adults they remain static; old dogs don't learn new tricks.	People constantly grow; it is never too late to learn; they enjoy learning and increasing their understanding and capability.
15. People need to be "inspired" (pep talk) or pushed or driven.	People need to be released and encouraged and assisted.

Source: From Douglas McGregor, *The Human Side of Enterprise* (New York: McGraw-Hill, 1961). Used by permission of the McGraw-Hill Companies.

FIGURE 2.23   Piaget's Model of Intellectual Development

Age 0–2	Sensorimotor stage	Trial-and-error learning based on organized motor activity
Age 2–7	Preoperational stage	Use of symbols to represent objects
		Development of language and use of dramatic play
Age 7–11	Concrete operations	Use of concepts, logical thinking
Age 11–15	Formal operations	Use of abstract as well as concrete thinking

Source: Adapted from Eli Ginsburg and Robert Opper, *Piaget's Theory of Intellectual Development,* 3rd ed. (Upper Saddle River, NJ: Prentice-Hall, 1988).

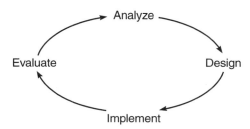

FIGURE 2.24   Tyler's Curriculum Cycle

Source: Adapted from Ralph W. Tyler, *Basic Principles of Curriculum and Instruction* (Chicago: University of Chicago Press, 1949).

THE RESEARCH BASE

A major resource for curriculum planners of the past thirty years has been the emerging research base in professional education. Focused primarily on instruction, this knowledge base is directly tied to curriculum through philosophy and purpose. Curriculum planners can use research knowledge to connect curriculum and instruction by designing more consistent and productive school programs.

Most educational research prior to 1970 is of limited value because it is both scanty and subject to procedural flaws. With the onset of federal funding for education, and the emergence of computers for data treatment (about 1970), research has proved more reliable. From 1970 to the present, research has been engaged in a long and sometimes frustrating process of "filling in" the gaps in our knowledge of teaching and learning. Although we do not yet possess a predictive database for designing school programs, we have become aware that combinations of instructional variables can lead to certain patterns of learning. This clarity in prescription means that curriculum intentions can be more accurately fulfilled using this knowledge.

The meta-analyses of the late 1980s and 1990s allow us to see more clearly how such combinations of instructional variables might form an instructional design to implement curricular priorities. Said another way, we are approaching a time in curriculum when we can build or "tailor" instruction for philosophical purposes.

This new era of "collected" knowledge can be said to have begun in 1969 with Barak Rosenshine and Norma Furst's review of previous research. Examining only those studies that focused on teacher variables and student gains in cognitive achievement, these researchers identified eleven areas that held promise for further study:

1. Clarity and teacher organization
2. Variation in activities, materials, and media
3. Enthusiasm of the teacher
4. Task orientation and academic focus
5. Student opportunity to learn (understanding of the task)
6. Use of student ideas in class
7. Justified criticism during instruction (later praise as well)
8. Use of structuring comments
9. Questions (high and low) appropriate to cognitive level
10. Probing or encouraging questions that allow student elaboration
11. Challenging instructional materials[1]

These early process–product and ethnographic (anthropological) studies sought to "prove" cause and effect in the classroom by isolating variables that could be manipulated by researchers:

> *The researcher is concerned with the discovery and building of principles—lawful relationships with a high degree of generalizability over several instances of class of problems—he seeks to understand the basic forces that interact whenever there is teaching and learning.*[2]

Although early studies seemed to reinforce a more structured kind of teaching, it soon became apparent that the outcome (standardized achievement gains in basic subjects) was highlighting some procedures at the expense of others. Eventually, these numerous research studies began to find that some techniques were effective under certain conditions and revealed teaching as the "multidimensional" act that it is:

> *These findings suggest that an intermediate amount of different kinds of teacher behavior are best for a particular goal and a particular group of pupils, but they don't begin to answer the question of the classroom teacher—how much a certain behavior is best for which goal for which pupil? What we have so far is an organizing principle (certain behaviors are functional for certain pupils with certain tasks) which can be used by the teacher and the researcher to begin thinking about effective teaching; we do not have specific answers for the teacher's question.*[3]

By 1976 a clear connection between means (teaching) and ends (the curriculum) had been established:

> *The practical object of research on teaching is to describe teaching effectiveness. This requires that we state a desired effect—a desired change in children—and the actions which produce it.*[4]

Teacher effectiveness research done in the 1980s showed more clearly the "patterns" of reinforcing variables and outcomes. Educational philosophies were supportive of either "high structure" in the classroom (perennialism, idealism, or realism) or of a greater flexibility and student-centeredness (experimentalism and existentialism). Given these orientations, and the accompanying goals and objectives, certain instructional patterns "reinforced" certain kinds of learning. In this manner, curriculum, as a design for learning, had reinforced instructional patterns that could be uncovered by research.

McNeil and Wiles identified three stereotypic patterns of instruction labeled direct, indirect, and self-directed and suggested that learning experiences could be designed based on existing research. A direct teacher, conveying subject matter, will be supported by on-task routines, structured comments, and questions; directional note-taking outlines; reinforcing testing procedures; and strict discipline to focus student behavior. By contrast, the indirect teacher will invest time in discovering student needs and previous knowledge and will be generally more flexible in the manipulation of classroom variables.[5]

From this conceptualization of curriculum and instruction, the instructional effectiveness is determined by the purpose of the curriculum. Curriculum planners must know the research on "what works" in order to prescribe and ensure a desired form of learning. The teacher may be the "final filter" for the curriculum, but the curriculum planner (through standards, goals, in-service training, and prescription of materials) can guide the teacher.

What follows is a summary of some of the critical areas of research that have accumulated over the past thirty years that could guide curriculum development in the coming decades. Both primary and recent source references are provided for the reader's further inquiry.

Research Summaries

Before Schooling (Presage Variables)

Schooling is a social experience in America and, all things being equal, the higher the socioeconomic status of the family the greater the educational achievement of the child.[6]

The social components that detract from or contribute to a child's success in school include social status, language abilities, level of parent education, and the parental involvement in a child's schooling. Improvement in any of these conditions will generally improve school performance.[7]

The Carnegie Foundation for the Advancement of Teaching identifies the following demographic problems impacting families:

> *Sixty percent of today's students live in families where both parents work. By 1995 two-thirds of all preschool children, and three out of four school-aged youngsters, will have mothers in the labor force. Nearly half of all white children live with a divorced mother, and an even higher percentage of black children live with a mother who was never married. For Hispanics, the latter proportion is one in three. Households headed by women have an average income of less than $12,000 per year. For many students, schools, for all practical purposes, are the family.*[8]

Family and parenting before school provide skills that are prerequisite for school success. Orientations to task structure, authority, time, standards, groups, and rewards are often taught in the home. Experience and language are formative in the preschool years, contributing to student readiness. It has been found that the planning and goal setting a parent does with a child influences school success more than parental participation (volunteer work).[9] However, parental involvement in general is associated with academic achievement, better attendance, reduced dropout rates, decreased delinquency, and fewer pregnancies while in school.[10]

In school, children of single-parent families were found to exhibit a number of significant personality differences including low self-esteem, low achievement motivation, poor peer relations, and high anxiety. Such children also were more likely to become juvenile delinquents, use drugs and alcohol at school, drop out, and become pregnant.[11] A study by the National Association of Elementary School Principals ($N = 18,000$) documented that such children will earn lower grades and account for 38 percent of all Ds and Fs given in school.[12]

Language and social maturity seem to be especially important presage variables. Of pressing importance are the 2.6 million non-English-speaking students in our public schools. Language and thought are linked, and linguistic confusion (nonmastery of bilingual instruction) is widespread. For English-speaking students, it has been documented that the dependence on verbal performance in the early years may be giving educators a false view of student capacity.[13] Finally, social immaturity (summer children) in the lower elementary grades is positively connected by research with retention, psychological referrals, placement in compensatory programs, and youth suicides.[14]

Finally, as a major preschool variable, research has identified home television as important. The average three to four year old in America watches television two to four hours per day, with boys watching significantly more than girls. Among other things, this medium seems to impact cognitive processing, attention span, intellectual symbol systems and, without question, the behavior of small children.[15]

Suggested Readings

Davidson, N., "Life without Father: America's Greatest Social Catastrophe," *Policy Review*, 51 (1990), 40–44.

Epstein, J., "Longitudinal Effects of Family–School Interaction on Student Outcomes," in A. Kerchoff (ed), *Research in Sociology of Education,* 59, No. 3 (1986), 171–189.

Guralnick, M., "The Next Decade of Research on the Effectiveness of Early Intervention," *Exceptional Children,* 58, No. 2. (1991), 174–181.

Havighurst, R., *Growing Up in River City* (New York: John Wiley & Sons, 1962).

Huston, A., "Development of Television Viewing Patterns in Early Childhood: A Longitudinal Investigation," *Developmental Psychology,* 26 (May 1990), 409–420.

McCartney, D., "Parallels between Research on Child Care and Research on School Effects," *Educational Researcher,* 19 (1990), 21–27.

Milne, A., "Single Parents, Working Mothers, and the Educational Achievement of School Children," *Sociology of Education,* 59 (14 July 1986), 139.

Schweinhart, L., "Significant Benefits: The High/Scope Perry Preschool Study," *Educational Research Foundation,* Ypsilanti, MI, 1993.

Compensatory Programs

It has been suggested by one set of researchers that the home has at least as much influence on student learning and behavior as do the teacher and the school.[16] If this is true, and if so many children enter school without parental support, then the school is faced with a choice between gross unfairness or a massive effort to compensate for such deficiency. Since 1965 public schools have operated programs (Comp Ed) to address this problem. Officially defined, compensatory programs seek to remedy deficiencies in disadvantaged students' backgrounds by providing specific curricula designed to make up whatever is lacking.

Although there is no evidence of long-term intellectual or cognitive gain resulting from these programs, there is substantial evidence that such programs work as long as resources are applied. Students in such programs evidence more academic motivation, are less likely to drop out of school, are less likely to be involved in acts of delinquency, and are less likely to go on welfare as adults. The Council on Economic Development estimates that for every dollar spent on such programs, seven dollars are saved down the road in higher tax distributions and lower expenditures for remedial education, welfare, and criminal justice programs.[17]

It is clear that these "extra services to low-achieving and economically disadvantaged students" must be maintained over time to be effective. It is true that the earlier these programs are begun, the greater the impact on achievement.[18] It is also clear that the cost of these programs cannot be directly related to student achievement gains.[19]

The kinds of compensatory programs vary with the populations served. The best known and longest running program is Head Start, a program for preschoolers. Heavily researched in the 1970s and 1980s, Head Start has been found to promote industry, initiative, dependability, social control, better reading and math skills, and a greater likelihood of promotion. A 1985 follow-up study of Head Start found that those attending were more likely to graduate from high school and less likely to be placed in special education classes.[20] Although research on this program has been challenged, no one disagrees with the idea that effects of the program evaporate rapidly when withdrawn. For this reason, some districts have a booster program called Follow Through.

A second major compensatory program in public schools is Chapter One or Title One (depending on the funding cycles and legislation renewal language). This program has served more than five million children in forty-five states at a cost in excess of $5 billion. Most recently, Chapter One has adopted a "whole school" approach rather than an "identified student" approach making it increasingly a supplement for low-income schools.

Ranging up to the eighth grade in some school districts, Chapter One uses five strategies to provide services to students: in-class assistance, pull-out programs, add-ons, replacement models, and school wide treatments. The pull-out model is shown by research to be most effective, but it is also the most disruptive pattern for the teacher and nonprogram students. The cost of this program has not been correlated with student achievement gains.[21]

A third major kind of compensatory program in public schools is provided for language-deficient children under such titles as English as a Second Language (ESL) and English for Speakers of Other Languages (ESOL). All of these programs are rationalized by the *Lau v. Nichols* U.S. Supreme Court decision that found that "it is the responsibility of schools to take action so that non-English speaking students have equal access to educational opportunity."

Research supports the idea that most language acquisition is accomplished prior to puberty (elementary school). It has also been found that speaking does not necessarily lead to language acquisition. Finally, it has been found that children who know one language well can more easily learn a second language.[22]

Ironically, the most common compensatory design, the immersion model, is shown by research to promote the least achievement. The very worst possibility, quite common, is to place a non-English-speaking student more than twelve years old and with poor language skills in his or her native language in a regular classroom.[23]

Suggested Readings

Crawford, J., *Bilingual Education: History, Politics, Theory and Practice*, 2nd ed. (Newark, NJ: Crane Publishing, 1991).

Hubbell, R., *A Review of Head Start Research Since 1970* (Washington, DC: U.S. Department of Health and Human Services, 1985).

Slavin, R., Karweit, N., and Madden, N., *Effective Programs for Students At-Risk* (Boston: Allyn & Bacon, 1989).

The Learning Environment

One of the near constants in American education has been the idea that schooling occurs in a building in which youth are congregated. This group instruction approach may wither in the twenty-first century with the availability of direct access to knowledge, epitomized by the Internet, but for the moment curriculum leaders need to understand the impact of environment on learning. Public school students spend about 1260 hours per year (15,000 total hours) in classrooms, and this space impacts the psychology, emotion, and even the physiology of learning.

Research has been conducted in great depth on the effects of space, light, noise, temperature, humidity levels, and color on student learning. Perhaps the most important lesson is that in the standard thirty- by twenty-eight-foot public school classroom, each student is allocated about nine square feet (three feet by three feet) of personal space. This space is akin to the amount of space provided for a short duration event, such as a call from a phone booth, not a six hour and fifteen minute instructional day.

The second most important research for planning instruction is the finding that the distance between speaker and listener determines the meaning of communication. Edward Hall has conceptualized these distances in terms of public (twelve plus feet), social (eight to twelve feet), personal (four to eight feet), near intimate (one to four feet), and intimate (zero to one foot). Because most classrooms are set up in a theater style (90 percent), the teacher is at a noncommittal social or public distance from most students.[24] Teacher interaction with students is limited to those within an "action zone" of the first two rows.[25] Seating patterns, whether rows, circles, or tables, will determine which students will communicate in a classroom.[26]

The ambience of the room is also important. Students in attractive rooms have better attitudes and work habits. Students in "ugly" rooms work faster, suffer fatigue, and evidence irritability.[27]

Suggested Readings

Bourke, S., "How Small Is Better: Some Relationships between Class Size, Teaching Practices, and Student Achievement," *American Educational Research Journal*, 23 (1986), 558–571.

Hathaway, W., *A Study into the Effects of Light on Children of Elementary School Age* (Edmonton: Alberta Department of Education, 1992). (ERIC ED 343 686)

Loo, C., "The Effects of Spatial Density on the Social Behavior of Children," *Journal of Applied Social Psychology*, 2, No. 4 (1972), 372–381.

Weinstein, C., "The Physical Environment of School: A Review of Research," *Review of Educational Research*, 49 (1979), 577–610.

Wiles, J. and Bondi, J., *Curriculum Development: A Guide to Practice*, 5th ed. (New York: Macmillan, 1998), pp. 49–75.

Selected Research Areas to Guide Curriculum Design

Over time (1970–2000), educational research has built up a body of research that provides clues about designing both curriculum programs and instruction to successfully implement those programs.

The reader should look at research in the following areas by the "weight of evidence." How much do we know? How much agreement is there among researchers in this area? If you were called to court as an educational expert, what could you say with confidence about this area of instructional planning?

In each following section, the reader is provided a summary and suggested readings for a "quick start" in learning about research in these knowledge areas.

Ability Grouping

This practice is found in 90 percent of American schools. The underlying assumption is that a student has "fixed" and measurable abilities that must be assessed and matched with appropriate teaching strategies. The practice originated in Boston public schools in 1908.

More than 1500 studies have been conducted on this practice with the vast majority advising against it. Studies fail to show academic gain or are unable to attribute such gain to the grouping process alone (influenced by such practices as smaller classes, teacher expectation, and teaching strategies). Many adverse byproducts, such as a decline in self-concept and lowered academic motivation, are documented in the lower-ability groups.

Most research in this area is concentrated on the effects of ability grouping on those in lower groups, and there is an absence of studies with high-ability students mixed in, making comparison of conditions difficult.

Suggested Readings

Hallihan, M., "The Effects of Ability Grouping in Secondary Schools," *Review of Educational Research,* 60 (1990), 501–504.

Kilik, J. and Kilik, C., "Meta-Analysis: Findings on Grouping Programs," *Gifted Child Quarterly,* 36, No. 2 (Spring 1992), 73–76.

Oakes, J., *Keeping Track: How Schools Structure Inequality* (New Haven: Yale University, 1985).

Slavin, R., "Achievement Effects of Ability Grouping in Secondary Schools: A Best Evidence Synthesis," *Review of Educational Research,* 60 (1990), 471–499.

Attribution Training

Research has documented that low achievers in school often have a condition called learned helplessness by which they attribute failure to factors beyond their control. It was found that the more successful students in school credit their personal success to internal factors, such as good study habits. Students with low motivation, by contrast, believe that effort is unrelated to outcomes.

Training such students to interpret failure as a natural stage in learning has shown promise. Specifically, the use of appropriate praise, a minimum of criticism, and giving feedback to students for effort is prescribed.

Suggested Readings

Dweck, C., "The Role of Expectations and Attributions in the Alleviation of Learned Helplessness," *Journal of Personality and Social Psychology,* 31 (1975), 674–685.

Graham, S., *Attribution Theory: Application to Achievement, Mental Health, and Interpersonal Conflict* (Hillsdale, NJ: Erlbaum and Associates, 1990).

Cooperative (Small-Group) Learning

Since the early 1970s research has accumulated on the use of small groups of mixed ability in the classroom. Most of this research is gathered under the name "cooperative learning," and this pattern suggests an alternative to the more pervasive "ability grouping" in schools. This research would include the various cooperative learning curriculum designs (student teams, games and tournaments, jigsaw learning together, and group investigation), as well as various forms of tutoring (peer, cross-age).

The majority of studies in this area have documented positive results in areas as diverse as standardized achievement test scores, improved race relations, better attendance, and smoother mainstreaming of special students. Most studies have been conducted in the lower grades, as opposed to high school, and many supply the caveat that these techniques work only under certain conditions, such as individual accountability by group members.

Critics of cooperative learning cite the emphasis on lower-level learning, an absence of success in urban environments, and the possibility that passive students could be "carried" by their peers. Overall, however, the research in this area represents one of the strongest mandates for change in public school patterns of instruction.

Suggested Readings

Battistich, V. et al., "Interactive Processes and Student Outcomes in Cooperative Learning Groups," *The Elementary School Journal*, 94, No. 1 (1993), 19–32.

Newmann, F. and Thompson, J., *Effects of Cooperative Learning on Achievement in Secondary Schools: A Summary of Research* (Madison, WI: National Center on Effective Secondary Schools, 1987).

Slavin, R., "Synthesis of Research on Cooperative Learning," *Educational Leadership* (Feb. 1991), 71–82.

Discipline

Defined as any student behavior that creates a competing vector or direction for the class, discipline has long been associated with control. The critical difference in approaches to undisciplined students is found in how much the student is involved in the process of disciplining. The range of teacher responses covers the philosophical spectrum from complete teacher control (perennial) to total student responsibility (existential).

Studies of effective and ineffective discipline activities found little difference in teacher response, but effective teachers had better preventive management strategies. Classroom climates have been found to determine teacher responses to student disruption.

By far the most widespread discipline program (assertive discipline used by more than 400,000 teachers) is no more effective than other approaches. A meta-analysis conducted in 1990 found "no significant differences" in results when this program was compared to other programs or no program at all.[28]

It does appear that certain discipline techniques work at certain levels of schooling. Lower elementary students respond to materialistic consequences, upper elementary students to social rules and norms, middle school students to peer pressure and individual responsibility, and high school students to freedoms.[29]

Suggested Readings

Cotton, K., "Schoolwide and Classroom Discipline," *School Improvement Research,* Series V (1990), 1–12.

Goldstein, W., "Group Process and School Management," in Wittrock, M. (ed.), *Handbook of Research on Teaching* (Chicago: Rand McNally, 1986), pp. 430–435.

Gender Bias

A major concern of educators in the 1980s and 1990s, gender bias in schools can and has been documented. This "inclination to give preference that interferes with an impartial judgment due to sex classification" appears to be a two-way street. Major studies have documented sex bias against boys in the elementary grades and against girls at all levels of schooling. Of chief concern is the low performance of girls on the Scholastic Aptitude Test (SAT) in upper elementary and secondary grades.

Theories of how boys overtake girls in math achievement include: (1) outright discrimination by male secondary teachers, (2) socialization patterns of females that value affiliation more than independence, (3) strong maturational growth by boys during the secondary years, and (4) the apparent belief that testosterone influences that part of the brain involved in math reasoning.[30]

Although great progress has been made in ensuring that materials are bias free and access is available to girls in all areas of school life, it appears that teacher perception and teacher behavior are the key to minimizing this fact of life in schools.

Suggested Readings

American Association of University Women, "Shortchanging Girls, Shortchanging America: A Call to Action," in *Initiative for Educational Equity,* Wellesley, MA, 1992.

Bennett, R. et al., "Influence of Behavior Perception and Gender on Teachers' Judgments of Student Academic Skills," *Journal of Educational Psychology,* 85, No. 2 (1993), 347–356.

Sadker, M. and Sadker, D., *Failing at Fairness: How America's Schools Cheat Girls* (New York: Charles Scribner, 1994).

Expectations of the Teacher

Research has demonstrated that variations in the way a teacher perceives a student determines the expectations of that student's performance and, incredibly, can predict that same performance. Studies dating back to the classic *Pygmalion in the Classroom* (1966) document that teachers act on their expectations and treat children differently, according to the teachers' perceptions, in the classroom setting.

Most studies have focused on discrimination in the case of "low" students and female students who are shown to be judged, ignored, compensated for, and disadvantaged based on teacher expectations. The validity of these expectations do not seem to affect the teacher behaviors, which include questioning, discipline, grading, grouping, and a host of other practices. Teachers have been found to reward students with the same learning style as the teacher and penalize those who have other styles. Even the measurable IQ of a student can be influenced by teacher expectation when teaching patterns are altered and intellectual growth is retarded.[31]

Suggested Readings

Good, T., "Two Decades of Research on Teacher Expectation: Findings and Future Directions," *Journal of Teacher Education,* 38 (1987), 32–47.

Rosenthal, R. and Jackson, L., *Pygmalion in the Classroom* (New York: Holt, Rinehart and Winston, 1968).

Sternberg, R., "Thinking Styles: Keys to Understanding Student Performance," *Phi Delta Kappan,* 71 (1990), 366–371.

Learning Styles

Learning styles are the mental processes and instructional settings a student uses most effectively while learning. Interest in this area is keen because of the obvious connection to more effective learning, but research is quite limited. Work in this area can be traced to the early study of Carl Jung in the 1920s which distinguished between two types of perceiving: sensation and intuition. He further hypothesized that people made decisions in two ways: logical and emotional. This work set the framework for most of today's learning style inventories.[32]

The idea of "matching student learning style with the various teaching styles" is exciting. Further, if curriculum intent is wed with teaching style (method pattern), then a connection between planning and implementing the curriculum is achieved. Unfortunately, most research in this topic area is tied to a specific instrument and therefore lacks the objectivity to document casual relationships through controlled study. Study has uncovered the type of style most often employed by different categories of students, thereby suggesting instructional approaches.[33]

Suggested Readings

Bellon, J. and Bellon, E., *Teaching from a Research Knowledge Base* (New York: Macmillan, 1992).

Titus, T., "Adolescent Learning Styles," *Journal of Research and Development in Education,* 23, No. 3 (Spring 1990), 165–170.

Use of Praise

Teachers use praise in the classroom assuming that if a pleasant consequence follows a behavior (reinforcement), that behavior is more likely to occur again in the future. Research conducted during the past thirty years does not support this widely held belief. Rather, research suggests that praise that is delivered in a certain form and at intervals can influence student behavior.

Research shows that praise in school classrooms occurs infrequently, with students experiencing such teacher approval only once or twice a day. Students for whom the teacher has high expectations receive more praise than students of low expectations. Regardless of the frequency, research suggests that certain patterns of praise work for certain students. High intelligence students and shy students may feel patronized or embarrassed by teacher praise.

It has been shown that students can elicit praise from the teacher by eye contact and smiling. Evaluative praise (good work, Johnny) is often rejected or counterproductive. The best praise practices, as suggested by numerous studies, is highly specific praise given contingent on a specific behavior observed by the teacher. Such praise should be delivered in private, if possible.

Suggested Readings

Brophy, J., "Teacher Praise: A Functional Analysis," *Review of Educational Research*, 51 (1981), 5–32.

Merrett, F., "Teachers Use of Praise and Reprimands to Boys and Girls," *Educational Review*, 44, No. 1 (1992), 73–79.

Morine-Dershimer, G., "Pupil Perception of Teacher Praise," *Elementary School Journal*, 82, No. 5 (1982), 421–434.

Questioning by Teachers

Questions asked by teachers in the classroom are often the intellectual link between the curriculum and student learning. Research since 1970 shows that most teacher questions (50,000 per year) are didactic or procedural and often produce listlessness in students.

Questions establish a level of cognitive activity on the part of the listener, although research has not conclusively documented the relationship between higher level questions and achievement. The meaning and the value of questions asked by the teacher are influenced by the "wait time" the teacher allows the student in responding. Longer intervals between question and answer allow more thought processing and result in longer and more complex answers by the student.

It has been observed that the level of questions tells the observer more about the cognitive processes of the questioner than the listener. Curriculum planners should note the connection between classroom teacher questions and the level of curriculum objectives as defined by Bloom's Taxonomy.

Suggested Readings

Carlsen, W., "Questioning in the Classroom: A Sociolinguistic Perspective," *Review of Educational Research*, 61 (1991), 157–178.

Redfield, D., "A Meta-Analysis of Experimental Research on Teacher Questioning Behavior," *Review of Educational Research,* 51, No. 2 (1981), 237–245.

Shiang, C., *The Effectiveness of Questioning on the Thinking Process,* Paper presented at the American Educational Research Association, San Francisco, 1989 (ERIC ED 013 704).

Retention

Of all the areas of research, the 800 studies on student retention or "flunking" are the most conclusive. Of these studies, few recommend this very common school practice.

Each year about 10 percent of all students are retained or asked to repeat a grade. The odds of being retained over a twelve-year period are about 50 percent, but not for all students. A highly identifiable population, male, poor, minority, and southern, are retained disproportionately. The annual cost of retaining these 2.4 million students is about $10 billion.

The prevailing notion among educators that retaining a student will lead to increased achievement is not supported. Although many retained students may initially excel in their second effort, they soon fall back and become indistinguishable in an academic sense from comparable students not retained.

The by-products of retention are many and all are unfavorable. Retention can be correlated statistically with low attendance, behavior problems, low self-esteem, and school dropout. The prison population of most states is dominated by retained students who dropped out of school and turned to crime.

Although there are many alternatives to retention, for example, transitional programs, compensatory programs, double promotions, and extending the school year, the practice seems a permanent fixture in American education and throughout the world.

Suggested Readings

Balow, I., *Retention: A Failed Procedure* (Riverside, CA: California Education Research Cooperative, 1990), pp. 1–35.

Holmes, C. and Matthews, K., "Grade Level Retention Effects: A Meta-Analysis of Research Studies," in L. Shepard and M. Smith (eds), *Flunking Grades: Research and Policies on Retention* (New York: Falmer Press, 1990), pp. 16–33.

Roderick, M., "Grade Retention and School Dropouts: Policy Debate and Research Questions," *Phi Delta Kappan,* 15, No. 3 (1995), 3–6.

Self-Concept Development

Academic self-concept, or a child's view of himself or herself as a learner, is regularly posited as an important predictor of school achievement. Teachers regularly hear that poor self-concept will deter academic performance. Further, the self-concept is thought to be important in attitudes toward school, motivation, participation, behavior control, and social adjustment. Research on this connection is, at best, mixed.

Self-concept has been shown to be multifaceted, hierarchical, and influenced by the age and development of the student. Self-concept as measured by scales drops, quite naturally, during the pubescent (middle school) years.

Academic self-concept is some combination of performance and reward (the grades), as well as attribution by the student for this success. Students who are secure experience feelings of confidence and well-being and possess higher expectations for future success. Personality factors, as well as support from outside the school, influence the self-concept. Negative self-concept can be reinforced by teacher expectation, failure, and retention.

Suggested Readings

Combs, A., (ed.), *Perceiving, Behaving, Becoming* (Alexandria, VA: Yearbook of the Association for Supervision and Curriculum Development, 1962).

Kurtz-Costes, B., "Self-Concept, Attributional Beliefs, and School Achievement: A Longitudinal Analysis," *Contemporary Educational Psychology,* 19 (1994), 199–216.

Marsh, H., "Relations among Dimensions of Self-Attribution, Dimensions of Self Concept, and Academic Achievement," *Journal of Educational Psychology,* 76, No. 6 (1984), 1291–1308.

Yawkey, T., *The Self Concept and the Young Child* (Provo: Brigham Young University Press, 1990), pp. 151–155.

Thinking Skills

The 1980s and 1990s have been exciting times as educators consider how to structure thinking skills in the classroom. Ongoing research focuses on the enhancement of memory as well as teaching behaviors that structure thinking patterns in learners, such as metacognition, semantic mapping, scaffolding, and schema development. It is apparent from these early efforts that the teacher can play an active role in teaching such skills to students.

Although student attention is related to teacher behavior, certain kinds of students are more attentive and have better memory processing. Students who are highly verbal and students who use certain cognitive strategies have higher attending behaviors. These skills can be taught. Girls are thought to be more attentive in school because they possess superior planning skills.

Metacognition is the process of being aware of your thinking patterns, and this can be modeled by the teacher. Associative learning of new material can be encouraged by tapping into prior experiences through semantic mapping techniques. Scaffolding refers to teachers providing "organizers" for students prior to inputting basic information. Finally, schema theory involves teaching new information in terms of old cognitive structures found in the child. Retention of information is greatly enhanced when teachers invest in exploring these structures.

Medical knowledge of the brain is growing rapidly, and educators who are responsible for student learning must keep abreast of this important work.

Suggested Readings

Alkon, D., "Memory Storage and Neural Systems," *Scientific American,* 261 (1989), 42–50.

Derry, S., "Designing Systems That Train Learning Ability: From Theory to Practice," *Review of Educational Research,* 56 (1986), 1–39.

"How a Child's Brain Develops: A Special Report," *Time,* February 3, 1997.

Thompson, R., "The Neurobiology of Learning and Memory," *Science,* 223 (1986), 941–946.

Technological Learning

Studies of technology-aided instruction vary greatly with the source selected. Years of studies on radio and television have little relevance to the impact of computer-assisted learning in schools. Nonetheless, the instructional landscape is rapidly being transformed, and researchers are conducting studies on these types of learning.

Little doubt exists that media, such as the television or the personal computer, impact the character of student learning. These instruments influence the rate of reading, attention spans, and may even breed a visual learning preference (as opposed to an auditory preference assumed by the old school). Specifically, technical learning introduces both a symbol system and specific learning processes as it interfaces with the learner. Such instruments also provide a textbase of knowledge as well as mental models of situations. In areas of new learning, visual clues and reward reinforcement establish basic frames of reference and primary understandings. In short, newer technologies have the capacities to take over many of the historic functions of the classroom teacher. Comparative studies of computers versus teachers suggest that such technology may act as a savant in many of these traditional functions.

Suggested Readings

Clark, R., "Reconsidering Research on Learning from Media," *Review of Educational Research,* 53, No. 4 (1983), 445–459.

Kozma, R., "Learning with Media," *Review of Educational Research,* 61, No. 2 (1991), 179–211.

Salomon, G. and Clark, R., "Reexamining the Methodology of Research on Media and Technology in Education," *Review of Educational Research,* 47, No. 1 (1990), 99–120.

Sullivan, E. and Rocco, T., Guiding Principles for Distance Learning in a Learning Society, 1996, www.lucent.com/cedl/ace.html.

The Use of the Research Base

Educators, specifically curriculum planners, possess professional knowledge they are not using. Many of the traditional practices, such as retaining 10 percent of all American students each year, simply do not stand up to objective inquiry. Educational leaders must know what is known, and they must begin to use this knowledge in shaping more effective school programs.

As an example of such use, let us look at what is available in this cursory review for the design of drop-out programs (about 30 percent of all secondary students quit school before completion):

Concern	*Research Tells Us*
Home and Family	Three-fourths of all schoolchildren have mothers in the labor force. Parents provide prerequisite skills for school success. Single-parent children are most likely to have difficulty. Language problems are a contributing factor to becoming a dropout. The television seems to misteach children before school.
Intervention Programs	Such programs work as long as resources are applied. Investment in early intervention lowers the drop-out rate. In school, the pull-out model is effective but disruptive to other students' learning.
The Classroom	Use of space in classrooms can cause disruption, and variables such as light can distract learners. Room ambience can affect student academic performance.
Expectation and Attribution	Many disadvantaged students come to school without confidence of success. Teachers often reinforce, negatively, the behavior of children by holding low expectations for success.
Praise	Praise is often misapplied by teachers and can lead to a downward spiral of academic self-confidence.
Ability Grouping	This contributes to loss of esteem in low-performing students. Students in low groups receive poorer service from the teacher.
Discipline	Discipline is usually oriented toward control. Teachers of students in lower grades are more successful using management to prevent discipline.
Questioning Techniques	Teachers tend to ignore lower pupils and ask them low-level questions. Cognition (thinking and

	learning) is tied directly to the act of questioning by the teacher.
Retention	Retention causes lowered self-concept and lowered student attribution.
Cooperative Learning	Cooperative learning has been found to be very promising for low-performing students and facilitates participation and social/racial inclusion.
Learning Styles	Learning styles are promising for adapting to cultural and linguistic differences and help teachers to see student strengths and intelligences.
Technology	Lower-performing students are those most successful with computer-assisted intervention.

The reader may wish to review these brief summaries to explore other instructional patterns for other types of students in school. How would this information help in designing a program for the gifted student? For middle school students? For girls? To enhance inclusion? Further reading is highly recommended.

SUMMARY

Curriculum specialists reference a body of common knowledge consisting of well-known school forms, documents, models, and research on teaching and learning. These referents provide a kind of professional shorthand for communication among curriculum persons and should be mastered by persons new to the field.

This chapter suggests fifteen schools, twenty documents, and sixteen models or paradigms that constitute common knowledge in curriculum. The reader may add or delete from these items as appropriate. In addition, research relating to preschool, the classroom environment, and in fifteen widely studied areas of teaching and learning is reviewed briefly. The chapter concludes by showing the application of such research to the curriculum knowledge base in planning a program for drop-out prevention. The reader is encouraged to make other such everyday applications.

SUGGESTED READINGS

Cunningham, Craig, *Curriculum Webs: A Practical Guide* (Boston: Allyn & Bacon, 2003).

McNeil, John, *Curriculum: The Teacher's Initiative,* 3rd ed. (Upper Saddle River, NJ: Prentice Hall, 2003).

Posner, George, *Course Design: A Guide to Curriculum Development,* 6th ed. (New York: Longman, 2001).

Wiggins, Grant and McTighe, Jay, *Understanding by Design: A Handbook* (Upper Saddle River, NJ: Prentice Hall, 2001).

ENDNOTES

1. Barak Rosenshine and Norma Furst, "Research on Teacher Performance Criteria," in *Research in Teacher Education* (Englewood Cliffs, NJ: Prentice Hall, 1969), pp. 43–51.

2. Robert Stake and Terry Denny, "Needed Concepts and Techniques for Utilizing More Fully the Potential of Evaluation," in *Educational Evaluation* (Chicago, NSSE Yearbook, 1969), p. 32.

3. Robert Soar, *Follow through Classroom Process Measures* (Gainesville, FL: Research and Development Council, University of Florida Project Report, 1970), p. 10.

4. Frederick MacDonald, "Report of Phase II Beginning Teacher Evaluation Study," *Journal of Teacher Education* (Spring 1976), 39.

5. John McNeil and Jon Wiles, *The Essentials of Teaching* (New York: Macmillan, 1990), pp. 30–33.

6. K. Jencks and B. Mayer, "Social Influences," in M. Aiken (ed.), *Encyclopedia of Educational Research,* 6th ed. (New York: Macmillan, 1992), pp. 562–567.

7. A. Friedkin and P. Necochen, "Social Influences," in M. Aiken (ed.), *Encyclopedia of Educational Research,* 6th ed. (New York: Macmillan, 1992), pp. 562–567.

8. E. Fiske, *Smart Schools, Smart Kids* (New York: Simon and Schuster, 1992), p. 203.

9. S. Scalover, "The Relationship between Parental Involvement and Academic Achievement in High School Students," Diss. Penn State 1988, pp. 21–30.

10. G. Greenwood, "Research and Practice in Parent Involvement," *Elementary School Journal,* 91 (3 Jan. 1993), 279–286.

11. C. Roy and D. Fuqua, "School Support System and Academic Performance of Single Parent Students," *School Counselor,* 30, No. 3 (1983), 183–192.

12. S. Darling, "Parents and Children Learning Together," *Elementary School Principal* (Nov. 1992), 10–13.

13. D. Larsen-Freeman, "Second Language Acquisition Research," in M. Aiken (ed.), *Encyclopedia of Educational Research,* 6th ed. (New York: Macmillan, 1992), p. 119.

14. J. Uphoff and J. Gilmore, "Pupil Age at School Entrance—How Many Are Ready for Success?" *Young Children* (Jan. 1986), 13–16.

15. R. Kozma, "Learning with Media," *Review of Educational Research,* 61, No. 2 (Summer 1991), 179–211.

16. G. Greenwood and C. Hickman, "Research and Practice in Parent Involvement," *Elementary School Journal,* 91 (3 January 1993), 279–286.

17. T. Toch, "Giving Kids a Leg Up: Educators Debate How to Best Help Deprived Kids Succeed in School," *U.S. News and World Report* (22 October 1990), p. 63.

18. F. Palmer, "The Effects of Minimal Early Intervention on Subsequent I.Q. Scores and Reading Achievement," Final Report, Educational Commission of the States, Denver, CO, 1976.

19. T. W. Fagan and C. Held, "Chapter One Program Improvement," *Phi Delta Kappan,* 72 (1991), 582–584.

20. A. Smith, The Impact of Head Start on Children, Families, and Communities. Final Report. U.S. Department of Health and Human Services, 1985.

21. T. W. Fagan and C. Held op. cit.

22. V. Collier, "A Synthesis of Research on Academic Achievement in Second Language," *TESOL Quarterly,* 23 (Sept. 1988), 509–530.

23. D. Larsen-Freeman, "Second Language Acquisition: Staking Out the Territory," *TESOL Quarterly, 25,* 2 (1991), 215–260.

24. E. Hall, *The Hidden Dimension* (Garden City, NY: Doubleday, 1966).

25. M. Dunkin and B. Biddle, *The Study of Teaching* (New York: Holt Rinehart, 1974).

26. J. Somers and K. Ross, "Study of Hospital Cafeterias," in E. Hall (ed.), *The Hidden Dimension* (Garden City, NY: Doubleday, 1966), p. 36.

27. W. Hathaway, *A Study into the Effects of Light on Children of Elementary School Age* (Edmonton: Alberta Department of Education, 1992), pp. 3–37.

28. E. Emmer and A. Ausikker, "School and Classroom Discipline Programs," in D. Moles (ed.), *Student Discipline Strategies: Research and Practice* (Albany, NY: SUNY Press, 1990).

29. N. Sprinthall, *Educational Psychology,* (New York: McGraw-Hill, 1990).

30. D. Kimure, "Sex Differences in the Brain," *Scientific American,* 267 (1992), 119–125.

31. S. Rodenbush, "Magnitude of Teacher Expectancy on Student I.Q.," *Journal of Educational Psychology,* 76 (1984), 85–97.

32. For example, three of the most widely used instruments in education are the Gregorc Instrument, the Myers-Briggs Personality Indicator, and the Hansen and Silver Learning Style Inventory.

33. M. Birely, "Teaching Implications of Learning Styles," *Academic Therapy,* (March 1987), 437–442.

3

THE DEVELOPMENT PROCESS

OVERVIEW

In this chapter the reader will look at the basics of curriculum development. Long ago curriculum development was likened to a cycle (Tyler, 1949), consisting of four basic steps: analysis, design, implementation, and evaluation. This development process is deductive, and fairly orderly, once the important value decisions have been made about purpose. The reader should conceptualize any curriculum as a design for learning. Each design has a different emphasis or approach to learning.

Curriculum work always contains assumptions that when formalized make up a philosophy. This philosophy, or set of premises, helps shape curriculum and establish the "criteria" for making decisions. Once a purpose is set, such as "preparing students for the world of work," then goals, objectives, and standards are used to give form to the curriculum. This form is shaped through curriculum maps, frameworks, and the alignment process.

Needs assessments are used to assess the relevance or efficacy of the curriculum. The form of the curriculum must be appropriate for the intended users. If needs assessments indicate an inappropriate level of difficulty or irrelevance, the curriculum must be altered.

Curriculum can be "packaged" in any number of forms. The author offers eight common designs for the reader to ponder. Every content organization, like every more general curriculum design, emphasizes some things over others for the student. Conceptual designs and mastery designs are not the same in their intent.

Finally, there needs to be clear linkage to the teacher who will deliver the curriculum. The curriculum intended and the curriculum experienced should be the same. Good curriculum documents and relevant training will increase the odds that the teacher will understand and follow the intentions of the curriculum designer.

THE DEVELOPMENT PROCESS

Unlike the disagreement that surrounds any discussion of philosophy in American education, curriculum specialists are in general agreement about the process of developing curriculum. Using a deductive logic, the process begins with the search for values or decision criteria that will indicate the basis for all decision making. These criteria can be acknowledged or inferred, but are generally spelled out in curriculum documents, such as philosophy statements, goals, objectives, standards, and even evaluation instruments. (See Figure 3.1.) With greater and greater detail, the curriculum takes form according to this set of priorities.

Nearly a century of work has contributed to this "cycle" or "system" of development. Luminaries, such as John Dewey, Ralph Tyler, and Hilda Taba, detailed the steps involved in making a curriculum complete. Tyler's (1949) list of questions established "feedback" in the process:

1. What educational purposes should the school seek to attain?
2. What educational experiences can be provided that are likely to attain those purposes?
3. How can these educational experiences be effectively organized?
4. How can we determine whether these purposes are being attained?

By 1962, Hilda Taba had refined the process further with her seven-step model:

1. Diagnosis of needs
2. Formulation of objectives
3. Selection of content
4. Organization of content
5. Selection of learning experiences
6. Organization of learning experiences
7. Determination of what to evaluate and the means of doing it

Philosophy
↓
Program Concept
↓
Broad Goals
↓
Objectives
↓
Program Design
↓
Evaluative Standards
↓
Needs Assessment
↓
Curriculum Alignment
↓
Program Design
↓
Course Frameworks
↓
Lesson Planning

**FIGURE 3.1   Deductive Curriculum
Development**

CRITERIA FOR DECISIONS

If philosophy establishes purpose in education, then goals, standards, frameworks, and objectives define the scope of that purpose. Without substance, structure, and strategy, curriculum development is aimless:

> *A society establishes and supports schools for certain purposes; it seeks to achieve certain ends or attain desired outcomes. Efforts of adults to direct the experiences of young people in a formal institution such as a school constitute preferences for certain human ends and values. Schooling is a moral venture, one that necessitates choosing values among innumerable possibilities. These choices constitute the starting point in curriculum planning.*[1]

The question of "how" to decide is one of critical importance for curriculum developers. The principle, or reason, for a decision is referred to as the "criteria" in curriculum work, and this has been a central concern of theorists for many years. Several possible criteria are suggested in the literature as a starting place for selection and decision making (inclusion/exclusion) in curriculum development.

Saylor and Alexander suggest that the criteria be one of "accepting responsibility":

> In selecting the basic goals which the school should seek to serve from among the sum total of ends for which people strive the curriculum planner faces the major issue: In the total process of human development what parts or aspects should the school accept responsibility for guiding?[2]

For John Dewey, another possible criteria in curriculum development would be "excellence." He describes the process in this manner:

> Every society gets encumbered with what is trivial . . . with what is positively perverse. The school has the duty of omitting such things from the environment which it supplies, and thereby doing what it can to counteract their influence in the ordinary social environment. By selecting the best for its exclusive use, it strives to reinforce the power of this best. As a society becomes more enlightened, it realizes that it is responsible not to transmit and conserve the whole of its achievements, but only such as to make for a better future society. The school is the chief agency for the accomplishment of this end.[3]

Yet a third possible criteria for selecting goals and outcomes would be the minimum essentials needed by students:

> If it is impossible to discover from educational theory fundamental tests for exclusion or inclusion, we are driven to the method of determining minimum essentials on the basis of the best current practices and experimentation which gives satisfactory results. Those results are satisfactory which meet adequately the common needs of life in society.[4]

There are also several well-known lists of questions addressing the criteria for selecting goals and content in curriculum development. A 1923 list by Charles McMurry included the following: What is the aim of education? What subject matter has the greatest pedagogical value? How is the subject matter related to instructional method? What is the best sequence of studies? How can the curriculum be best organized?[5]

A 1926 list by Thomas Briggs was more comprehensive:

1. What is the desired end of education?
2. What is the good life?
3. To what extent shall education modify character and the actions of future citizens?
4. For what ends are the schools responsible?

5. What subject areas are most vital in attaining these ends?
6. What should be the content of these subject arrangements?
7. How should the material be organized?
8. What is the responsibility of each level of schooling?
9. What is the relative importance of each course of study?
10. How much time should be allotted for each subject?
11. How long should education be continued at public expense?
12. What is the optimum length of the school day? School year?
13. What is the optimum workload for each pupil?
14. What are the probable future needs of the pupil?[6]

Finally, for John McNeil, in 1976, those critical questions included the following:

1. Is the purpose of school to change, or adapt to, or accept the social order?
2. What can the school do better than any other agency or institution?
3. What objectives should be common to all?
4. Should objectives stress cooperation or competition?
5. Should objectives deal with controversial issues or only established knowledge?
6. Should attitudes be taught? Fundamental skills? Problem-solving strategies?
7. Should teachers emphasize subject matter or create behaviors out of school?
8. Should objectives be based on local needs, society in general, or student needs?[7]

McNeil, continuing in 1996, asked if goals and objectives are meeting the following conditions that would make them more acceptable:

1. Are the goals congruent with values and functions of the controlling agency?
2. Are goals comprehensive, encompassing a single powerful purpose?
3. Are goals consistent with one another?
4. Are goals attainable, capable of being reached without major changes?[8]

Without a criteria, the process of curriculum development breaks down. There is no rule, no guiding principle. Daniel and Laurel Tanner have noted the problem in this way:

> *In the absence of a holistic conception of curriculum, the focus is on the piecemeal and mechanical functions . . . the main thrust in curriculum development and reform over the years has been directed at micro-curricular problems to the neglect of the macro-curricular problems.*

ROLE OF PHILOSOPHY

Educational philosophy guides all curriculum development by setting priorities and answering value-laden questions. Philosophies set the parameters of definitions of curriculum, thereby defining the scope of the curriculum development process.

For John Dewey, a philosophy served as a general theory of educating. Boyd Bode, a progressive educator, saw philosophies in education as a source of reflective consideration. Ralph Tyler, a leading curriculum theorist throughout much of the twentieth century, perceived educational philosophy as a screen for selecting educational objectives for programs.

Philosophy has been a large part of the curriculum literature, and in the twenty-first century, it is important to realize that schools are purposeful places that do prescribed things to children. The choices of what to do are many.

There are many labels for various educational beliefs. For the sake of simplicity, five generic philosophies are described, compared and contrasted, and applied in a school setting (see Figure 3.2). Each philosophy represents a different set of underlying values that would structure the curriculum development process:

Perennialism

The most conservative, traditional, or inflexible of the five philosophies is *perennialism,* a philosophy drawing heavily from classical definitions of education. Perennialists believe that education, like human nature, is a constant. Because the distinguishing characteristic of humans is the ability to reason, education should focus on developing rationality. Education, for the perennialist, is a preparation for life, and students should be taught the world's permanencies through structured study.

For the perennialist, reality is a world of reason. Such truths are revealed to us through study and sometimes through divine acts. Goodness is to be found in rationality itself. Perennialists favor a curriculum of subjects and doctrine, taught through highly disciplined drill and behavior control. Schools for the perennialist exist primarily to reveal reason by teaching eternal truths. The teacher interprets and tells. The student is a passive recipient. Because truth is eternal, all change in the immediate school environment is largely superficial.

Idealism

Idealism is a philosophy that espouses the refined wisdom of men and women. Reality is seen as a world within a person's mind. Truth is to be found in the consistency of ideas. Goodness is an ideal state, something to strive to attain.

Idealists favor schools that teach subjects of the mind, such as are found in most public school classrooms. Teachers, for the idealist, would be models of ideal behavior.

For idealists, the schools' function is to sharpen intellectual processes, to present the wisdom of the ages, and to present models of behavior that are exemplary. Students in such schools would have a somewhat passive role, receiving and memorizing the reporting of the teacher. Change in the school program would generally be considered an intrusion on the orderly process of educating.

FIGURE 3.2   The Five Philosophies Compared

	Perennialism	Idealism	Realism	Experimentalism	Existentialism
Reality Ontology	A world of reason and God	A world of the mind	A world of things	A world of experience	A world of existing
Truth (Knowledge) Epistemology	Reason and revelation	Consistency of ideas	Correspondence and sensation (as we see it)	What works What is	Personal, subjective choice
Goodness Axiology	Rationality	Imitation of ideal self, person to be emulated	Laws of nature	The public test	Freedom
Teaching Reality	Disciplinary subjects and doctrine	Subject of the mind—literary, philosophical, religious	Subjects of physical world—math, science	Subject matter of social experiences— social studies	Subject matter of choice— art, ethics, philosophy
Teaching Truth	Discipline of the mind via drill	Teaching ideas via lecture, discussion	Teaching for mastery of information— demonstrate, recite	Problem-solving, project method	Arousing personal repsonses— questioning
Teaching Goodness (Values)	Disciplining behavior (to reason)	Imitating heroes and other exemplars	Training in rules of conduct	Making group decisions in light of consequences	Awakening self to responsibility
Why Schools Exist	To reveal reason and God's will	To sharpen the mind and intellectual processes	To reveal the order of the world and universe	To discover and expand the society we live in to share experiences	To aid children in knowing themselves and their place in society
What Should Be Taught	External truths	Wisdom of the ages	Laws of physical reality	Group inquiry into social problems and social sciences, method and subject together	Unregimented topic areas
Role of the Teacher	Interprets, tells	Reports, person to be emulated	Displays, imparts knowledge	Aids, consultant	Questions, assists student in personal journey
Role of the Student	Passive reception	Receives, memorizes	Manipulates, passive participation	Active participation, contributes	Determines own rules
School's Attitude toward Change	Truth is eternal, no real change	Truth to be preserved, anti-change	Always coming toward perfection, orderly change	Change is ever-present, a process	Change is necessary at all times

Source: Jon Wiles and Joseph Bondi, *Curriculum Development: A Guide to Practice,* 5th ed. (New York: Macmillan, 1998), pp. 41–44. Used by permission.

Realism

For the *realist,* the world is as it is, and the job of schools is to teach students about the world. Goodness, for the realist, is found in the laws of nature and the order of the physical world. Truth is the simple correspondences of observation.

The realist favors a school dominated by subjects of the here-and-now world, such as math and science. Students would be taught factual information for mastery. The teacher would impart knowledge of this reality to students or display such reality for observation and study. Classrooms would be highly ordered and disciplined, like nature, and the students would be passive participants in the study of things. Changes in school would be perceived as a natural evolution toward a perfection of order.

Experimentalism

For the *experimentalist,* the world is an ever-changing place. Reality is what is actually experienced. Truth is what presently functions. Goodness is what is accepted by public test. Unlike the perennialist, idealist, and realist, the experimentalist openly accepts change and continually seeks to discover new ways to expand and improve society.

The experimentalist favors a school with heavy emphasis on social subjects and experiences. Learning would occur through a problem-solving or inquiry format. Teachers would aid learners or consult with learners who would be actively involved in discovering and experiencing the world in which they live. Such an education program's focus on value development would factor in group consequences.

Existentialism

The *existentialist* sees the world as one personal subjectivity, where goodness, truth, and reality are individually defined. Reality is a world of existing, truth subjectively chosen, and goodness a matter of freedom.

For existentialists, schools, if they existed at all, would be places that assisted students in knowing themselves and learning their places in society. If subject matter existed, it would be a matter of interpretation such as the arts, ethics, or philosophy. Teacher–student interaction would center around assisting students in their personal learning journeys. Change in school environments would be embraced as both a natural and necessary phenomenon. Nonschooling and individually determined curriculum would be a possibility.[9]

A modern example of existentialism can be found in the Sudbury Schools in the United States (see Figure 3.3).

FIGURE 3.3   Existentialism—The Sudbury Philosophy

Alpine Valley School is one of a growing number of schools around the world based on the Sudbury Valley School, located in Framingham, Massachusetts. Founded in 1968, Sudbury Valley has pioneered a unique approach to education, based on the premise that people learn best when they retain control over their own learning.

In a nutshell, the Sudbury philosophy is as follows:

- **Freedom *with* responsibility.** Students are free to spend their time however they please, as long as they do not impinge on the right of other students to do the same.

- **Self-motivation, self-regulation, self-evaluation.** Students initiate all their own activities; they are never told what they should do (or how), and they are not given any formal evaluation. It is up to them to determine for themselves what they want and need, and to request assistance in this quest if they wish.

- **Democracy.** In order to direct their own educations, students' opportunities to shape the decisions made at their school must be real and meaningful.

- **Trust.** A student's freedom is undermined unless the adults associated with the school, staff and parents, believe in it and support it by their actions. This can be difficult, but it is necessary.

These core beliefs rest on a number of assumptions, among them the following:

- We are all born with an intense drive to understand and master our environment.
- Learning happens all the time in whatever we do.
- No one can decide for another what they should learn (or when or how) or what constitutes a good use of their time.
- The only way a young person can learn to be responsible is by being given real responsibility from the youngest age.

As a consequence, learning assumes a multitude of very different forms at a Sudbury school. Some of the more visible features are as follows:

- **Age-mixing.** Because students are not grouped arbitrarily, they are free to associate with (and learn from) people of all ages, however they see fit. The benefits of this—educational, social, and more—make it the "secret weapon" of a Sudbury school.

- **Play and conversation.** It is difficult to exaggerate the importance of play and conversation in people's efforts to build conceptual models of the world. Because this model building also happens to be enjoyable, some of the most common activities at Sudbury schools are things that most people would label as simply playing and talking.

- **Open campus.** Students' freedom would be incomplete if it did not include freedom of movement. Consequently, students are free to come and go from campus as they please, as long as they meet their commitments to the school.

- **All activities are valued equally.** Because students are free to spend their time however they choose, it is no one's place to tell them that they are "wasting" their time, or that they should move on from one activity to another. Because we believe that people learn in all sorts of ways, from whatever they do, there is also no bias toward traditional academic subjects.

HOW PHILOSOPHY IMPACTS THE CURRICULUM

Curriculum planners look to the major ideas within philosophy for structuring school experiences for students. Although the names of the philosophies may vary over time, the issues they contest are lasting. To the author, the time-orientation of the philosophy (past, present, future) is very important. In philosophies that look backward (perennial, conservative, reactionary), the past is all-important and the transmission of that cultural heritage is the curriculum. Philosophies that are focused on the here and now (realism, middle of the road) are more practical and concerned with the application of that tested wisdom from the past. For those philosophies that are future oriented (progressive, experimental, liberal), the past serves as a guide but is not considered sacrosanct. Change is embraced as natural, and there is an openness to the environment (see Figure 3.4).

For the author, use of a continuum of "structured" and "flexible" can help to explain philosophies as applied in schools. In the highly structured school, there is a strong attempt to control the environment and the student so that a more perfect transmission of the "known curriculum" can occur. By contrast, in schools in which student differences are acknowledged or where there is an "in the future" orientation because students are seen as clients, the environment and interactions are more flexible.

Philosophy in the School Setting: Ten Variables

The following list defines ten areas that can be observed in a school and that indicate that school's philosophy.*

Community Involvement. Schools with a predetermined mission seek to limit interaction with the community, perceiving it as either an inconvenience or an interference with the process. By contrast, schools with an expansive curriculum see the community as an extended learning environment. Issues: physical access to the school building; legal access for participation; intellectual access to the curriculum.

School Buildings and Grounds. School facilities and properties are used to a lesser or greater degree depending on the definition of curriculum. Restricted learning areas suggest control, whereas total use of physical resources indicates a broad definition of learning. Issues: the use of outside properties (grounds); traffic patterns within the building; treatment of visitors; noise levels.

Classrooms. How the classroom is arranged and the use of space in the classroom can indicate the philosophy of the resident program. Order and uniformity would suggest a prescribed curriculum, whereas diversity and flexibility

---

*For additional treatment of this topic, see Wiles, J. and Bondi, J. *Curriculum Development: A Guide to Practice*, 5th ed. (New York: Macmillan, 1998), pp. 49–73.

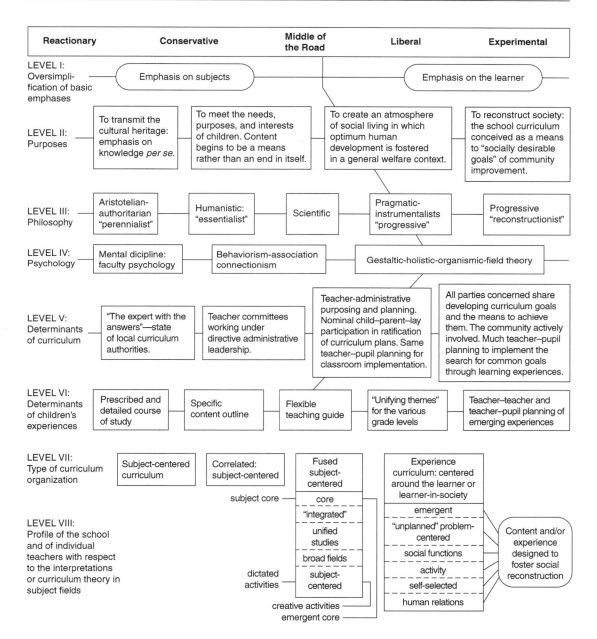

FIGURE 3.4   How Philosophy Impacts Curriculum

Source: Jon Wiles, *Promoting Change in Schools* (New York: Scholastic, Inc., 1993), p. 16. © 1993, Scholastic, Inc. Reprinted by permission of Scholastic, Inc.

would suggest a more loosely defined curriculum. Issues: seating patterns; degree of personal items displayed or allowed; verbal interaction patterns.

Organization of Knowledge. The pattern in which information is introduced or presented may reveal the philosophy of the school. Sequential material or skill-mastery learnings suggest control. Interdisciplinary, minicourses, or conceptual learnings suggest an orientation toward real-world applications. Issues: degree of textbook dependence; elective choices available for learning; questions and student verbal interaction.

Learning Materials. The variety of sensory stimulation can reveal the working philosophy in a classroom or school. A controlled or structured curriculum will limit media and narrow cognitive focus. Issues: variety of media and materials; cognitive focus of instruction; time orientation of lesson (past, present, future).

Teaching Strategies. Teacher behaviors may reveal the definition of curriculum within the school. Structuring techniques, such as lecture and didactic questioning, suggest that the teacher is the focus. Student interaction in group work or discussion broadens the focus of learning. Issues: interactive distances and body language; degree of diversity allowed by teacher; motivational techniques.

Staffing Patterns. Deployment of teachers suggests whether interaction is desired and how teachers are to work with students. Organization of students often parallels such deployment. Issues: job description of teacher; organization of teachers (solitary or teamed); how students are grouped for instruction.

Administrative Conditions. Administrators in traditional curriculums exhibit more controlling behaviors toward both teachers and students. When administrative presence is less obvious, the curriculum can gain flexibility. Issues: rules and regulations in the building; treatment of disciplinary measures; method of recording student progress.

Climate. Highly structured curriculums create efficiency-oriented work climates. Less structured curriculums encourage a generally more relaxed work relationship. Issues: decision-making patterns (formal/informal); mediums of communication in building; rewards in evidence in building.

Roles of Participants. The uniformity of roles for administrators, teachers, and students suggests structure. In contrast, any one group playing other roles indicates flexibility. Issues: dress patterns of administrators and teachers; kinds of leadership opportunities for students; variety of special events and non-scheduled activities.

In conclusion, it can be said that an overall measure of the philosophy of any school is the degree of structure or flexibility present or observed. A curriculum that is highly defined and predetermined (perennialist, idealist, realist) will use structure to control deviancy and diversity. Efficiency will be a preoccupation with such a curriculum because "speed over material" is the only true planning variable. By contrast, curriculums that are open ended, applied, or student centered (the experimentalist and existentialist) will encourage flexibility because they are seeking applied learning in an ever-changing real world.

GOALS AND OBJECTIVES

The United States is unique in having a decentralized education system. Because education was not mentioned in our Constitution, and because education is a state responsibility, there are no national goals such as those displayed in Figure 3.5 to serve as general organizers in the development of curriculum. The first real attempt to develop true national goals for public schools in America came in 1990 when the president of the United States and all fifty governors signed the Goals 2000 document (see Chapter 2). General or global goals are important in curriculum work because they link intentions (the philosophy or concept statement) with the more detailed planning process. Detailed goals (objectives) continue the deductive logic of curriculum analysis and design.

Even without national directives, there are numerous lists of goals to be reviewed. In the documents section in Chapter 2, lists by the Committee on the Reorganization of Secondary Education (1918) and the Educational Policies Commission (1944) are featured.

FIGURE 3.5   Sample National Goals from Other Nations

Australia
1. Fulfilling lives and active citizenship
2. Joining the workforce
3. Overcoming disadvantage and achieving fairness in society

Taiwan (Republic of China)
1. The three principles: geography, history, and economy (the meaning of nation)
2. Utilization of group life (operation of democracy)
3. Productive labor (livelihood)
4. Eight moral virtues: loyalty, kindness, love, faith, righteousness, harmony, peace, fidelity

People's Republic of China (Red China)
1. Develop good moral character
2. Develop love of motherland
3. Literacy and intellect
4. Healthy bodies
5. Interest in aesthetics

Source: Adapted from national documents from respective state education departments. Also from C. Postlethwaite, *Encyclopedia of Comparative Education and National Systems of Education* (Oxford: Pergamon Press, 1988).

Because goals represent intended outcomes or results, they come in many forms. In the 1980s and 1990s, school systems increasingly stated their goals for education in terms of student behaviors (see Figure 3.6). These goals can be assessed in terms of "things students can do."

Goals can be thought of as having increasing levels of detail. Global goals are nearly philosophical statements. In a more specific form, goals may be broken down into subparts like a conventional outline with Roman numerals. Finally, in greater detail, the goals may be stated in terms of instructional or behavioral outcomes. The following questions may serve as criteria for any goal statements in curriculum development:

1. Are the goals realistic? Can they be attained and will teachers relate to them?
2. Are the goals specific, implying behaviors to be changed?
3. Are the goals performance related?
4. Are the goals suggestive of involvement, allowing individuals to see themselves connected to the goal by action?
5. Are the goals observable or measurable? Could the results of this goal be shown after attainment?

Finally, sometimes goals are found in the form of belief statements that serve to define a philosophy or core value. In the following example, individualizing instruction is broken down into statements that can focus program development:

We Believe in Individualized Instruction

1. We believe that students are individuals with unique characteristics and interests.
2. We believe students learn best in an environment tailored to their needs.
3. We believe the role of the teacher is a facilitator or learning assistant to students.
4. We believe the content must be made relevant to the lives of the students.

Objectives and Taxonomies

The scope of educational programs can be determined from the goal statements, but it is the objectives (detailed goal statements) that define the true purpose of the curriculum. When goals reach the classroom level, they usually become behavioral and focus on what the student learns as opposed to what the teacher does. Such a linkage is necessary for program evaluation to be viable and for instructional accountability to exist.

An example of this reduction can be given using "thinking skills" as a focus. At the general level (global) the goal might be "Highest priority will be given to the development of sensitive, autonomous, thinking human beings." More specifically, this goal may be targeted or defined (platform goal) as "Critical thinking skills will be mastered by all students prior to graduation." Even more specific (behav-

FIGURE 3.6 Goals as Behavioral Outcomes

Academic Goals

Achievement

Maintain or improve test scores
Reduce failures and parental notices
Reduce retentions and dropouts
Produce better grade point averages
Increase honor roll (based on grades)
Institute new honor rolls in nonacademic areas
    (based on nonacademic achievement)
Meet needs of high achievers

Responsibility

Arrive on time
Decrease vandalism cases
Decrease discipline counts
Admit to wrongdoing
Take care of academic areas

Respect for Others

Decrease sarcasm and put-downs
Increase sensitivity to needs of others
Increase their role in helping others
    (peer learning)

Behaviors

Healthy Habits

Monitoring self
Exhibit smoking and drug awareness
Exhibit awareness of physical growth
Walk for health
Participation in intramural sports

Higher Self-Esteem

Increase openness to new experiences
Eliminate self-abusive behaviors
Increase ability to self-reveal
Exhibit school pride

Attendance and Participation

Increase daily attendance count
Increase club memberships
Decrease make-up work

Stress and Misbehavior

Decrease visits to counselor
Decrease outbursts in class
Decrease aggressive behaviors
(Teachers) distribute homework more evenly

Organization

Bring materials to class
Complete homework frequently
Maintain personal calendar
Bring gym clothes
Manage time wisely
Ask questions to clarify responsibilities

Problem Solving

Possess analysis skills
Solve word problems
Apply subjects to "real world"
Possess creative thinking skills
Learn in hands-on manner

Love of Knowledge

Belong to an academic club
Read designated books
Meet with adult tutor/mentor
Develop a personal library
Exhibit awareness of state, national, and
    world events

Attitudinal Goals

Positive Attitude

Exhibit enthusiasm about learning
Participate in school activities
Volunteer/join school service clubs

Mannerly and Courteous

Exhibit ability to introduce self to adults
Dress neatly and appear well groomed
Know etiquette

Source: Life Skills Curriculum, Jon Wiles, 1990.

ioral) goals, now an objective, would be "Students will evidence critical thinking by demonstrating the ability to classify, compare and contrast, follow directions, and reason using both inductive and deductive logic on completion of the course." At this point, curriculum development can address specific experiences to accomplish goals in this area. Objectives can do the following for curriculum developers:

1. Identify specific student behaviors to be changed by designed experiences.
2. Increase communication among teachers about purpose and specific activities.
3. Direct and order instructional activities at the school and classroom level.
4. Provide a meaningful basis and focus for program evaluation.

Specifically, the flow from goals to objectives to instructional plans is aided by "behavioral objectives." These objectives are operational statements that describe the desired outcome of an educational program. Such objectives must be derived from global and platform goals to remain within the "scope" of the program and to aid in "sequencing."

Sometimes schools become bogged down in writing behavioral objectives, resulting in simplistic and mechanical targets. Philosophically, many educators resist such a level of clarity in planning because it ignores the possibility of concomitant learning (spontaneous) and often prohibits alternatives for teachers.

Behavioral objectives always contain required parts to be complete and measurable, and use of the ABCD rule (audience, behavior, condition, and degree) assists in writing useful objectives at the classroom level. For example

> *Given equations containing two unknowns (condition), the learner (audience) will solve nine out of ten (behavior) problems within twenty minutes (degree).*

The use of behavioral objectives is greatly aided by addressing the three learning taxonomies (cognitive, affective, and psychomotor) found in the documents section of this book (see Bloom in Chapter 2) In addition, identified behaviors (see Figure 3.7) help curriculum developers identify the specific behavior they are seeking as well as to think about the instructional process as a continuum or hierarchy of de-

FIGURE 3.7   Descriptive Verbs for Writing Objectives

Logical/Critical	Creative	Social/Qualitative
Name	Predict	Accept
Define	Design	Join
List	Imagine	Agree
Trace	Suggest	Help
Identify	Pretend	Praise
Order	Propose	Expand
Demonstrate	Assess	Save
Classify	Rearrange	Support
Summarize	Change	Compliment
Defend	Invent	Contribute
Distinguish	Manipulate	Aid
Determine	Elaborate	Thank

velopment. For example, most classroom instruction in public schools occurs at the lower end of Bloom's cognitive levels (basic knowing, comprehension) and not at the upper levels (analysis, evaluation). Likewise, in the Krathwohl taxonomy of affective behaviors, low-level behaviors, such as responding, are more common than higher-level behaviors, such as "valuing."

It is interesting to consider both the cognitive and affective taxonomies in tandem because it is widely accepted that "feelings" influence "thinking." If the curriculum planner wishes to move the student up the ladder from a comprehending and responding student to an analyzing and valuing student, two things must occur: First, the student must become more involved in the learning act (because feelings are individual) and, second, the teacher must act to involve the student. The use of behavioral objectives to "order" the curriculum makes instructional methodology (and staff development activities) highly specific. Figure 3.8 shows how objectives affect student behaviors.

STANDARDS

Following the statement of Goals 2000 in 1990, the United States embarked on an outcome-based education model that featured standards and testing to structure curriculum. It should be noted that such standards were also popular in the 1920s (see Callahan's *Education and the Cult of Efficiency*) and in the 1950s. National, subject matter, and state achievement standards for education were generated and

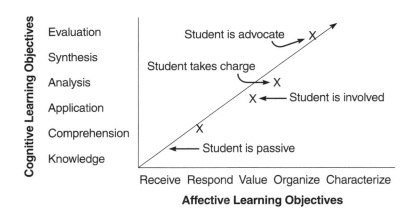

FIGURE 3.8   How Learning Objectives Affect Student Behavior

Note: The use of the cognitive and affective taxonomies lets the teacher plot expectations for student behavior in the classroom. When responding and comprehending, for example, the student's role is passive. At higher-level combinations, the student gets involved, then takes charge of his or her learning, and finally becomes an advocate of the lesson. It is important to understand that teachers with low-level objectives (recite, list) will not get active student involvement.

Source: Jon Wiles. Notes taken while working with Dade County Schools, Florida.

measured by both norm-referenced and criterion-referenced national and state tests. The underlying rationale for this movement was that such standards were the key to both national and individual economic readiness.

Figure 3.9 identifies standards generated by various professional associations in math, science, language arts, reading, writing, civics, social studies, economics, and geography. Most of these lists were adopted or modified by individual states and tied to achievement and promotion testing programs. Such testing programs, in many states, are now used to control curriculum and teaching. The critical issue is teachers' reactions to a standards-based curriculum. As John McNeil observes,

FIGURE 3.9   World Class Standards—Subject Areas

World Class Standards

What Secondary Students Abroad Are Expected to Know, Defining World Class Standards. American Federation of Teachers (AFT), 1995.

Language Arts

Standards for the Assessment of Reading and Thinking. Urbana, IL: National Council of Teachers of English, 1994.
NAEP Reading Standards. Washington, DC: National Assessment of Education Progress (NAEP), 1995.
NAEP Writing Standards. Washington, DC: National Assessment of Education Progress (NAEP), 1994.
Reading Standards. Newark, DE: International Reading Association, 1995.

Mathematics

Curriculum and Evaluation Standards for School Mathematics. Reston, VA: National Council of Teachers of Mathematics (NCTM), 1989.
Professional Standards for Teaching Mathematics. Reston, VA: National Council of Teachers of Mathematics (NCTM), 1991.
NAEP Mathematics Standards. Washington, DC: National Assessment of Education Progress (NAEP), 1994.

Social Science

NAEP Social Studies Standards. Washington, DC: National Assessment of Education Progress (NAEP), 1995.
National Content Standards for Civics. Calabasas, CA: Center for Civic Education, 1995.
National Content Standards for Economics. National Council of Economic Education (NCEE), 1995.
National Content Standards for Geography. National Geographic Society, 1994.
National Content Standards for History. National Center for History in the Schools, 1995.
National Content Standards for Social Studies. National Council on Social Studies (NCSS), 1995.

Science

Benchmarks for Science Literacy, Project 2061, American Association for the Advancement of Science (AAAS). New York: Oxford University Press, 1993.
National Science Education Standards. National Research Council. Washington, DC: National Academy Press, 1996.
NAEP Science Standards. Washington, DC: National Assessment of Education Progress (NAEP), 1995.
Science Performance Standards. New Standards Project, 1995.

Note: For updates of this compilation see www.ascd.org.

"teachers respond in different ways . . . ; some try to ignore it, carrying on as usual. Some turn into grim 'test factories,' abdicating control over the curriculum to the test contractors and 'teaching to the test.' Still others pursue the high-quality standards of the professional associations and engage students in meaningful activities related to the disciplines."[10]

At the program development level, standards can be used to establish validation checkpoints. In Figure 3.10, basic checkpoints in the curriculum are presented

FIGURE 3.10   Standards Can Be Used for a Status Check

Mapping Worksheet with Standards

Curriculum Area: Computer Education

Purpose: The overall goal in the educational use of computers is to integrate computer literacy into all content areas of the middle school curriculum, thus providing an additional tool for interdisciplinary curriculum development. In addition, elective computer courses in application and programing provide for personal development and the reinforcement of essential skills.

Program Descriptors	Status		
	Yes	No	Action Plan to Achieve
1. Microcomputers, either permanently located in all classrooms or on mobile carts, are available for classroom use.			
2. Additional mobile computers will be available to move into classrooms when necessary or to develop a minilab when desired.			
3. Each school will have at least two qualified full-time computer education teachers.			
4. Each school will have at least two complete computer labs containing a minimum of sixteen microcomputers and have a ratio of two students per computer. Each lab will include necessary computer system hardware, software, and peripheral equipment to meet current and future trends and developments. The complete computer lab will consist of necessary space, lighting, seating, air cooling system, electrical system, and security plus access to telecommunications.			
5. Daily lab schedules should include time set aside for independent student use.			
6. All students in grades 6 and 7 will be scheduled into one of the computer labs for a minimum of three hours a week in order to meet the state requirements for computer literacy.			
7. A minimum of two computers with needed peripherals will be located in the teachers' work area for teacher use (i.e., grading, software review, word processing, etc.).			

Note: The standard establishes an observable and verifiable target that can focus planning efforts.

Source: Jon Wiles and Joseph Bondi, *Curriculum Development: A Guide to Practice,* 5th ed. (New York: Macmillan, 1998), p. 192. Used by permission.

in standards format, allowing the validation of a minimal program for all students in the district. Standards also can be used as targets for future development. (See Figure 3.11.)

CURRICULUM DESIGNS

Curriculum designs are most observable as "programs" and as content organizers. Sometimes schools or districts adopt a "label" program such as the "middle school" design. As the reader can observe in Figure 3.12, this program is based on a human development rationale (as opposed to a content rationale) and has a three-part curriculum emphasis: academics, personal learning, and skills for continued learning. Although the internal components of the design may vary, they all promote flexibility to serve the diversity of preadolescent learners.

Designs are also found in the way content is organized and treated. If the curriculum does not clarify for the teacher what the intended outcome is to be, it is unlikely the implementation of the program will be successful. Curriculum developers "skew" the subject matter toward certain ends by the way they organize it. A good organizer to understand the "pole positions" in this regard is to ask whether the curriculum seeks to standardize student response or whether it seeks to individualize the response. Generally speaking, the more "structure" that is found in the curriculum (a text, a test, etc.), the more standardized the outcome will be. If the curriculum introduces choice in learning, if it promotes flexibility, the student learning will be more individualized.

The author presents for the readers' consideration eight common curriculum designs found in American schools. Each of these designs could be applied to the same subject matter, but with different results. Content designs, of course, are the most structured design found in schools, whereas problem-solving and creative designs encourage more student input into the learning experience. (See Figure 3.13.)

Curriculum Alignment

As the various programs, subjects, and objectives are delineated, it becomes necessary to order the curriculum. This process can be accomplished in several ways. A traditional way is to construct content columns or continuums that show the flow of the subject through each consecutive grade. Figure 3.14 takes the subject of science from kindergarten through the twelfth grade and shows it as largely "loosely connected" knowing. Districts that allow their textbooks to serve as the curriculum organization often follow an outline such as this. In the worst-case scenario, different textbook adoptions at different levels or at different times (based on cost) lead to a badly fragmented or redundant outline.

A second traditional way to align the curriculum is to construct a "scope and sequence" chart that gives both a vertical (through the grades) and horizontal (across the subjects in same grade) look at instruction. If done well, such a grid will reveal inconsistency and suggest curriculum maintenance activities. Like the

FIGURE 3.11   K–12 Technology Literacy Standards (NETS Standards for Schools)

Performance Indicators for Technology Literate Students

Grades Pre-K–2

Prior to completion of grade 2, students will

1. Use input devices (e.g., mouse, keyboard, remote control) and output devices (e.g., monitor, printer) to operate computers, VCRs, audiotapes, telephones, and other technologies.
2. Use a variety of media and technology resources for directed and independent learning activities.
3. Communicate about technology using developmentally appropriate and accurate terminology.
4. Use multimedia resources (interactive books, educational software, elementary multimedia encyclopedias) to support learning.
5. Work cooperatively and collaboratively with peers, family members, and others when using technology in the classroom.
6. Demonstrate positive social and ethical behaviors when using technology.
7. Practice responsible use of technology systems and software.
8. Create multimedia products with support from teachers, family members, or student partners.
9. Use technology resources (e.g., puzzles, logical thinking programs, writing tools, digital cameras, drawing tools) for problem solving, communication, and illustration of thoughts, ideas, and stories.
10. Gather information and communicate with others using telecommunications, with support from teachers, family members, or student partners.

Grades 3–5

Prior to completion of grade 5, students will

1. Use keyboards and other common input and output devices (including adaptive devices) efficiently and effectively.
2. Discuss common uses of technology in daily life and advantages and disadvantages those uses provide.
3. Discuss responsible uses of technology and information and describe personal consequences of inappropriate use.
4. Use tools and peripherals to support personal productivity, to remediate skill deficits, and to facilitate learning throughout the curriculum.
5. Use technology tools (e.g., multimedia authoring, presentation, Web tools, digital cameras, scanners) for individual and collaborative writing, communication, and publishing activities to create knowledge products for audiences inside and outside the classroom.
6. Use telecommunications to access remote information to communicate with others, and to pursue personal interests.
7. Use telecommunications and on-line resources (e.g., e-mail, on-line discussions, Web environments) to participate in collaborative problem-solving activities.
8. Use technology resources (e.g., calculators, probes, videos, educational software) for problem-solving, self-directed learning, and extended learning activities.

Continued

FIGURE 3.11   *Continued*

9. Determine when technology is useful and select the appropriate tools and technology resources to address tasks and problems.

10. Evaluate the accuracy, relevance, appropriateness, comprehensiveness, and bias of electronic information sources.

Grades 6–8

Prior to completion of grade 8, students will

1. Apply strategies for identifying and solving routine hardware and software problems.

2. Demonstrate knowledge of current changes in information technologies and the effect those changes have on the workplace and on society.

3. Exhibit legal and ethical behaviors when using information and technology and discuss consequences of misuse.

4. Use content-specific tools, software, and simulations (e.g., environmental probes, graphing calculators, exploratory environments, Web tools) to support learning and research.

5. Apply multimedia tools and peripherals to support personal productivity, group collaboration, and learning throughout the curriculum.

6. Design develop, publish, and present products (e.g., Web pages, videotapes) using technology resources that communicate curriculum concepts to audiences inside and outside the classroom.

7. Collaborate with peers, experts, and others using telecommunications and collaborative tools to investigate curriculum-related problems, issues, and information and to develop solutions or products for audiences inside and outside the classroom.

8. Select and use appropriate tools and technology resources to accomplish tasks and to solve problems.

9. Demonstrate an understanding of concepts underlying hardware, software, and connectivity and of practical applications to learning and problem solving.

10. Research and evaluate the accuracy, relevance, appropriateness, comprehensiveness, and bias of electronic information sources concerning real-world problems.

Grades 9–12

Prior to completion of grade 12, students will

1. Identify capabilities and limitations of contemporary and emerging technology resources and assess the potential to these systems and services to address personal, lifelong learning, and workplace needs.

2. Make informed choices among technology systems, resources, and services.

3. Analyze advantages and disadvantages of widespread use and reliance on technology in the workplace and in society as a whole.

4. Demonstrate and advocate legal and ethical behaviors regarding the use of technology and information.

5. Use technology tools and resources for managing and communicating personal or professional information (e.g., finances, schedules, addresses, purchases, correspondence).

6. Evaluate technology-based options, including distance and distributed education, for lifelong learning.

7. Routinely and efficiently use on-line information resources for collaboration, research, publications, communications, and productivity.

8. Select and apply technology tools for research, information analysis, problem solving, and decision making in content learning.

FIGURE 3.11   *Continued*

9. Investigate and apply expert systems, intelligent agents, and simulations in real-world situations.

10. Collaborate with peers, experts, and others to contribute to a content-related knowledge base by using technology to compile, synthesize, produce, and disseminate information, models, and other creative works.

Source: National Educational Technology Standards for Students: Connecting Curriculum and Technology (Eugene, OR: ISTE (International Society for Technology in Education), copyright © 2000, ISTE.

FIGURE 3.12   The Middle School as a Program Design

I. Philosophy
  A. Child-centered
  B. Holistic knowledge structure is developed
  C. Thinking skills are priority goals
  D. Safety is essential
  E. Students' developmental needs are important

II. Curriculum
  A. Academic excellence/social competence
    1. Academic core
    2. Exploration and developmental programs
  B. Personal development
  C. Mastery of continuous learning skills

III. Organization
  A. Interdisciplinary teams
  B. Advisement program
  C. Block scheduling and flexible scheduling within blocks
  D. Team planning and shared decision making
  E. Exploratory and developmental experiences
    1. Elective classes
    2. Wheels and exploration credits
    3. Minicourses
    4. Clubs, activities, interest groups, intramurals
  F. Integrated curriculum
  G. In-service education and professional development

IV. Implementing Strategies (delivery systems)
  A. Cooperative learning
  B. Interdisciplinary teaching
  C. Learning styles
  D. Student services and career planning systems
  E. Home–school partnerships and communications

Source: Jon Wiles and Joseph Bondi, *Curriculum Development: A Guide to Practice,* 5th ed. (New York: Macmillan, 1998), p. 183. Used by permission.

FIGURE 3.13   Eight Common Curriculum Designs

Type	Purpose	Activity
Critical/ Creative Thinking	Construction of new knowledge and forms	Model-building Free imagination
Problem-Solving	Issues analysis Skills application	Current events Futurism
Cooperative Learning	Social skill development Shared decision making	Cooperative activity Group work
Interdisciplinary	Connecting information	Organizing, ordering
Conceptual Learning	Understanding	Big ideas, familiarity
Inquiry Approach	Awareness, interest	Stories, unknowns
Skill-Based Instruction	Manipulation, patterns	Rules, practice, ordering
Content-Based	Knowledge acquisition	Facts, representative form

Source: Adapted from Michele Keating, Jon Wiles, and Mary Piazza, *Learning Webs: Curriculum Journeys on the Internet* (Columbus, Ohio: Merrill Publishing, 2002).

simple content columns discussed previously, this form of curriculum alignment assumes that subject matter is the curriculum.

A more useful approach to instructional design is the construction of a curriculum map or framework that *details the curriculum in terms of purpose.* In this technique, the curriculum is outlined in terms of not only content but also concepts and learning outcomes (skills, behaviors, attitudes). Using a form like that shown in Figure 3.15, each program component is plotted by intent, large and smaller learnings, and outcomes. Some authorities include a third dimension, the "taught" curriculum. If the curriculum is tested by state or normed tests, those tests can be "keyed" to the curriculum, thereby ensuring that what is tested is also taught. If behavioral objectives are developed for the curriculum, this mapping experience will reveal their natural inclusion or exclusion in the curriculum.

Finally, even subject areas can be mapped and aligned for greater logic and clarity. Figure 3.16 illustrates how the dimensions of the various social studies are integrated and connected.

Needs Assessments

The assessment of needs serves as a reality check on curriculum planning. As goals and objectives are established, questions about their appropriateness may arise. Are our goals realistic? Are they specific enough to measure? Can they be observed? Can they be attained by our students? The needs assessment process addresses these questions and provides data that allow curriculum planners to answer these and other questions. In many cases, following the needs assessment, program structures and organization may be revised.

Focusing the curriculum through the needs assessment process amounts to an inquiry into the status of the school or district. The real overarching question is

FIGURE 3.14   A K–12 Content Outline in Science

Kindergarten

Weather and seasons (observations)
Interrelationships of plants and animals
The sun—our principal source of energy
Classification of living things
Simple measurements
How plants are alike and different

Farm animals
Care of pets
Observing animals
Indoor plants
Earth, moon, and stars

Grade 1

Animals and pets
  Farm animals
  Zoo and circus animals
  Woodland animals
  Common birds
Where plants live
Where animals live
Grouping and classification

Air and water
Seeds, bulbs, plants, and flowers
Day and night
Sun, moon, stars
Seasons and weather
Fire and temperature
Simple machines

Grade 2

Animals of our neighborhood
Useful and harmful animals
Birds and insects in winter
Animal babies
How plants and animals get their food
Plant reproduction
How animals protect themselves and their young
Effects of seasons on lives of people, animals, and plants
Weather and how it affects our earth

Heat and temperature
The sun
The moon
The earth and sky
Simple constellations
Gravity
Air and atmosphere
Magnets and forces
Exploring space

Grade 3

How the face of the earth changes
The atmosphere
Motions of the earth
Earth satellites
Stars and moon
Energy and its sources
Sound
Weather and climate
Rocks and soil
How animals serve people

Plants and animals of the desert
Plants and animals of the sea
Life cycle of animals
Common birds, trees, and flowers
Forest plants
Conservation of plants and animals
Ocean life
Magnets and electricity
Great names in science

Grade 4

Environment of local state
Measurement systems (including metric)
Plants and animals of the past
Earth and its history
Balance of nature
Classification systems
Structure of plants
How weather influences physical life
Causes of seasons
Solar system and the universe

Oceans and the hydrosphere
Climate
Rocks and minerals
Plants and seeds
The insect world
Biological organization
Living in space
Air and water pollution
Great names in science

Continued

FIGURE 3.14   *Continued*

Grade 5

How living things adapt themselves	The Milky Way
Plants and their food	Great names in science
Properties of air	Use and control of electricity
Properties of water	Magnetic fields
Chemical systems	Latitude and longitude
Time and seasons	Space and space explorations
Molds	Conservation
Bacteria	Biotic communities
Trees	Biological adaptations
Sun	

Grade 6

Helpful and harmful insects	Elements of sound
Improvement of plants and animals	Light and heat
Classification of living things	Heat engines
Food for growth and energy	Equilibrium systems
Microbes	Atom and nuclear energy
Algae and fungi	Inventions and discoveries
Energy and simple machines	Great names in science
Climate and weather	Space and space travel
Motors and engines	Ecology and environment
Electricity and its uses	Recycling of resources
Simple astronomy	Energy futures
Elementary geology	Conservation

Grade 7

Scientific method	Atmosphere
Scientific classification	Energy crisis
Bacterial mutations	Alternative energy sources
The cell	Conservation
Life cycle of insects	Properties and uses of water
Anatomy and physiology	Effects of weather and climate
Genetics	Changes and uses of materials
Rocks and soil	Ecology and environment
Minerals	Famous scientists and their contributions
Air pressure	

Grade 8

Scientific method	Conservation
Science nomenclature	Contributions of scientists
Scientific measurement	Astronomy
Water and its uses	Heat
Magnetism and electricity	Light
Composition of the earth	Machines
The earth's movement	The atom
Weathering and erosion	Chemical changes
The ocean	Wave energy
The atmosphere	Mechanical energy
Weather	Electrical energy
The universe	Nuclear energy
The Milky Way	Ecology and environment
Space and space travel	Recycling of resources

FIGURE 3.14   *Continued*

Grade 9

General science
Air and air pressure
Heat and fuels
Weather and climate
Air masses and fronts
Erosion
Nature and uses of light
Water and its uses
Air and water pollution
Electricity and electronics
Solar energy
Nuclear energy
Molecular theory

Earth science
Ecology and environment
Space and astronomy
Space travel
Metals and plastics
Sound and music
Nature and causes of disease
Health and safety
Nature and uses of chemicals
Simple and complex machines
Transportation and communication
Effects of alcohol and narcotics on the
     human body
Careers in science

Grade 10

Biology
Characteristics of life
Vetebrate life
Mammals and birds
Conservation of human resources
Plant life
Behavior
The scientific method
Disease and disease control
Genetics
Heredity
Biology of humans

Humans—a changing organism
Microscopic life
Classification
DNA–RNA
Nutrition and digestion
History of plants and animals
Reproduction and growth
Biology and space travel
Environmental issues
Energy in ecosystems
Careers in biology

Grade 11

Chemistry
Matter and its behavior
Carbon and its compounds
Formulas and chemical equations
Acids, bases, and salts
Atomic theory
Periodic law
Water and solutions
Oxidation–reduction

The nonmetals
Ionization and ionic solutions
The metals and alloys
Colloids, suspensoids, and emulsoids
Electrochemistry
Equilibrium and kinetics
Nuclear reactions
Radioactivity
Careers in chemistry

Grade 12

Physics
Mechanics
Heat
Electricity and magnetism
Sound and acoustics
Light and optics
Wave motion
Nuclear physics

Electronics
Force
Work, energy, and power
Space, time, and motion
Relativity
Solid state physics
Careers in physics

FIGURE 3.15 Curriculum Map or Framework

Curriculum Area:	Music
Subject:	Discover Music (General Music)

Grade Level:	6
Grading Period:	1—Page 1

Major Topics/ Content	Generalizations/ Concepts	Intended Outcomes	Specific Skills/ Standards
Rhythm Beat Meter metric accent Duration Relationship to beat—long, short, same	Music is organized by an underlying pulse. Music includes patterns of long and short sound and silences.	Aurally and visually identify and physically respond to beat and duple and triple meter—2/4, 3/4, 4/4. Recognize relationship of pattern to the beat of music they hear and see. Patterns will include these note values:	Identify and demonstrate beat and meter through movement and playing instruments in response to music heard and/or seen. Read rhythmic patterns independently; perform patterns vocally and instrumentally. Improvise and compose rhythmic accompaniments using these patterns.
Melody Contour ascending descending repeating Tonality tonal, atonal	Melody is a succession of pitches that can ascend, descend, and repeat. Some melodies are organized by tonal centers; some melodies have no tonal center.	Aural and visual identification of melodic contour. Aural recognition of presence or absence of tonal center.	Improve and demonstrate melodic contour through bodily movement. Describe tonality of music heard. Perform music that is tonal and music that is atonal with voices and recorders.
Harmony Texture thick, thin homophony (chordal)	Two or more sounds can be combined to make harmony. Chords can be used to accompany a melody.	Aurally recognize density of music. Aurally recognize chord changes. Select chords to accompany melodies.	Identify texture (thick, thin) of music heard. Move in response to chord changes in music. Play chordal accompaniments using I, IV, V^7 in at least one key by reading chord symbols and by ear (use autoharp).

FIGURE 3.16 Curriculum Connections in Social Studies

	Course of Study	Theme	Link to Vision	Connections						
				Sociology	History	Geography	Economics	Political Science	Ethics	Humanities
K	My Family and Others	Observations of self and other families in the world	Begin to locate self in space	Variations in the human family	Songs/stories about other cultures	Basic physical geographic skills and concepts	Concepts of needs, wants, scarcity, choices	Personal responsibilities; rules at home and school	Codes of behavior followed by all people	Celebrations and expressions of creativity
1	Families Near and Far	Continued observations of self and other families in the world	Enrich personal and social sense of identity	Social interactions of diverse groups	Music, legends, stories about other cultures	Relationships between humans and environment	Choice, opportunity cost, specialization	Community rules and cooperation among groups	Characteristics of good citizens all over the world	Celebrations and expressions of creativity
2	Our Cultures: Past and Present	Ethnicity, customs, traditions, and values of the United States	Associate new experiences with past; build allusionary base	Customs and values of diverse cultures	American heroes, holidays and symbols	Physical geography skills, map keys, symbols	Producer/consumer, property, risk-takers	Symbols of freedom; government for people	Role models who displayed traditional values	Expressions of diverse cultural heritages
3	Beginnings: People, Places and Events	Critical events from the past that helped shape our world	Personal and social identity; associate present and past	Interactions between cultures; spread of ideas	Narrative study of critical events from the past	Physical geography; influence on civilizations	Basic needs, trade, banking, specialization	Democracy, participatory government; codes of conduct	People who display universally valued traits	Developments, art, language, dance, music
4 5	History and Geography to 1880 / U.S. and Florida History and Geography Since 1880	Specific topics in the history and geography of the United States and Florida	Associate new experiences with the past; gather information about people in time, in space, and in culture	Movement; interaction of people/ideas; relationship of events to present/future U.S. and Florida problems	Narrative/biographical history placed within a chronological/thematic frame of reference	Physical geography, exploration, settlement, transportation, expansion, migration, environment	Economic concerns related to exploration and trade; lifestyles, entrepreneurship, and multiple work skills	Documents of democracy; levels/branches/purposes/functions of government; local and state study	Responsibilities of citizens for general welfare; ideals valued by Americans; group participation	Various forms in arts, literature, music, drama, and fine arts
6 7	Geography: Asia, Oceania, and Africa / Geography: Europe and the Americas	Systematic observation and analysis of people and their world using the geographic themes of location, place, human–environment interactions, movement, and region	Expand personal sense of identity; provide additional information about people in space and in culture	Interaction of people/ideas; ways in which group dynamics influence norms and mores	Draws on relevant historical understandings related to each place	Human and physical geography placed within time and space	Interrelatedness of economics to the social and political order; concept of economic decision making	Connections between political institutions, the economy and society	Values and belief systems of many different cultures and how they can affect worldviews	Art, architecture, literature, music, language that displays cultural differences and similarities

Continued

FIGURE 3.16 *Continued*

Course of Study	Theme	Link to Vision	Connections						
			Sociology	History	Geography	Economics	Political Science	Ethics	Humanities
8 Florida: Challenges and Choices	Systematic analysis of contemporary Florida people and issues	Prepare students to explain, sympathize, judge, decide, and act	Personal, social responsibility of individual/group	Study of events that created modern Florida	Five geographic themes as they relate to Florida	Personal/social /local/global decision making	Interconnectedness of political, economic issues	Value of ethical behavior in contemporary society	Art, literature, music, folkways of life in Florida
9 Eastern and Western Heritage	Chronological, topical study of civilization to the Renaissance	Expands common knowledge, values, and cultural allusions	Interaction between cultures; spread of ideas		Influence on cities and cultural development	Division of labor; barter, banking, cash economy	Foundations for several forms of government	Universal nature of social order; responsibilities	Art, literature, music of past civilizations
10 Visions and Their Pursuits: An American Tradition	Chronological, thematic study of U.S. history to World War I	Identification in time, space, culture; aware of human condition	Social interaction; development of group norms	Narrative, cultural history placed within a chronological framework	Factors influencing development of certain regions	Economic concepts used to interpret history	Specific foundation of U.S. political system	Values affecting the treatment of specific groups	American art forms, music, folk/fine arts
11 Visions/Countervisions: Europe, U.S., and the World	Chronological, topical study of modern U.S. and world history	Awareness of cultural heritage of the U.S.; sense of time/space/ culture	Interactions of people/society in modern world		Influence on political, economic world events	Comparing economic systems and effects	Emergence of political systems and their effects	Responsibilities of all citizens for ethical behavior	Art, literature, music as responses to events
12 The American Political and Economic Experience	Application of political and economic principles to the individual	Prepare for participation in social, political, and economic life	Development of norms. Interaction of people	Spread of political and economic ideas/systems	Influence on political, economic, and human behavior	Distribution and redistribution of resources	Relationship between people and their government	Ways to ensure ethical behavior	Examples of economic/political philosophies

Source: Connections, Challenges, Choice—A Report of the Florida Commission on Social Studies Education: A Commitment to the Students of Florida (Tallahassee: Florida Department of Education, 1991), pp. 1–126.

"Does this program meet our expressed needs?" If not, the goals, the instructional design, or even student expectations may call for redesign.

Needs assessments are unique in that they are internally designed and implemented. Outside opinion and expertise are not usually a part of the process. In most cases, schools or districts decide on categories of data that they would like to review and the procedures for gathering and assessing this information. A standard needs assessment framework is provided in Figure 3.17.

Rather than being a judgmental process of good and bad, or right and wrong, data is viewed as a "condition." In Figure 3.18, for example, it appears that corporal punishment is being unevenly applied in the fifteen schools assessed. Whether corporal punishment is an appropriate practice, or how much behavior is excessive, is not the issue. Simply, the application of this practice is quite uneven.

Needs assessments, because they are internal tools for "correcting" the curriculum, often use subjective data as well as objective data. Surveys and opinionnaires are common (see Figure 3.19) and can provide a look at the discrepancy between where we are and where we say we would like to be. If the discrepancy revealed by the needs assessment is too large, our goals and objectives may need to be adjusted.

Finally, needs assessments do not lead to judgments or sanctions of school curriculum efforts. They are exclusively for the use of curriculum planners.

Content Design and Structure

The power of curriculum development to guide teaching cannot be overstated. In-service training can provide teachers with skills and instructional approaches; the curriculum rationalizes such acts. By determining how content is to be treated, the curriculum developer skews the curriculum toward certain ends. Obviously, the content design should be an extension of philosophy, program concept, goals, and the various-level objectives.

In all teaching, there is a tension between philosophies that lead to conformity and those that lead to diversity. The curriculum can seek to standardize student responses by increasing environmental "structure" in the classroom, or it can seek flexibility in the classroom with the intent of meeting perceived differences by individualizing instruction (see Gibbons model, Chapter 2). The position of the curriculum designer on this continuum of choosing should be a product of three factors: philosophy, learning theory, and knowledge of the research bases for instruction.

The timeless concept of horizontal and vertical articulation (coordination) is applicable in making a selection from among many standardized curriculum structures. To the degree that the designer seeks to constrain learning within a highly defined scope (parameter), most focus will be on vertical connectedness of the same subject. If, by contrast, the philosophy and goals are broad (e.g., Seven Cardinal Principles), then horizontal articulation (connection of subjects) will be the supreme focus. In the case of existentialism, such efforts to define the curriculum (focusing) will be moot; simple access to the curriculum will be the primary concern.

FIGURE 3.17   Needs Assessment Framework

I.   General Information
    a. Location of school district
    b. Demographic characteristics of immediate area
    c. Natural resources of region
    d. Commercial–industrial data
    e. Income levels of area residents
    f. Special social–economic considerations
II.   General Population Characteristics
    a. Population growth patterns
    b. Age, race of population
    c. Educational levels of population
    d. Projected population
III. School Population Characteristics (Ages 3–19)
    a. School enrollment by grade level
    b. Birthrate trends in school district
    c. In-migration, out-migration patterns
    d. Race/sex/religious composition of school district
    e. Years of school completed by persons more than twenty-five years of age
    f. Studies of school dropouts
IV.   Programs and Course Offerings in District
    a. Organization of school programs
    b. Programs' concept and rationale
    c. Course offerings
    d. Special program needs
V.   Professional Staff
    a. Training and experience
    b. Awareness of trends and developments
    c. Attitudes toward change
VI.   Instructional Patterns and Strategies
    a. Philosophical focus of instructional program
    b. Observational and perceptual instructional data
    c. Assessment of instructional strategies in use
    d. Instructional materials in use
    e. Decision-making and planning processes
    f. Grouping for instruction
    g. Classroom management techniques
    h. Grading and placement of pupils
    i. Student independence
    j. Evaluation of instructional effectiveness
VII. Student Data
    a. Student experiences
    b. Student self-esteem
    c. Student achievement
VIII. Facilities
    a. Assessment of existing facilities and sites
    b. Special facilities
    c. Utilization of facilities
    d. Projected facility needs
IX.   Summary of Data

FIGURE 3.18   Displaying Needs Assessment Data

Preliminary Needs Assessment Data from Fifteen Pilot Middle Schools 1988–1989
Middle Schools Comparison of Factors Affecting School Achievement in Dade Co. 6/88

	Age of School	Assigned Cap.	# of Students	# Stud. Trans.	% New Teachers	% Staff Attend.	Ratio W–B–H	% Limit. Eng.	% F/R Lunch	% St. Mobility	% St. Attend.	Suspension 86/7	Corp. Pun. 86/7	St. Not Promoted over no. grades	St. Dropout/Yr.	# Comp Ed St.
Lake Stevens	1975	1292	1088	312	14	96.8	8/59/33	2.5	48.5	36	90.7	268	4	11.2/3	4.1	247
Palm Springs	1957	1222	1169	0	0	97.1	8/0/91	10.4	17.5	36	92.1	269	0	23.7/4	6.0	125
Charles Drew	1967	1220	876	35	14.6	97.1	0/99/1	0	53.9	42	90.2	118	71	21.0/2	10.8	266
Madison	1955	1007	841	31	10.9	96.9	3/73/24	5.7	48.3	39	91.6	84	8	35.3/3	9.1	197
Citrus Grove	1924	1417	1358	154	9.4	96.5	4/9/87	17.9	55.2	38	91.9	233	0	15.3/3	6.9	321
Citrus Ridge	1969	1120	1107	189	5.1	96.7	26/39/32	2.8	25.0	28	92.7	157	0	1.8/3	5.7	74
Mays	1951	1050	733	300	13.5	94.8	10/54/35	4.1	68.3	41	90.0	158	0	24.3/3	4.5	114
Redlands	1926	1290	1281	1155	8.1	97.7	58/16/24	1.5	27.6	31	91.4	354	1	20.0/3	5.8	131
Campbell Dr.	1976	1516	1266	721	8.5	96.8	20/28/51	2.1	50.3	37	86.3	373	0	18.3/3	5.2	168
Filer	1956	1355	1372	146	9.4	96.7	3/10/86	9.5	51.0	28	92.6	50	1	4.7/3	9.1	237
Nautilus	1949	1243	1327	999	12.5	97.0	22/18/59	10.8	48.5	40	90.0	267	0	17.1/2	14.6	265
Norland	1960	1348	1377	360	4.5	96.6	19/67/13	0.9	25.1	25	95.5	170	99	8.7/3	1.3	161
Shenandoah	1926	1436	727	8	3.0	96.4	4/2/94	17.9	55.2	34	91.9	99	0	11.8/2	10.3	138

Note: The reader should note the variance in areas such as corporal punishment, drop-out rates, transfers, and socioeconomic levels of students. All of these suggest program development or curriculum renewal.

Source: Middle School Progress Report, Dade County, Florida, 1989. Editor Jon Wiles.

Among the most highly defined curriculum structures are simple content chains that must be mastered in an order predetermined by the teacher or tradition (such as geometry). Here, systems of thought, standardized procedures, chronology, or representative outlined material forces the student to learn the material in "order." In Figure 3.20, the path for teaching about population growth is presented as an outline of content topics.

A second highly structured ordering of content is the "spiral" design. In this configuration, content expands in scope and builds on learnings over the years. Although this reinforcement can be conceptual, it is more likely an enlarged "revisiting" of previous material, knowledge, and ideas. In Figure 3.21, learning about living things is portrayed from first grade to high school biology.

A third type of curriculum content design seeks to relate knowledge within an area of study by establishing connectedness. In the correlational approach, common

FIGURE 3.19 Sample Opinionnaire

Middle School (Grades 6–8) Opinionnaire, Parent Form

Please rate each of the following ideas about middle schools to show how important each one is to you and your child. Choose the answer that you feel is best and place the corresponding number in the blank space. Use the key below to show your feelings.

1 Very Important	2 Important
3 Fairly Important	4 Not Very Important
5 Not Important at All	

Example: If having guidance and counseling service available for each student is "Fairly Important" to you, you would place a "3" in the blank space.

_____ 1. Guidance and counseling services should be available for each student.

_____ 2. Each student should have at least one teacher who knows him/her well.

_____ 3. Small group and individual guidance should also be provided by a classroom teacher under the direction of the school counselor.

_____ 4. Opportunities for after-school social activities (such as dances, athletic games, boosters) should be provided for students.

_____ 5. Opportunities should be provided to help students develop good attitudes and standards for themselves.

_____ 6. Club activities should be scheduled during the day to provide opportunities for group work in areas of common interest.

_____ 7. Students should expand and discover their individual interests and aptitudes through exploratory and enrichment courses (such as home economics, band, creative writing).

_____ 8. Remedial instruction should be available to assist students who have difficulty in mastering basic skills.

_____ 9. A wide variety of intramural activities (team competition within the same school) should be offered to allow all students to participate.

_____10. Physical education should emphasize health, physical fitness, and lifetime sports.

_____11. Students should have an opportunity to express creativity through student newspapers, drama, and music.

_____12. A variety of teaching methods and materials should be utilized rather than a single textbook approach.

_____13. Students should use and apply basic skills through projects and "hands-on" activities.

_____14. Students should proceed at their own rate according to their abilities.

_____15. Behavior problems should be handled, when possible, by teachers and parents without the involvement of the administrators.

_____16. Major disciplinary problems should be handled by the school administrators.

_____17. An alternative program to suspension should be provided for students having behavior problems (in-school suspension program).

_____18. Opportunities should be provided for parents to have a conference with all of their child's teachers at the same time.

Note: Responses will tell planners which of these items is most important to the client parent.

Source: Jon Wiles and Joseph Bondi, *Making Middle Schools Work* (Alexandria, VA: ASCD). Used by permission of the Association for Supervision and Curriculum Development. Copyright © 1985 by ASCD. All rights reserved.

FIGURE 3.20   Simple Content Structures—Outlines

Population Explosion

I.   Population Crisis
   A. Different population growth rates in developed and nondeveloped countries
   B. Greatly increased numbers of youth
   C. Stress on resources
      1. Energy/natural resources
      2. Food
      3. Housing
      4. Employment
      5. Environment

II. Dynamics of Population Growth
   A. Population growth curves
   B. Birth/death rates
   C. Fertility rate
   D. Migration
   E. Zero population growth

III. Limits to Population Growth: Pros and Cons
   A. Theory of Thomas Malthus
   B. Family planning/birth control
   C. Health
   D. Education
   E. Urbanization
   F. Family structure
   G. Tradition
   H. Force

IV. Case Studies
   A. United States
   B. Bangladesh
   C. China
   D. Japan

relationships between two or more subjects are displayed while maintaining the subject matter separation. Biology and chemistry could be treated in such a manner without reorganizing their structures into biochemistry. Another connecting design that maintains the subject integrity is the minicourse. In the example given in Figure 3.22, general science is treated as a series of subjects that maintain their disciplinary integrity.

FIGURE 3.21   Spiral Designs—"Living Things"

First grade	Children grow plant in cup, study effect of light and water.
Fourth grade	Students take field trip to pond to observe interdependence of life forms and food chains (ecology).
Seventh grade	Students dissect frog to identify common body parts of amphibians.
Tenth grade	Students in biology study taxonomies of living things.

FIGURE 3.22   Connecting Designs—The Minicourse

Anatomy

This course covers cellular structure, organization of the body in terms of cells, tissues, organs and systems, and anatomical terminology. Special attention will be paid to the effects of alcohol, drugs, and tobacco on the systems of the body.

Ecology

This course studies our relationship to the total environment. Students will learn how we have changed our environment and the type of actions needed to preserve our environment.

Rock and Minerals

This course will help the student understand the materials that make up the earth's crust. The actual identification of rocks and minerals will be accomplished through field study.

Microbiology

This course is designed to study all microscopic forms of life, such as algae, fungi, mold, bacteria, and protozoans. With the aid of the teacher all students will grow their own cultures for study.

A fourth and ever more flexible content structure is the conceptual approach. Here, larger organizing ideas and principles are extracted from the body of content and serve as organizers for future learning. Three common labels in this category are core, broad fields, and thematic. Core structures often overlap two or more subjects and show their commonality while still treating their distinctiveness as an organizer. Major topics may be covered from each perspective (see Figure 3.23). Broad fields designs are usually more restricted to branches of knowledge, such as social studies and the arts. Thematic structures take topics such as problem solving, culture, family, power, or ritual, and weave subject matter into them without great effort to relate those subjects to one another.

Finally, a fifth curriculum content structure can be called integrated because content disciplines lose their pure identities. In this category would be fused and

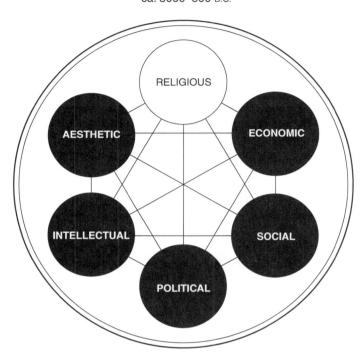

EGYPT
ca. 3000–500 B.C.

Some Historic Characteristics of Ancient Egypt

RELIGIOUS   ◯
• Polytheistic
• Immorality for the
  "good"

AESTHETIC   ⬤
• Monumental art
• Freestanding statues
• Murals

INTELLECTUAL   ⬤
• Hieroglyphic writing
• Engineering—pyramids

ECONOMIC   ⬤
• Intensive irrigation
  farming
• Copper mining, quarrying,
  brick making

SOCIAL   ⬤
• Classes:
    Nobility and priests
    Merchants and artisans
    Laborers and peasants

POLITICAL   ⬤
• Economy controlled
  by the pharaoh
• Theocratic government

FIGURE 3.23   Conceptual Designs—Core

Source: Adapted from John D. McNeil and Jon Wiles, *The Essentials of Teaching: Decisions, Plans, Methods* (New York: Macmillan, 1990), p. 380. Our thanks to Professor Oliver Ivey, Auburn University, for this conception.

interdisciplinary designs. Fused designs merge two or more previously independent subject areas (biology and chemistry) into a new area (biochemistry).

Interdisciplinary content designs erase old structures and create overlapping content presentations organized around problems, needs of students, or outcomes, such as skill development and application. Usually, the curriculum is mapped to identify contributions (Figure 3.24) and then the subjects are loosely woven together (Figure 3.25).

The reader should see these designs as reinforcing philosophy (tight content designs for highly structured beliefs, such as perennialism and idealism) and more loosely structured content for philosophies concerned with application (realism) or the diversity of students (experimentalism or existentialism). As the content structure is formed and handed to the teacher, its design would suggest methodology and material development. Appropriate teaching behaviors, perhaps reinforced in staff development, color or skew the meaning of the content: These choices are summarized in Figure 3.26.

Instructional Linkage

Curriculum planning cannot cease after creating documents because the final curriculum form results from teacher planning. Although curriculum workers can structure the learning environment with goals and objectives and intended outcomes, even with the selection of materials, they must follow the teacher into the classroom with instructional design in order to be effective. Researcher David Berliner stated the case for such classroom involvement in this way:

> *A set of complex decisions must be made, primarily before instruction takes place. Teachers need to be acutely aware of the power they have when making certain decisions to facilitate or retard achievement, to affect the attitude of students, and to control classroom behavior. . . . Teachers who must choose between recitation, lecture, discussion, reading circles, computer-mediated instruction, television, and so on, must also learn that each activity limits or enhances certain factors that affect instruction. . . . Teachers usually do not know how to make these kind of cost/benefit decisions when choosing activity structures (methods).*[11]

DeCharm and Kluender echo this theme by observing:

> *Many teachers, veterans of ten years or more, often in the same school, sometimes with the same subject matter, conduct classes as though they were following an invisible script. They demonstrate the craft of teaching but little artistry.*[12]

How is the teacher to decide which of the many strategies to employ (Figure 3.27) when teaching? Only a full and complete understanding of the purpose and intent of the planned curriculum will allow such classroom curriculum work to be successful.

FIGURE 3.24 Interdisciplinary Mapping

Grade	Six
Grading Period	Second nine weeks
Title of Interdisciplinary Unit	The Physical Earth
Goal of Unit Content	To acquaint students with the structure of the physical earth and its effects on life.

Subject	Topics	Generalization/Concepts
Math	Addition and Subtraction Decimal Addition and Subtraction Multiplication Division Decimal Multiplication and Division	Math has an internal consistency and predictability. Decimals are the foundation of our number system.
Language Arts	Reading Writing Thinking Speaking Listening	Sharing common human experiences assists in defining one's own humanity and in developing a positive self-concept. Literature is a reflection of its historical era. Personal values are enhanced through exploring the values of others. Functional literature provides the skills necessary and/or relevant to business and personal management.
Science	Earth Climate Space	Earth is our home and we have a responsibility to understand and maintain it for future generations. Learning about the types of resources (renewable/non-renewable) clarifies the need to recycle or conserve. Understanding and predicting weather are important to organisms interacting with the environment.
Social Studies	The Middle Ages The Rise of Modern Civilization Map and Globe Skills	Charts and graphs assist people in understanding information. Maps and globes assist people in understanding spatial relationships on the earth. Physical characteristics of the earth influence the way people live.
Health	Interpersonal Relationships Personal Health Practices Substance Abuse Human Growth and Development Disease/AIDS Education Safety/First Aid/CPR	Relationships within the family and among peers affect potential well-being. Information about the classification and effects of tobacco, alcohol, and other drugs is needed to make healthy decisions.

PERSPECTIVE: Will our students see school experiences as a unified whole applicable to a successful life or as a collection of apparently unrelated presentations?

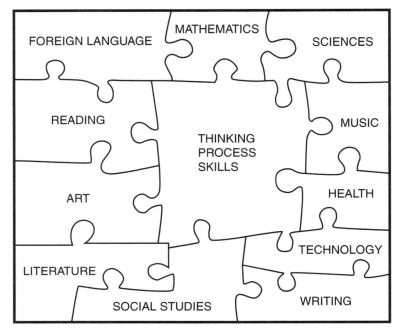

A holistic knowledge structure, or confusion over relevancy.

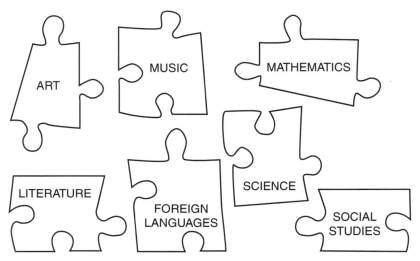

FIGURE 3.25   Interdisciplinary—"Weaving Subjects"

Source: Middle School Progress Report, Dade County, Florida, 1992.

FIGURE 3.26   Content Organization Options

Content	
Outlines	Traditional representations
Systems	Fixed and unchanging
Fixed procedures	Knowing
Chronologies	
Spiral	
Repeating patterns of knowledge	Repetition of patterns
Systematic unfolding of content	Foundational and higher learning
Fragmented	
Minicourse approach	Relational learning
Correlational	
Conceptual	
Core	Flexible
Broad fields	General understanding
Thematic	
Integrated	
Fused	Applied
Interdisciplinary	Loosely organized
	Focused on students

Curriculum developers should envision a "cycle within a cycle" for the classroom where the same analyze–design–implement–evaluate cycle used in large-scale planning is repeated by the teacher. In the instructional paradigm shown in Figure 3.28, the teacher begins planning by reviewing curriculum plans, objectives, and content organization and ends the cycle by verifying the efficacy of the plan.

It is vital that the curriculum developer communicate to the teacher the purpose or intent of the curriculum. Just as there are different philosophies of education, there are different conceptions of instruction. Even in the same building, with the same teacher and children, addressing the same content, there can be different reasons for teaching.

Teachers have a series of questions to be answered by their planning procedures, and those questions can only be addressed in the context of the curriculum intent. Figure 3.29 lists twenty questions that can help the classroom teacher fine-tune the curriculum. Such questions can also serve as an evaluative feedback loop for curriculum designers in assessing teacher performance.

In the end, the rationale for the lesson (curriculum purpose) should determine both instructional design and strategies employed by the teacher. The other planning variables (time, material) should support this curriculum and instruction link.

FIGURE 3.27   Instructional Choices: Possible Strategies for the Teacher

1. *Comparative Analysis*—A thought process, structured by the teacher, that employs the description, classification, and analysis of more than one system, group, or the like in order to ascertain and evaluate similarities and differences.

2. *Conference*—A one-to-one interaction between teacher and learner where the individual's needs and problems can be dealt with. Diagnosis, evaluation, and prescription may all be involved.

3. *Demonstration*—An activity in which the teacher or another person uses examples, experiments, and/or other actual performance to illustrate a principle or show others how to do something.

4. *Diagnosis*—The continuous determination of the nature of learning difficulties and deficiencies, used in teaching as a basis for the selection, day by day or moment by moment, of appropriate content and methods of instruction.

5. *Directed Observation*—Guided observation provided for the purpose of improving the study, understanding, and evaluation of that which is observed.

6. *Discussion*—An activity in which pupils, under teacher and/or pupil direction, exchange points of view concerning a topic, question, or problem to arrive at a decision or conclusion.

7. *Drill*—An orderly, repetitive learning activity intended to help develop or fix a specific skill or aspect of knowledge.

8. *Experimentalism*—An activity involving a planned procedure accompanied by control of conditions and/or controlled variation of conditions together with observation of results for the purpose of discovering relationships and evaluating the reasonableness of a specific hypothesis.

9. *Field Experience*—Educational work experience, sometimes fully paid, acquired by pupils in a practical service situation.

10. *Field Trip*—An educational trip to places where pupils can study the content of instruction directly in its functional setting, e.g., factory, newspaper office, or fire department.

11. *Group Work*—A process in which members of the class working cooperatively, rather than individually, formulate and work toward common objectives under the guidance of one or more leaders.

12. *Laboratory Experience*—Learning activities carried on by pupils in a laboratory designed for individual or group study of a particular subject-matter area, involving the practical application of theory through observation, experimentation and research, or, in the case of foreign language instruction, involving learning through demonstration, drill, and practice. This applies also to the study of art and music, although such activity in this instance may be referred to as studio experience.

13. *Lecture*—An activity in which the teacher gives an oral presentation of facts or principles, the class frequently being responsible for note-taking. This activity usually involves little or no pupil participation by questioning or discussion.

14. *Manipulative and Tactile Activity*—Activity by which pupils utilize the movement of various muscles and sense of touch to develop manipulative and/or perceptual skills.

15. *Modeling and Imitation*—An activity frequently used for instruction in speech, in which the pupils listen to and observe a model as a basis upon which to practice and improve their performance.

16. *Problem Solving*—A thought process structured by the teacher and employed by the pupils for clearly defining a problem, forming hypothetical solutions, and possibly testing the hypothesis.

17. *Programmed Instruction*—Instruction utilizing a workbook or mechanical and/or electronic device which has been programmed by (a) providing instruction in small steps, (b) asking one or more questions about each step in the instruction and providing instant knowledge of whether each answer is right or wrong, and (c) enabling pupils to progress at their own pace.

FIGURE 3.27 *Continued*

18. *Project*—A significant, practical unit of activity having educational value, aimed at one or more definite goals of understanding and involving the investigation and solution of problems.

19. *Reading*—Gathering information from books, periodicals, encyclopedias, and other printed sources of information, including oral reading and silent reading by individuals.

20. *Recitation*—Activities devoted to reporting to a class or other group about information acquired through individual study or group work.

21. *Role-Play*—An activity in which students and/or teacher take on the behavior of a hypothetical or real personality in order to solve a problem and gain insight into a situation.

22. *Seminar*—An activity in which a group of pupils, engaged in research or advanced study, meets under the general direction of one or more staff members for a discussion of problems of mutual interest.

Source: Jon Wiles and Joseph Bondi, *Curriculum Development: A Guide to Practice,* 3rd ed. (Columbus, OH: Charles Merrill, 1989), pp. 185–186. Used by permission.

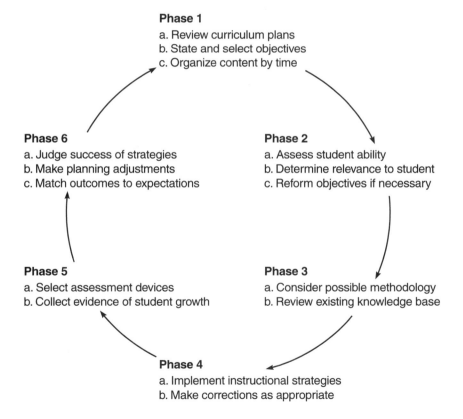

Phase 1
a. Review curriculum plans
b. State and select objectives
c. Organize content by time

Phase 6
a. Judge success of strategies
b. Make planning adjustments
c. Match outcomes to expectations

Phase 2
a. Assess student ability
b. Determine relevance to student
c. Reform objectives if necessary

Phase 5
a. Select assessment devices
b. Collect evidence of student growth

Phase 3
a. Consider possible methodology
b. Review existing knowledge base

Phase 4
a. Implement instructional strategies
b. Make corrections as appropriate

FIGURE 3.28   Instructional Planning as a Cycle

Source: Adapted from Jon Wiles and Joseph Bondi, *Supervision: A Guide to Practice,* 4th ed. (New York: Macmillan, 1996), p. 110. Used by permission.

FIGURE 3.29   Questions That Help Focus Instruction

1. Is the classroom physically prepared? Is the furniture arranged in ways that promote the desired learning? Is the environment conducive to what I intend to teach?

2. Do I have a plan for getting students into the room and settled in their seats?

3. Have I thought of a "motivational opener" to smooth the transition from the last class to the next one?

4. Can I give students a preview (advanced organizers) of what we will be doing during the period so that they will know what to expect?

5. Have I estimated the time required for each activity in this period?

6. Are the major concepts for this lesson covered by my planned activities?

7. Do the materials to be used contain the essential facts I want to teach?

8. Have I planned for the appropriate level of affect desired?

9. Have I planned so to allow each student to participate at his or her appropriate level of learning?

10. Are the necessary and appropriate materials present in the classroom?

11. Do I have a plan for discussion? Have I clarified what kinds of discussion will contribute most to the lesson objectives?

12. Have I planned for relevance? Do I have some real-life examples to present?

13. Have I considered handout procedures and steps for collecting homework?

14. How will I involve special students in this lesson?

15. What is my plan for grouping? What directions will I give?

16. Do I have a plan for possible deviant behavior?

17. Do I want to emphasize a certain format or standard for today's homework or assignment?

18. What kind of test questions will I ask about today's material? Do I want to share these expectations with students?

19. What technique will I use for closing today's lesson?

20. What is my procedure for class dismissal?

Source: Jon Wiles and Joseph Bondi, *Curriculum Development: A Guide to Practice,* 5th ed. (New York: Macmillan, 1998), p. 143. Used by permission.

SUMMARY

Curriculum development in American schools is a highly refined process beginning with a conceptualization and based on some agreed-on criteria. Armed with these directives, the curriculum designer can create programs to meet the needs of most students through a deductive process of planning. In this chapter the reader has reviewed illustrations of the major components, including philosophy and goal statements, objectives, program designs, program standards, course frameworks, and various means to instructional linkage.

Regardless of the level of instruction, this kind of procedural flow produces plans that will allow instruction to be more effective and to be delivered as intended. Also, the more compatible the curriculum and instructional designs, the more powerful the curriculum is as experienced by the student.

In reality, the linear logic of the development process is often interrupted by variables in our "open system of education." The following chapter details how curriculum specialists can increase the odds of successful implementation.

SUGGESTED READINGS

English, Fenwick, *Deciding What to Teach and Test: Developing, Aligning, Auditing* (Newbury Park, CA: Corwin Press, 1992).

Morrison, Gary, *Designing Effective Instruction* (New York: John Wiley, 2001).

Reiser, Robert, *Instructional Planning: A Guide for Teachers,* 2nd ed. (Boston: Allyn & Bacon, 1996).

Senge, Peter, *The Fifth Discipline: The Art and Practice of the Learning Organization* (New York: Doubleday, 1990).

Whitehead, Bruce, *Planning for Technology: A Guide* (Thousand Oaks, CA: Corwin Press, 2003).

ENDNOTES

1. Galen Saylor and William Alexander, *Curriculum Planning in Schools* (New York: Holt, Rinehart and Winston, 1974), p. 6.

2. G. Saylor and W. Alexander, op. cit.

3. John Dewey, *Democracy and Education* (New York: Macmillan, 1916), p. 246.

4. "Minimum Essentials in Elementary Subjects," in *Subject Matter and the Curriculum,* Fifteenth National Society for the Study of Education Yearbook (Bloomington, IL: Public School Publishing, 1915), p. 16.

5. Charles McMurry, *How to Organize the Curriculum* (New York: Macmillan, 1923), p. 76.

6. Thomas Briggs, *Curriculum Problems* (New York: Macmillan, 1926).

7. John McNeil, *Designing Curriculum* (Boston: Little Brown, 1976), pp. 91–92.

8. John McNeil, *Curriculum,* 5th ed. (New York: HarperCollins, 1996), p. 130.

9. Jon Wiles and Joseph Biondi, *Curriculum Development: A Guide to Practice,* 5th ed. (New York: Macmillan, 1998), pp. 41–44. Used by permission

10. John McNeil, *Curriculum: The Teacher's Initiative* (Upper Saddle River, NJ: Merrill Publishing, 2003), pp. 235–236.

11. David Berliner, "The Half-Full Glass: A Review of Research on Teaching," in *What We Know about Teaching* (ASCD Yearbook, 1984), p. 57.

12. E. DeCharm and M. Kluender, "Good Teachers in Good Schools," *Educational Leadership* (Oct. 1986), 43–46.

4

LINKS FOR CURRICULUM IMPROVEMENT

OVERVIEW

Success in curriculum work requires more than a simple logic and a deductive refinement of ideas. Curriculum workers reach out to knowledge bases across the social sciences and employ these links in implementing programs. These "tools of the trade" make curriculum work more efficient, and knowing these links will make the reader more aware of the process of curriculum development.

Leaders in curriculum operate in an "open" system that is heavily influenced by forces outside of education. These workers must understand the interrelatedness of many variables that affect their work. A systems perspective explains many of the complexities of this condition.

Curriculum development is always a process of changing or improving, going from one condition to another. The large number of variables requires managerial skills on the part of the curriculum planner. Much curriculum work is carried on by committees and groups in order to promote common goals and values among diverse populations. Because curriculum developers are most often staff persons (not line administrators), establishing a work climate is critical to "leading without formal authority."

Staff development is a useful tool for helping teachers understand and identify with the goals of any curriculum. Staff development should be tied closely to personnel and program evaluation because it is the classroom teacher who mediates between curriculum plans and classroom programs.

Finally, in an age dominated by new interactive technologies, curriculum work is changing. Leaders must understand the "substance" of these changes and use these new communication devices to make curriculum work more easily and efficiently.

LEADERSHIP IN SCHOOL SETTINGS

Leadership has been studied extensively in any number of environments. Leadership is a critical tool for curriculum development because values must be clarified, plans developed and implemented, and the performance of organizational members assessed. It can be said that leadership is the intangible driving force in curriculum development. Leadership results from some combination of four key variables:

1. The characteristics of the leader
2. The characteristics of the organization
3. The nature of tasks to be performed
4. The social, economic, and political conditions

Over time, the study of leadership has revealed that to be a leader, an individual must possess the characteristics or traits needed by followers, be in the correct situation to apply those characteristics, and be recognized by those being led as the leader. It is especially important that the reader understand the "transaction required" (communication) between the leader and the followers. Without any one of these three ingredients, leadership will not be established. Wiles and Lovell have summarized the findings of research about leaders:

1. Leadership is a group role.
2. Leadership, other things being equal, depends on frequency of interaction.
3. Status position or title does not necessarily give leadership.
4. Leadership in any organization is widespread and diffuse.
5. The norms of the group determine the leader.
6. Leadership and follower qualities are interchangeable.
7. Persons who try too hard to persuade or control are rejected as leaders.
8. Feelings about the leader determine selection of a leader.
9. Leadership shifts from situation to situation.[1]

There are many definitions of leadership. Examples include the following:

> The leader is the focus of group processes.
> The leader is the one who exerts influence.
> The leader induces compliance (power).
> The leader initiates structure in the organization.
> The leader accomplishes goals for the organization.[2]

In educational leadership, all of these definitions are possible, but in most curriculum work, leadership is a sharing and group-oriented phenomena. Said another way, curriculum leaders get power from (power with) others in the organization rather than by forcing compliance (power over). It has been observed that the situation can make a leader a hero, villain, or fool.[3]

Because education is knowledge work, as opposed to manual work, the orientation of leaders is different. In a knowledge industry, the effect, rather than efficiency, is a criteria for success. Democratic leadership, rather than bureaucratic leadership, is needed to produce such effects or outcomes. Drucker observes five realities in such organizations:

1. Knowledge work is not defined by quantity, nor is it defined by costs. Knowledge work is defined by its results.
2. In knowledge organizations there are people who manage no one and yet are executives because they make decisions that have significant impact on the performance and results of the whole.
3. Effective executives build on strengths—their own, their staff, the situation—and not on weaknesses or impossibilities.
4. Effective executives gear efforts to results . . . rather than with the work to be done.
5. In knowledge work executives concentrate on a few major areas where superior performance will produce outstanding results.[4]

There are recurring tasks in curriculum work, and Figure 4.1 briefly describes eight areas that are common to most work. The specific curriculum task, of course, varies from organization to organization and work situation to work situation.

A major variable in determining the "style" of a leader, defined as the sum of perceived behaviors evidenced by that leader, is whether he or she sees the role as one that is dynamic or maintenance oriented. Arguing for a technical assistance role would be the idea that curriculum change is rarely lasting and that curriculum leaders are most helpful when they are assisting and serving where needed. The counterargument, for a dynamic and intellectual role, is made by Bruce Joyce who observed

> *In the past, curriculum planners have been technically weak, (unable to clarify ends or engineer means). . . . curriculum workers have defined themselves as*

FIGURE 4.1   Recurring Leadership Tasks

1. **Developing an Operating Theory.**   Leaders must be able to conceptualize tasks and communicate the approach to those tasks to others in the organization. The pattern of task identification and response forms the basis of an operating theory.

2. **Developing Organization and a Work Environment.**   Curriculum tasks are often non-permanent responses to needs. In such cases, the way in which people, resources, and ideas are organized is left to the leader. An important task is to structure an organization and work environment that can respond to those needs.

3. **Setting Standards.**   Because curriculum problems often involve diverse groups of individuals with different needs and perceptions, an important task for a curriculum leader is to set standards and other expectations that will affect the resolution of problems. Such standards may include work habits, communication procedures, time limitations, or a host of related planning areas.

4. **Using Authority to Establish an Organizational Climate.**   Persons assigned to leadership positions generally are able to structure organizations by suggesting changes and initiating policies. One of the most important tasks for a curriculum leader is using such authority to establish a desirable work climate. Such a climate, discussed later in this chapter, is made up of the collective perceptions of persons affected by the structure of the organization.

5. **Establishing Effective Interpersonal Relations.**   Because leadership is a product of human exchanges or transactions within organizations, it is essential that interpersonal relationships contribute to the attainment of desired ends. The way in which a curriculum leader interacts with others in the organization can assist in the establishment of a pattern of effective interpersonal relationships.

6. **Planning and Initiating Action.**   The curriculum leader is sometimes the only person with the authority to plan and initiate actions. Deciding when and how to initiate action is a strong leadership activity. Failure to lead planning or initiate action can undermine other leadership functions.

7. **Keeping Communication Channels Open and Functioning.**   Many times the curriculum leader is in a unique position of being able to communicate with others in an organization when lateral and horizontal communication is limited for most members. The leader can use his or her position to facilitate the matching of persons who need to communicate with one another. The leader can also make changes in communication patterns, where necessary, to ensure that such communication channels are functioning.

8. **Assessing Achievement.**   Periodically, every leader must ask, "Are we accomplishing what we intend to achieve in this organization?" The establishment of structure to evaluate and assess progress is a recurring task of leadership. These tasks, in combinations, are used to promote planned change for improving curriculum in schools.

Source: Jon Wiles and Joseph Bondi, *Curriculum Development: A Guide to Practice,* 5th ed. (New York: Macmillan, 1998), pp. 216–218. Used by permission.

helpers, not leaders, letting the community and teachers make decisions and then assisting in the implementation of those decisions.

By focusing on schools and teachers in schools, curriculum is being forced to operate within the parameters of the institution . . . by far the most paralyzing ef-

fect of the assumptive world in which the curriculum specialist lives is that it tends to filter out all ideas which might improve education but which fit awkwardly into the school pattern.[5]

Leaders in curriculum development may play many roles in pursuing an improved condition in the learning environment. Among those roles might be expert, counselor, instructor, adviser, manager, trainer, modeler, observer, evaluator, advocate, analyzer, confronter, and linker. The correct role for leading would be determined by the situation and needs of those to be led.

Suggested Reading

Stogdill, R. M., *Handbook of Leadership: A Survey of Theory and Research* (New York: Free Press, 1974).

CURRICULUM AS A SYSTEM, DEVELOPMENT AS A CYCLE

Systems theory, a product of the social sciences, provides curriculum planners with the critical concept of "interdependence" in organizations and helps to explain how one part of an organization influences the other parts. A system, by definition, is simply a grouping of objects that are treated as a unit. In a school setting, a system might be defined in a manner that constrains action toward the accomplishment of a goal. Curriculum development as a process, for example, seeks to improve the learning experiences of students.

For the curriculum leader, the value of studying a system (see Figure 4.2) is to identify noncontributing conditions or bottlenecks in the flow of activity. Once identified, these obstacles can be overcome using planning tools and the manipulation of organizational structures. Models of an ideal condition for school improvement can be constructed from studying the system.

Ralph Tyler, in his cyclical model of curriculum improvement (analyze, design, implement, evaluate) is credited with bringing a systems perspective to education. The Tyler model forces planners to think about both the efficiency and the product of their labor. An example of the cycle is presented in Figure 4.3.

An early advocate of a systems orientation in curriculum work, Kathryn Feyereisen, defined the development process in this manner:

basically a plan of structuring the environment to coordinate, in an orderly manner, the elements of time, space, materials, equipment, and personnel.[6]

Another definition from the systems perspective found that

The purpose of curriculum development is to research, design, and engineer the working relationships of the curricular elements that will be employed during the instructional phase in order to achieve the desired outcome.[7]

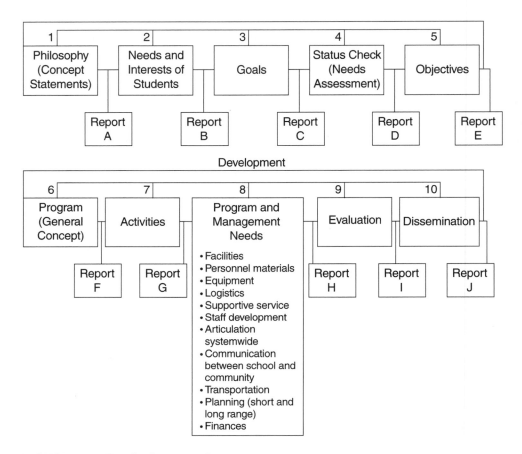

FIGURE 4.2   Curriculum as a System

Source: Jon Wiles and Joseph Bondi, *Curriculum Development: A Guide to Practice,* 3rd ed. (Columbus, OH: Charles Merrill, 1989), p. 128. Used by permission.

In educational contexts, systems models have three phases: the input, the process, and the output. The input phase is concerned with goal setting, needs assessments, and the development of strategies. The process phase includes all of the activities needed to implement, manage, and monitor program development. The output phase, of course, is concerned with evaluation and correctional feedback efforts. Because a system channels efforts to accomplish organizational purposes, this perspective allows a curriculum designer or developer to be a problem solver who organizes by function and manages by product.

In public schools, systems thinking is encouraged by three types of review: accreditation visits, surveys, and the needs assessment. Accreditation reviews establish

FIGURE 4.3   Curriculum Development as a Cycle

Analysis Stage

1. Identify Denver public schools' philosophy.
2. Identify board policy relative to middle schools.
3. Superintendent (public) statement on middle schools.
4. Outline time frame for implementation.
5. Formation of centralized coordinating group.
6. Delineation of tasks + appointment of subcommittees.
7. Develop "definition" of Denver Middle Schools.
8. Structure awareness/orientation campaign.
   a. Administrators
   b. Teacher groups

Design Stage

9. Translate philosophy into goal statements.
10. Project preliminary budget/resource base.
11. Prioritize goal statements.
12. Translate goal statements to objectives format.
13. Block out three- to five-year plan for implementation.
14. Establish management/information system to monitor progress of implementation (external audit).
15. Establish evaluation targets, time, responsibilities, resources; identify baseline data needed.
16. Conduct needs assessment.
17. Develop final management system (Program Evaluation Review Technique: PERT).

Implementation or Management Stage

18. Provide advanced organizers (simple plan) to all interested persons.
19. Provide each school with resource kits, glossaries, data bank from needs assessment (local planning/decision-making data).
20. Formation of teams in each school to serve as
    a. Study group for mapping curriculum/skills.
    b. Planning group/house plan.
    c. Team/cooperative teaching unit.
21. Provide preliminary staff development (demonstration teaching) in all schools on
    a. Advisor/advisee program.
    b. Continuous progress curriculums.
    c. Team planning and teaching.
22. Require school-by-school development plan including curriculum, staff development, evaluation, community involvement.
23. Provide local budget supplement based on plan.

Evaluation Stage

24. Conduct formative evaluation (external audit) every six weeks, to monitor management outline.
25. Conduct major review after six months—revise time line, goals, needs, etc.
26. Develop master evaluation plan (sum of all schools) for three-year period.

Source: Author's notes. Denver, Colorado.

global standards and then bring a team of educators to measure the school or district by those standards. Surveys, by contrast, tend to import teams of experts who "judge" according to their expert opinion. A needs assessment, covered more thoroughly in Chapter Five, assesses the performance of the school or district by some subjective criteria established internally by those being assessed.

The use of systems thinking, and seeing curriculum work as a loop or cycle, contributes by forcing a macroperspective of changing rather than the more common and traditional layering of change on top of the old program.

Suggested Reading

Feyereisen, K., *Supervision and Curriculum Renewal: A Systems Approach* (New York: Appleton-Century-Croft, 1970).

CHANGE IN EDUCATION

Change is a given in American society in the twenty-first century. The past thirty years (see Figure 4.4) have been hectic in terms of both the pace and the type of change occurring. Schools, although seemingly impervious to permanent change, nonetheless are constantly shifting their form. Understanding how change occurs in an educational environment is a basic skill for curriculum leaders.

Curriculum development means change! As we improve school programs, educators move programs from some condition to an improved condition. As has been emphasized in this book, the vision of where we are trying to go may be as important as the method of changing. For years the author has used a technique known as developmental staging to envision change over time (Figure 4.5).

There are many kinds of change—including planned change, coercive change, natural change, interactive change, and technological change. Most change in education requires a normative change (values are changed) because of the human and decentralized nature of our work. Coercive change does not work well because workers (teachers and any subordinates) cannot be closely supervised. In the end, people in education change because they believe the change is right.

Educators use models of change from other walks of life to understand how change occurs in education. Following are five stereotypical models:

Agricultural Model. Using a change agent approach, change is demonstrated in the field for firsthand observation.

Medical Model. Action research is used to proceed from clinical study to developmental studies to dissemination and adoption.

Business Model. Incentives are used to entice change or compliance.

Military Model. Authority and coercion are used to "force" change.

Religious Model. Unchallengeable beliefs and authority are imposed, resulting in only superficial change.

FIGURE 4.4   Changes in American Society, 1965–2000

Affirmative action
Animal-to-human organ transplants
Antibiotic failures
Biotechnology
Breakup of industrial monopolies (AT&T)
Cable TV
Cellular phones
Civil rights movement
Cloning of animals
Collapse of savings and loan industry
Computer data exchanges
Deregulation of industry
Disappearance of union power
Emergence of Japan
Energy conservation
Environmentalism
Exercise boom
Facsimile (fax) machines
Fall of Communism
Family declines
Fiber optics
Gay liberation
Genetic engineering
Greenhouse effect
Human rights movement
Inflation
Internet
Loss of respect for major institutions
Militancy and fundamentalism on rise
Negative campaign advertising
Organized peace movement
Political correctness
Racial tensions
Reunification of Germany
Safe sex
Satellite communication
Superconductivity
Terrorism
TV shopping networks
VCRs
Women's movement

Source: Dr. John C. Lundt, University of Montana, School of Education; President, Educational Leadership Associates, Inc. Used by permission.

FIGURE 4.5 Developmental Staging—Seeing the Change

	Stage 1: Present Condition	Stage 2: Awareness	Stage 3: Experimentation	Stage 4: Adoption	Stage 5: Desired Condition
The School Philosophy	Either no formal statement or a written document on file in the school office.	School staff share beliefs, look for consensus, restate philosophy and objectives in terms of expected behavior.	Staff begins use of goals as guide to evaluating school practices. Begin to involve students and community in planning.	Philosophy and goals used to shape the program. Formal mechanism established to monitor program and decision making.	Philosophy a living document. Guides daily decisions. The program is a tool for achieving desired educational ends.

The Learning Environment

	Stage 1: Present Condition	Stage 2: Awareness	Stage 3: Experimentation	Stage 4: Adoption	Stage 5: Desired Condition
Use of the Building	Only uniform instructional spaces. Little use of the building spaces for educational purposes.	Some deviation from traditional space utilization (classroom learning center). Possibly a complete demonstration class for bright ideas.	Limited building conversion (knock out walls). Begin to identify unused spaces. Planning for large learning spaces.	Development of a comprehensive plan for use of grounds and building. Total renovation of spaces.	Tailor-made learning environment—all spaces used to educate. Building facilitates the learning intention.
Use of Materials	Classrooms are dominated by a grade-level text. Library with a limited offering. Used as a study hall for large groups.	Use of multilevel texts within classroom. Materials selected after an analysis of student achievement levels. Supplemental resources made available to students.	Diverse materials developed for the students. Resource centers established. Cross-discipline selection of materials. More multimedia used. Some independent study.	Materials purchasing policies realigned. Common learning areas established as resources centers. More self-directed study built in.	Diversified materials. Something for each student. Integrated subject materials. Portable curriculum units (or carts). Heavy multimedia. Active learning centers.
Use of Community	Little or no access to school. Information about programs scanty. Trust low.	Some school program ties to community. Token access via PTA and media. School perceived as island in neighborhood.	Preliminary uses of community as learning environment. Identification of nearby resources. Use of building for community functions.	Regular interchange between school and community. Systematic communication. A network of services and resources established.	School program outwardly oriented. Community seen as a teaching resource. Systematic ties with service and resource around school.

Administrative Conditions

	Stage 1: Present Condition	Stage 2: Awareness	Stage 3: Experimentation	Stage 4: Adoption	Stage 5: Desired Condition
Organization of Student	Uniform patterns. One teacher, thirty students in six rows of five in each row in each period of each school day.	Understanding that organization of students should match curricular intentions. Some initial variation of group sizes in classroom.	Limited organization to facilitate the grouping of students. Begin use of aides and parents to increase organizational flexibility.	Full administrative support for a reorganization of students. Building restructured where necessary. An increase in planning for effectiveness.	Group sizes vary according to the activity planned. Full support given to eliminate any problem areas.
Report of Student Progress	"Progress" is defined narrowly. Letter grades or simple numerals represent student learning in the subject areas.	Recognition of broader growth goals for student. Use of philosophy to evaluate the existing practices.	Experimentation with supplemental reporting procedures. Involvement of student and parent in the process.	Development of a diverse and comprehensive reporting procedure for student progress.	Descriptive medium used to monitor individual student progress. Broadly focused evaluation. Team of teacher, student, and parents involved.
Rules and Regulations	High degree of regimentation. Many rules, most inherited over the years. The emphasis on enforcement and on control.	Staff and students identify essential rules. Regulations matched against the school philosophy.	Rules and regulations streamlined. Used as a teaching device about life outside of school. Increased student self-control.	Greater use of student and staff input into regulation of the school environment. Rewards built in for desirable performance.	Moving toward minimal regulation and increased student self-control. Regulations a positive teaching device.

FIGURE 4.5 *Continued*

Discipline	Reactive pattern ranging from verbal admonishment to expulsion. Recurring offenders.		Staff analysis of school policies. Shift of emphasis to causes of the problems. Some brainstorming of possible solutions.	Establishment of a hierarchy of discipline activity. Begin implementing preventive strategies.	Program of the school eliminates most sources of discipline problems. The procedure for residual problems clear to all.
Instructional Organization					
Staffing Patterns	Building teachers isolated in self-contained classrooms. Little or no lateral communication or planning present.	Limited sharing of resources. Some division of labor and small-scale cooperation in teaching. Informal communication about student progress.	Regular cooperative planning sessions. Some curricular integration via themes. Students rotate through subject areas. Problems of cooperation identified.	Interdepartmental organization. Use of common planning time. Administrative support such as in scheduling. Use of philosophy as curricular decision-making criteria.	Teaching staff "team" working toward common ends. Staff patterns reflect instructional intentions. Administration in support of curricular design. Coursework integrated for students.
Teaching Strategy	Some variety but lecture and teacher-dominated question-answer session the norm. Homework used to promote day-to-day continuity.	Observation of other teaching models. Skill development via workshops. An identification of staff strengths and weaknesses. Some new patterns.	Building-level experiments by willing staff members. "Modeling" of ideas. On-site consultant help made available for skill development.	School day divided according to the teaching strategy employed. Faculty evaluation of the effectiveness of new ways after a trial period.	Great variety of methods used in teaching, uses of media, dealing with students. The curricular plans determine strategy.
Staff Development	Staff development is global, rarely used to attack local needs and problems. Occurs as needed.	Staff identifies in-service needs and priorities. Philosophy assists in this process. Local staff skills and strengths are recognized.	Staff development realigned to serve needs of teachers. Opportunities for personal growth are made available.	Formal procedures for directing staff development to needs established. Staff development seen as problem-solving mechanism.	Staff development an ongoing process using available resources. An attempt to close theory-practice gaps.
Roles of Participants					
Student Roles	Passive recipient of knowledge. Instruction is geared to average student. Reactive communication with the teacher.	Investigation of new student roles by teacher. Limited hierarchy of trust established in the classroom. Needs and interests of students investigated.	Ground rules for increased student independence set. Student involvement in planning. Role of student connected to philosophy of the school.	Periodic review of student roles. Roles linked to school wide rules and regulations. Philosophy guides role possibilities.	Students involved in planning and conducting program. Increased independence and responsibility. Use of "contracts" to maintain new understandings.
Teacher Roles	Defined by the subjects taught. Perceived as the source of all knowledge. Other roles peripheral.	Perceiving roles as suggested by the philosophy. Roles accepted at verbal level. Limited experimentation with new roles.	Investigation of new roles—trying on new relationships. Goal-setting for individual teacher. Skill development through in-service.	Administrative reorganization for role support. Sharpened planning and action skills needed to serve the students according to the philosophy.	Teacher role is defined by student needs. Teacher the organizer of the learning activities. Teacher talents used more effectively.
Principal Roles	Solely responsible for school operation. The "boss," enforcer of all rules. The linkage to all outside information and resources.	Awareness of role limitations. An awareness of real leadership potential. A setting of role priorities.	Limited sharing of decision making in area of curriculum. Limited joint planning with the faculty. Review of existing policy according to the philosophy.	Role perception changes to manager of resources. Emphasis on development (active) rather than order (static). Increase in curriculum leadership functions.	Instructional leader. Administrative acts support the curriculum. Philosophy guides the decision making.

Source: Jon Wiles, *Planning Guidelines for Middle School Education* (Dubuque, IA: Kendall Hunt, 1976).

133

It is probable that of these five models, the agricultural and religious come closest to an educational model. In schools the "assumptive world" that Joyce speaks of keeps educators from thinking beyond the "boundaries" of buildings, books, and teachers in seeking change. Further, the long history of a teacher as the "solitary artisan" working with students makes that teacher a resistant and somewhat suspicious consumer of change.

In schools and educational environments, there are good reasons why change is resisted. Among these reasons are the following:

Fear.   The individual has had a previous experience with the change that was unpleasant or the individual fears failure in changing.

Conservatism.   Most teachers come from lower-middle-class backgrounds and are fearful of losing their newly gained status or making a major mistake in their employment.

Obligation.   The subject of change may be committed to a previous pattern and sees changing as a conflict.

Identification.   The individual may not see the change as reinforcing his or her needs or values.

Awareness.   The individual may not be able to assess a change because of habit, tradition, or ignorance.

In Figure 4.6, Goodwin Watson identifies conditions under which planned change has a better chance of succeeding. Wiles, in Figure 4.7, summarizes the findings of a Florida research project that sought to identify "good bets" for spending money on change projects. In that model, the lower the risk, the better the "bet."

In general, there are conditions in most school districts that preclude successful curriculum change. Nine problem areas in this category are as follows: an absence of clear goals, unpredictable power sources interfering from outside, a consistent dependence on money as a moving force, the absence of systems thinking in problem solving, an operational orientation to the past and present, decentralized decision making without policy guidance, the absence of evaluative feedback, inadequate training of staff, and administrative turnover. Each of these conditions would have to be considered, if not neutralized, for change to succeed in school districts. At the school building level, additional impediments might include too little planning time for teachers, underfunding, task overload, and failure to understand site-specific differences among schools.

Promoting planned changes, the nature of curriculum improvement, should rest on understandings of how to "implement" or manage change. As the subject of many books, planning change in education is essentially a response to the practice environment (the schools). The author offers twenty points (Figure 4.8) for consideration in designing a change strategy.

FIGURE 4.6   Overcoming Resistance to Change

Goodwin Watson posited the following observations on the reception of change in formal organizations based on the early findings of the Cooperative Project for Educational Development (COPED):

1. Resistance will be less if administrators, teachers, board members, and community leaders feel that the project is their own—not one devised and operated by outsiders.
2. Resistance will be less if the project clearly has wholehearted support from top officials of the system.
3. Resistance will be less if participants see the change as reducing rather than increasing their present burdens.
4. Resistance will be less if the project accords with values and ideals that have long been acknowledged by participants.
5. Resistance will be less if the program offers the kind of new experience that interests participants.
6. Resistance will be less if participants feel that their autonomy and their security is not threatened.
7. Resistance will be less if participants have joined in diagnostic efforts leading them to agree on the basic problem and to feel its importance.
8. Resistance will be less if the project is adopted by consensual group decision.
9. Resistance will be reduced if proponents are able to empathize with opponents to recognize valid objections and take steps to relieve unnecessary fears.
10. Resistance will be reduced if it is recognized the innovations are likely to be misunderstood and misinterpreted, and if provision is made for feedback of perceptions of the project and for further clarification as needed.
11. Resistance will be reduced if participants experience acceptance, support, trust, and confidence in their relations with one another.
12. Resistance will be reduced if the project is kept open to revision and reconsideration if experience indicates that changes would be desirable.
13. Readiness for change gradually becomes a characteristic of certain individuals, groups, organizations, and civilizations.

Source: Adapted from R. Lippitt, J. Watson, and B. Wesley, *The Dynamics of Planned Change* (New York: Harcourt, Brace & World, 1958), p. 340.

A very useful idea in planning school change is related to the idea that norms govern school change. This idea probably explains why educators so often use committees to solve problems. Group norms result from the interaction of individuals (as does leadership), and when a norm becomes a majority belief, change is enhanced. The early model of this phenomenon by Lionberger (see Figure 4.9) addresses the "tip over" effect in educational change. Stated simply, when a majority of support is achieved, the change process gains momentum. Strategies to gain the support of the early majority are critical to successful change.

FIGURE 4.7   Educational Change Probability Chart

	Higher Risk ←			→ *Lower Risk*	
Source of Innovation	Superimposed from outside	Outside agent brought in	Developed internally with aid	External idea modified	Locally conceived, developed, implemented
Impact of Innovation	Challenges sacrosanct beliefs	Calls for major value shifts	Requires substantial change	Modifies existing values or programs	Does not substantially alter existing values, beliefs, or programs
Official Support	Official leaders actively oppose	Officials on record as opposing	Officials uncommitted	Officials voice support of change	Enthusiastically supported by the official leaders
Planning of Innovation	Completely external	Most planning external	Planning processes balanced	Most of planning done locally	All planning for change done on local site
Means of Adoption	By superiors	By local leaders	By representatives	By most of the clients	By group consensus
History of Change	History of failures	No accurate records	Some success with innovation	A history of successful innovations	Known as school where things regularly succeed
Possibility of Revision	No turning back	Final evaluation before committee	Periodic evaluations	Possible to abandon at conclusion	Possible to abort the effort at any time
Role of Teachers	Largely bypassed	Minor role	Regular role in implementation	Heavy role in implementation	Primary actor in the classroom effort
Teacher Expectation	Fatalistic	Feel little chance of success	Willing to give a try	Confident of success	Wildly enthusiastic about chance of success
Workload Measure	Substantially increased	Heavier but rewarding	Slightly increased	Unchanged	Work load lessened by the innovation
Threat Measure	Definitely threatens some clients	Probably threatening to some	Mild threat resulting from the change	Very remote threat to some	Does not threaten security or autonomy
Community Factor	Hostile to innovations	Suspicious and uninformed	Indifferent	Ready for a change	Wholeheartedly supports the school

Shade the response in each category that most accurately reflects the condition surrounding the implementation of the middle school. If the "profile" of your school is predominantly in the high-risk side of the matrix, substantial work must be done to prepare your school for change.

Source: From Jon Wiles, *Planning Guidelines for Middle School Education*, p. 30. Copyright 1976 by Kendall/Hunt Publishing Co.

FIGURE 4.8   Twenty Points to Consider in Designing Educational Change

1. Positive change and innovation are not synonymous. Isolated change, random change, scheduled change, and bureaucratic change are not always positive.
2. Positive change is never an isolate; it is always defined in terms of system or a larger purpose.
3. Until the target of change is clearly identified, change cannot be purposeful.
4. A first step in changing is to establish a reality among those affected by the change. Use of numbers (counting) is more expedient than use of philosophy to establish such a reality.
5. Change in a school or district must fit the external system in which the school or district operates.
6. The language, techniques, and strategies of changing must be tailored to fit the culture of the school or district.
7. Positive changes do not last if they are not structural or institutional; they cannot last as an extension of a personality.
8. Change must be perceived as a solution to a problem or it will succumb to the "busy school" syndrome of everyday demands.
9. Money and politics are the stream in which change flows.
10. True decision makers in education are often not educators but rather persons external to the school or district.
11. The thirst for recognition is a very powerful lever for promoting positive change in a school world without extrinsic rewards.
12. Money always brings an innovative bloom in schools.
13. Outside money is always tied to a value or norm of the supporting source.
14. A lot of innovation is simply common sense, and common sense needs a forum in schools promoting positive change.
15. Use of ideas from other walks of life (institutions) is an almost untapped source of renewal and innovation in public schools.
16. Categorical money offered to schools or districts usually distorts purposeful change in those institutions and should be accepted in context.
17. Creating an atmosphere for changing often means borrowing the influence (businesses, government, politicians) of outsiders.
18. In any school district, understanding the past is useful in explaining the present condition.
19. Changing schools is always big business, and the larger the district the bigger the business implications.
20. Politics is a part of change in schools, in fact, it is the cornerstone of meaningful changes.

Source: Jon Wiles, *Promoting Change in Schools: Ground Level Practices That Work* (New York: Scholastic, 1993), pp. 100–101.

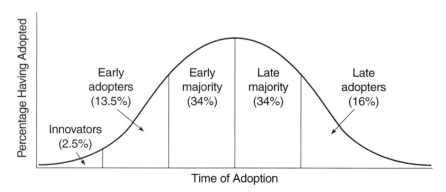

FIGURE 4.9   Lionberger's Change Curve Model

Source: Adapted from Herbert I. Lionberger. *Adoption of New Ideas and Practices* (Ames: Iowa State University Press, 1961).

CURRICULUM MANAGEMENT PLANNING

Curriculum Management Planning (CMP), developed during years of field applications by Jon Wiles and Joseph Bondi, superimposes a management system on top of the traditional curriculum development cycle. The CMP constrains curriculum development efforts toward point-to-point goals and thereby increases the efficiency of such work.

The CMP views curriculum development as a flow of steps that begins with a statement of purpose and ends in the dissemination of findings from evaluation efforts (Tyler cycle). (See Figure 4.10.) The intention of the CMP is to introduce a regular and predictable process of changing in what otherwise can be a disruptive (open) environment.

CMP substitutes data analysis for the more traditional arguments about philosophy, such as are found in accreditation and surveys, thus sharpening the focus to outcomes. CMP relies heavily on committees (both ad hoc or temporary and standing or permanent) to force value clarification and a commitment to changing. Figure 4.11 shows the use of the ad hoc committees to force movement along the curriculum cycle to analyze, design, implement, and evaluate.

The CMP works to minimize political activity and special pleading by existing interest groups through a kind of "separation of powers." By targeting goals in each stage, it guarantees a continuity of effort in each sphere. It coordinates and

FIGURE 4.10   Curriculum Development Flow

1. **Purpose Statement.** Describes the specific problem or need addressed by this curriculum change.
2. **Philosophical Position.** Identifies the beliefs (students, teachers) that undergird this approach. What assumptions are being made?
3. **Supporting Documentation.** Uses statistics, research, or other authoritative documents to support this project and this approach.
4. **Critical Elements.** Programmatic areas to be addressed.
5. **Program Objectives/Learning Objectives.** In each programmatic area, what is to be accomplished?
6. **Observable Standards.** What will be seen by anyone viewing this project?
7. **Facility Needs.** What physical resources are needed to succeed?
8. **Equipment/Communication Needs.** Necessary tools for success.
9. **Material/Transportation Needs.** Undergirding curriculum structure.
10. **Area of Needs to Be Assessed during Design.** Curriculum areas to be addressed.
11. **Time Line for Implementation.** How long will the planned change take?
12. **Budget (include categories and estimates).** How much will the planned change cost?
13. **Evaluation/Validation Checkpoints.** Establish time line to evaluate status of planned change.
14. **Task/Responsibility Chart.** Who will be responsible for each part?
15. **Dissemination Plan.** How will information be shared with others?

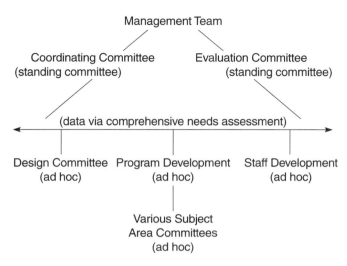

**FIGURE 4.11   A Curriculum Management
                Committee Structure**

Source: Jon Wiles and Joseph Bondi, *Curriculum Development: A Guide to
Practice,* 5th ed. (New York: Macmillan, 1998). Used by permission.

manages the critical elements of time and resource allocation. Most importantly,
CMP can structure a thoughtful and long-lasting effort to produce meaningful improvement in schools.

Suggested Reading

Association for Supervision and Curriculum Development, *Making Middle
Schools Work* (Alexandria, VA: ASCD, 1986).

Curriculum Management Tools

Curriculum planners can push the process of development along by using tools or
"activating instruments" at appropriate times. Such tools help manage change efforts and include, for example, defining the path of change, placing activities in
time frames (calendars), assigning responsibilities to others, making general cost
estimates, and developing school-level implementation plans.

The Path

All organizations have a way of working, but not all schools work the same way.
Figure 4.12 shows a fairly typical 11-step decision path to activate the development process. The school board, in this example, authorizes the superintendent to
form a structure by which a long-range improvement plan will be established. A
simple calendar (estimated) is projected for these steps. The reader should note
that to bypass any of these steps would lead to delays down the road.

FIGURE 4.12   Typical Decision Path

Time Line	Development Activities
October	• Board authorizes preliminary assessment.
November	• Board directs superintendent to form committee structure. • Superintendent forms basic planning structure. • Coordinating committee, curriculum task force, and business advisory groups are formed.
December	
January	• Priorities and "best practice" standards are established. • Needs and discrepancies are identified; study groups are formed. • Organization; facilities; staff development.
February	• Recommendations formatted into a district strategic plan.
March	• Board approves proposed district strategic plan.
April	• Evaluation and monitoring group is established. • School-based action commences.

The Calendar

The use of a planning calendar serves as a communication device to all involved in the development process, focusing on the timing of events. In large projects, a calendar can help planners spread out the workloads (Figure 4.13). In some cases, the complexity of events and the volume of changes may call for a creative way to think about the changes. In Figure 4.14, the author created a calendar using the Dewey decimal classification of retrieval found in most libraries. IBM and other computer companies sell software that monitors complex change programs in organizations.

Responsibilities

The basic responsibility chart identifies an agency or individual who is to be responsible for some part of a development process. A classic error for educational leaders is to assume responsibility (no delegation) for all aspects of a change process. Most complex change is geometric in nature as tasks interact, and without delegation the leader will discover no one to turn to when things don't work. Responsibility charts normally have columns that name the person, the activity, the completion date, and sometimes the allotted budget.

Cost Estimates

Although it is logical to assume that the cost of curriculum development is calculated prior to activation, this is often not the case. School boards mandate changes,

THE PROJECT CALENDAR

	August			September								October							November							December				
	22	26	27	5	6	12	13	19	20	26	27	10	11	17	18	24	25	31	1	7	8	14	15	21	22	5	6	10	12	13
Teachers				1		2		3				4		5		6		7			8	9		10						
Leadership Group											1		2					3	4		5		6		7	8				
Principals									1								2						3							
Assistant Principals				1								2						3				4								
Management Team	1											2													3					
School Visits (as needed)					1				2											3			4			5	6	7	8	
School Board																											1			
Coordinating Committee																1										2				
Staff Development													1																	
Grant															1							2					3			
Evaluation Committee										1											2	3			4	3				
Program Consultant				1								2						3				4								
Public Relations Committee					1																	2								

FIGURE 4.13   The Project Calendar

Source: Jon Wiles and Joseph Bondi. *Making Middle Schools Work* (Alexandria, VA: ASCD). Used by permission of the Association for Supervision and Curriculum Development. Copyright © 1985 by ASCD. All rights reserved.

and responsibilities are assigned. However, unanticipated costs or increasing costs can doom a project. Creating a cost estimate up front (Figure 4.15) may help decision makers identify priorities and construct realistic budgets for changing.

School-Based Plans

Finally, in medium and large districts, providing for school site implementation plans can assist leaders in seeing their responsibility. The total of all school site plans should be equal to the overall plan, thereby making district-level planning easier to follow (Figure 4.16).

Finally, although no formula exists for promoting desired changes in schools, there does seem to be a series of steps necessary to overcome predictable obstacles to changing. These steps would "set the course" for change and, hopefully, neutralize regularly anticipated resistance.

Create a Vision.   The numerous distractions of an "open" system cannot be overcome without clear goals and objectives. Priorities and sequencing and time lines spell out what might result from an investment of effort.

Become Legitimate.   Curriculum leaders can become legitimate leaders in a number of ways: wrapping the effort in law, soliciting the support of key

FIGURE 4.14   Improvised Planner's Calendar—"Library Model"

Fall 1998

140—Facility modifications identified, scheduled 86/87, 87/88

240—Complete curriculum delivered to all teachers

340—Begin seminar series for potential middle school leaders

440—PR emphasis on curriculum (target parents) design

640—Teachers assess own school by new curriculum

740—Resource assessment by building against curriculum needs

741—Total resource budget developed for 97/98

840—Data processing pilots new student evaluation in one school

940—Board Report V delivered by Coordinating Committee

The 40 Series Fall 2002

Calendar of Events

	Summer 0–9	Fall 10–19	Spring 20–29	Summer 30–39	Fall 40–49
Facilities and Special Programs Placement (100–199)	100			130	140
Curriculum (200–299)	200 201 202	210 211 212	220 221 222 223 224	230	240
Administrator/Supervisor Training (300–399)		310	320	330 331	340
Public Relations (400–499)			420		440
Transportation and Redistricting (500–599)				530	
Teacher Training (600–699)			620 621 622		640
Instructional Materials (700–799)					740 741
Evaluation (800–899)	800 801	810 811 812	820 821 822		840
Board Reports (900–999)	900	910	920	930	940

Source: Jon Wiles, *Promoting Change in Schools* (New York: Scholastic, 1993), p. 156.

FIGURE 4.15   Cost Estimate by Program

Item	Cost Start-Up	Continuing
1. Personnel		
a. 10 Regular teachers		$ 600,000
b. 20 Instructional aides		400,000
c. 1 Program coordinator		60,000
d. 1 Secretary/bookkeeper		40,000
2. Fixed Charges		
Social Security and teacher retirement @ 20% of 1,000,000		220,000
3. Materials		
Continuous cost—10 teachers @ $2,000/teacher	$ 30,000	20,000
4. Equipment		
Cots, chairs, tables, learning center equipment, playground equipment	40,000	8,000
5. Facilities		
Renovation of the cafeteria and auditorium on the present high school site	300,000	
6. Maintenance and Operation of Plant		
10 teachers @ $4,000/teacher		40,000
7. Staff Development		
a. Consultant honorarium and travel	10,000	20,000
b. Materials		1,000
Subtotal	$380,000 +	$1,409,000
Total Cost of Kindergarten School Program		$1,789,000

decision makers, gaining endorsement from authorities, promoting supportive policies, or projecting a media image that becomes magnetic. Legitimacy does not occur because a plan has been formulated.

Provide Definition.   Many change efforts fail because only a "general orientation" is provided. People affected by change want to know what is happening. To a change model, add an implementation schedule, responsibility chart, and all the additional structures that take away anxiety. Regular progress using data, not jargon, will increase confidence.

Attaining Buy-In.   People are willing to change if they understand why and how, and if they see the change benefiting them as individuals. Educators underestimate how badly a staff of all college graduates wish to be perceived as competent. Presenting change as a challenge and success as a reward brings results.

FIGURE 4.16   School-Based Development Plans

School Goal #2:   The school will develop a technology plan that will provide students and staff with the skills necessary to be productive, successful members of our technologically advanced society.

Objectives

1. Each teacher in our school will be provided with a computer.
2. Our staff will work to develop a vocational technology lab.
3. Our staff will work to develop a comprehensive computer lab with equivalent computer and technology courses.
4. A network of computers will be developed so that they can be used by the instructional and administrative staff.

Strategies

1. Computer in-service training will be provided for all staff.
2. Proposals will be submitted to county, business/community partners, and corporations (for grant purposes) to secure necessary funding and/or equipment.
3. Appropriate instructional materials will be secured to establish the technology curriculum.

Resources Needed

1. The school's technology committee will develop a technology plan and grant proposals to secure equipment and funds.
2. District staff will be needed to provide assistance in securing and developing grant proposals.
3. District staff and school-based staff will provide in-service training for the staff at school.
4. Educational partnerships with business/community leaders will continue to be developed.

Time Line

1. Every teacher will be provided with a computer by June, 2003.
2. Phase 1 of vocational technology lab and appropriate curriculum operational by 2001–2002 school year.
3. A computer lab will be operational by 1998–2000 school year.
4. Technology and computer curriculum will be implemented by the end of the 1999–2000 school year.
5. Networking capabilities for faculty and staff will be implemented by the end of the 2001–2002 school year. Networking of existing computer labs will be completed by the end of the 2001–2002 school year.
6. Progress will be assessed to determine success of this plan during the 1996–97 school year.

Evaluation

1. Monthly reports will be submitted by the technology committee to assess the progress of each objective.
2. School-based technology committee will meet on a regular basis to review progress and implement specific procedures needed to meet objectives.
3. SAC committee members will review by site visitations and staff surveys and assess the progress of the technology plan.
4. Parent and employee responses on the County Parent and Employee surveys will show an improved awareness of the school's technology.

Gaining Control.   Positive change in schools results from gaining control of the process and overcoming the natural and unforeseen barriers. Reducing the change effort from a goal to a series of observable activities makes change real to those affected by it. Management of curriculum change ensures results.

Sustaining Momentum.   Most change in schools comes from the idea of an individual or from a money source. Take away either of the stimuli and you have failed change. The goal of any change project is to "institutionalize" the process with policy and record keeping and evaluative reports. Using a point-to-point orientation keeps the project from getting bogged down.

Tactics

Specific tactics can be used to move the process through the change cycle:

Analysis

1. Set the stage by introducing change within context.
2. Introduce changes as an extension of past activity.
3. Project positive outcomes, such as reducing workload.

Design

1. Institutionalize the change (no personalities).
2. Provide a clear buy-in theme for the overall effort.
3. Always define the change in terms of the system.
4. Make the language of changing culturally appropriate.
5. Present the change in distinct stages.

Implement

1. Provide both a destination and a duration for the project.
2. Keep the planning of change visible through the project life.
3. Make change appear manageable by using an "if–then" logic.

Evaluate

1. Clearly identify the target so change is a positive thing.
2. Remember that counting is more productive than debating.
3. Determine the odds for changing and be flexible.

COMMITTEES AND GROUPS

As the agent responsible for activating the planned curriculum, a worker in curriculum often meets with others in committees and small groups. The role of this specialist at a meeting is defined by the leadership perspective (active or passive), but among the common tasks in a meeting are the following:

Initiating Activities.   Suggesting ideas, helping to define old and new problems, reordering ideas and materials, and proposing possible solutions.

Coordinating.   Relating activities of various subgroups, cross-pollinating ideas, defining relationships.

Summarizing.   Assembling data, providing ways to report findings, restating ideas in a more general form, pulling together related data.

Testing.   Examining the practicality of ideas, evaluating procedures, eliminating faulty practices.

There are things that have been learned through research that can guide a curriculum leader in these sessions. Figure 4.17 provides a series of conclusions about what makes any given group productive.

As the status leader in a group (possesses title), the curriculum leader will often be called on to conduct meetings. Figure 4.18 provides some of the essential elements of an effective (results in a product) meeting.

In such meetings, the leader may encounter individuals who do not want the meeting to succeed and who employ "blocking" behaviors. Such negative behaviors are contrasted with more positive behaviors in Figure 4.19.

A very important skill for a meeting and group leader is to be a good listener. Communication is a lot like an iceberg, with 85 percent of the real effort below the surface. The leader should ask herself or himself the following questions as the meeting progresses:

1. What does the speaker want to say?
2. What does the speaker want to conceal?
3. What does the speaker reveal without knowing it?
4. What does the listener want to hear?
5. How will the listener's perception of the speaker distort the message?
6. How is the physical environment influencing this communication?

Finally, because thought is faster than talk (by a magnitude of four), it is common to drift off during a long discussion. The leader must be prepared to paraphrase and summarize all communication, thus attention while listening is an important skill. Figure 4.20 identifies ten steps to keep focused during group discussions.

ESTABLISHING POSITIVE CLIMATES

When a curriculum leader is unable to personally supervise all persons contributing to a development effort, investing in climate formation is a good idea. The theory behind climate engineering is, stated simply, that motivation is aroused by the environment in which we work and the tasks we encounter.

FIGURE 4.17   What Research Says Makes Any Group Effective

If a group is to be productive, the individuals in question must first become a group in a psychological sense through acquiring the feeling of group belongingness that can come only from a central purpose, which they all accept.

If a group is to be productive, its members must have a common definition of the undertaking in which they are to engage.

If a group is to be productive, it must have a task of some real consequence to perform.

If a group is to be productive, its members must feel that something will actually come of what they are expected to do; said differently, its members must not feel that what they are asked to do is simply busywork.

If a group is to be productive, the dissatisfaction of its members with the aspect of the status quo to which the group's undertaking relates must outweigh in their minds whatever threats to their comfort they perceive in the performance of this undertaking.

If a group is to be productive, its members must not be expected or required to attempt undertakings that are beyond their respective capabilities or that are so easy for the individuals in question to perform that they feel no sense of real accomplishment.

If a group is to be productive, decisions as to work planning, assignment, and scheduling must be made, whenever possible, on a shared basis within the group, and through the method of consensus rather than of majority vote; in instances in which these decisions either have already been made by exterior authority or in which they must be made by the group leader alone, the basis for the decisions made must be clearly explained to all members of the group.

If a group is to be productive, each member of the group must clearly understand what is expected and why, accept his or her role, and feel himself or herself responsible to the group for its accomplishment.

If a group is to be productive, its members must communicate in a common language.

If a group is to be productive, its members must be guided by task-pertinent values that they share in common.

If a group is to be productive, it is usually necessary for its members to be in frequent face-to-face association with one another.

If a group is to be productive, its members must have a common (though not necessarily a talked-about) agreement as to their respective statuses within the group.

If a group is to be productive, each of its members must gain a feeling of individual importance from his or her personal contributions in performing the work of the group.

If a group is to be productive, the distribution of credit for its accomplishments must be seen as equitable by its members.

If a group is to be productive, it must keep on the beam and not spend time on inconsequential or irrelevant matters.

If a group is to be productive, the way it goes about its work must be seen by its members as contributing to the fulfillment of their respective issue and social-psychological needs, and, by extension, of those of their dependents (if any) as well.

If a group is to be productive, the status leader must make the actual leadership group centered, with the leadership role passing freely from member to member.

If a group is to be productive, the task it is to perform must be consistent with the purposes of the other groups to which its members belong.

If a group is to be productive, the satisfactions its members expect to experience from accompanying the group's task must outweigh in their minds the satisfactions they gain from their membership in the group *per se.*

Source: Adapted from Kimball Wiles and John Lovell, *Supervision for Better Schools,* 5th ed. (Englewood Cliffs, NJ: Prentice-Hall, 1983), pp. 65–67.

FIGURE 4.18   Essentials of an Effective Meeting

    A. Convene on time
    B. Good opening/warm-up exercise
    C. Well-planned agenda (prioritized)
    D. Clear roles (leader, recorder, participants)
    E. Appropriate environment (comfortable)
    F. Materials/equipment
    G. No outside interruptions
    H. Define adjournment time
I. Premeeting Checklist [ ]
    A. Precise purpose—objective
    B. Written announcement (time, purpose, location, etc.)
    C. Tentative agenda distributed with vital backup materials
    D. Predetermined adjournment time
    E. Identify audience
    F. Identify materials (visuals, equipment) needed
    G. Who can help? Advise in advance
    H. Plan ingredients—all points to be made
    I. Estimate time for each agenda item
    J. Plan opening
    K. Integrate impact features
    L. Examine texture (variety)
    M. Dry-run visuals/equipment
II. Role of Chairperson [ ]
    A. Begin on time
    B. Provide overview
    C. Keep on target
    D. One agenda item at a time
    E. Cut off redundant debate
    F. Neutralize "dominator"
    G. Draw out the "timid/perplexed"
    H. Encourage full discussion
    I. Keep climate relaxed/wholesome
    J. Use rules for brainstorming
    K. Use rules of order
    L. Tap resources of audience
    M. Delegate to "volunteer"
    N. Serve as negotiator, arbitrator, neutral, compassionate listener—shift role
    O. Keep calm
    P. Adjourn on time

FIGURE 4.18   *Continued*

III. Role of Meeting Participant [ ]
  A. Do advance preparation
  B. Be on time
  C. Raise questions for clarification—"Gate opening for expertise"
  D. Demonstrate responsible (attitude/behavior) good manners
  E. Accept share of work—offer to help
  F. Stick to point
  G. Help others to stay on topic
  H. Be sensitive to others' feelings (particularly chairperson)
  I. *Listen actively—listening with warmth is contagious*
IV. Postmeeting Checklist [ ]
  A. Minutes or record distributed—twenty-four hours
  B. Clear follow-up assignments and time line
  C. Evaluation
  D. Next meeting (date/time)
  E. Location
  F. Tentative agenda
  G. Responsibilities
V. Meeting Record [ ]
  A. Purpose—to provide
    1. Minutes of meeting to participants
    2. Concise, right-to-the-point notes
    3. Opportunity for recorder to be active participant
    4. Basis for summarizing the meeting
    5. Critical elements and decisions made
    6. Immediate dissemination
  B. Objective—to provide
    1. Date, time convened, and time terminated
    2. Name of recorder
    3. Names of participants
    4. Specific topics covered
    5. Time spent on each topic
    6. Decisions reached and actions to be taken
    7. Responsibilities for follow-up
    8. Deadlines for action to be taken
    9. List of handouts distributed at the meeting

Source: As cited in Jon Wiles and Joseph Bondi, *Curriculum Development: A Guide to Practice,* 5th ed. (New York: Macmillan, 1998), p. 226. Used by permission.

FIGURE 4.19   Negative and Positive Meeting Behaviors

Negative Behaviors	Positive Behaviors
1. A person aggressively expresses disapproval of ideas of others.	1. A person brings the discussion back to the point.
2. A person attacks the groups or ideas under consideration that have not had a full hearing.	2. A person seeks clarification of meaning when ideas expressed are not clear.
3. A person tries to reintroduce an idea into the discussion after it has already been rejected.	3. A person questions and evaluates ideas expressed in objective manner.
4. A person tries to assert authority by demanding.	4. A person challenges reasoning when the soundness of logic is doubtful.
5. A person introduces information to the meeting that is obviously irrelevant to the discussion at hand.	5. A person introduces a new way of thinking about topic.
6. A person tries to invoke sympathy by a depreciation of self or his or her position.	6. A person makes a summary of points.
7. A person uses stereotypes to cover his or her own biases and prejudices.	7. A person underscores points of agreement or disagreement.
8. A person attempts to downgrade the importance of the group's role or function.	8. A person tries to resolve conflict or differences of opinion.
9. A person tries to interrupt the group process by speaking tangentially or citing unrelated personal experiences.	9. A person introduces facts or relevant information.
10. A person seeks to call attention to himself or herself by excessive talking, using extreme ideas, or displaying unusual behavior.	10. A person evaluates progress of the group.

Source: Jon Wiles and Joseph Bondi, *Supervision: A Guide to Practice,* 4th ed. (Columbus, OH: Charles Merrill, 1996), p. 228.

FIGURE 4.20   Guidelines for Improved Listening

Nichols identifies ten guidelines for improving listening:
1. Focus on areas of interest in the speaker's message.
2. Judge the content of the message and not the delivery.
3. Learn to hold your fire and not reveal your bias.
4. Focus on central ideas and the flow of the message.
5. Remain flexible in thinking by concentrating on various ways to remember what is being said.
6. Take notes only for specifics, not for an outline.
7. Give the speaker your conscious attention and fight back distractions.
8. Tune out distractions over which you have no immediate control.
9. Keep your mind open by avoiding blind spots and personal prejudices.
10. Capitalize on thought speed—we think four times faster than we talk.

Source: Ralph Nichols, "Listening Is a Ten-Part Skill," *Managing Yourself, Nation's Business* (May 1995), 44.

Research by George Litwin and Robert Stringer of Harvard University revealed nine critical variables that can be influenced by the leader (Figure 4.21). According to this work, climate affects work in the following way:

1. Individuals are attracted to work climates that arouse their dominant needs.
2. Such on-the-job work climates consist of both experiences and incentives.
3. These climates interact with worker needs to arouse motivation toward need satisfaction.
4. Climate represents the most powerful lever available to managers in bringing about change in individuals.

In their work, Litwin and Stringer looked at a number of organization types (hospitals, business, military, schools) and documented that certain emphasis by leaders using these nine variables produced either achievement, affiliation, or power motivation. Figure 4.22 summarizes the findings of this important research.

The reader may look on climate in one of two ways. Either climate is used to establish an orientation of an organization toward certain ends (high-achieving

FIGURE 4.21   Nine Variables That Constitute a Climate

1. **Structure.**   The feeling that employees have about the constraints in the group, how many rules, regulations, procedures there are; is there an emphasis on "red tape" and going through channels, or is there a loose and informal atmosphere?
2. **Responsibility.**   The feeling of being your own boss; not having to double-check all your decisions; when you have a job to do, knowing that it is your job.
3. **Reward.**   The feeling of being rewarded for a job well done; emphasizing positive rewards rather than punishments; the perceived fairness of the pay and promotion policies.
4. **Risk.**   The sense of riskiness and challenge in the job and in the organization; is there an emphasis on taking calculated risks, or is playing it safe the best way to operate?
5. **Warmth.**   The feeling of general good fellowship that prevails in the work group atmosphere; the emphasis on being well-liked; the prevalence of friendly and informal social groups.
6. **Support.**   The perceived helpfulness of the managers and employees in the group; emphasis on mutual support from above and below.
7. **Standards.**   The perceived importance of implicit and explicit goals and performance standards; the emphasis on doing a good job; the challenge represented in personal and group goals.
8. **Conflict.**   The feeling that managers and other workers want to hear different opinions; the emphasis placed on getting problems out in the open, rather than smoothing them over or ignoring them.
9. **Identity.**   The feeling that you belong to a company and you are a valuable member of a working team; the importance placed on this kind of spirit.

FIGURE 4.22   Summary of Findings of Climate Research

The Relationship of Climate Dimensions and Achievement Motivation

Climate Dimension	Hypothesized Effect on Achievement Motivation	Findings	Hypothesis Support	Revised Hypothesis
Structure	reduction	mixed	moderate	—
Responsibility	arousal	consistent positive	weak–moderate	—
Warmth	no effect	some negative	moderate	—
Support	arousal	positive	moderate	—
Reward	arousal	consistent positive	strong	—
Conflict	arousal	mixed	very weak	—
Standards	arousal	mixed	weak	—
Identity	no effect	negative	none	arousal
Risk	arousal	some positive	weak–moderate	—

The Relationship of Climate Dimensions and Affiliation Motivation

Climate Dimension	Hypothesized Effect on Affiliation Motivation	Findings	Hypothesis Support	Revised Hypothesis
Structure	reduction	consistent negative	strong	—
Responsibility	no effect	zero order	strong	—
Warmth	arousal	consistent positive	strong	—
Support	arousal	positive	strong	—
Reward	arousal	consistent positive	strong	—
Conflict	reduction	weak negative	moderate	—
Standards	no effect	some negative	very weak	reduction
Identity	arousal	positive	strong	—
Risk	no effect	some negative	very weak	reduction

The Relationship of Climate Dimensions and Power Motivation

Climate Dimension	Hypothesized Effect on Power Motivation	Findings	Hypothesis Support	Revised Hypothesis
Structure	arousal	strong positive	very strong	—
Responsibility	arousal	positive	strong	—
Warmth	no effect	weak negative	moderate	—
Support	no effect	weak positive	moderate	—
Reward	no effect	zero order	strong	—
Conflict	arousal	consistent positive	strong	—
Standards	no effect	weak positive	moderate	—
Identity	reduction	weak positive	none	no effect
Risk	no effect	negative	very weak	reduction

Source: Adapted and reprinted by permission of Harvard Business School Press from George H. Litwin and Robert A. Stringer, Jr., *Motivation and Organizational Climate.* Boston: Division of Research, Harvard Business School, 1968, exhibits 5.9, 5.10, and 5.11, p. 100. Copyright © 1968 by the Harvard Business School Publishing Corporation; all rights reserved.

school), or climate can be used to connect certain individuals with tasks that they will be personally motivated to fulfill.

These variables, translated into educational settings, allow the curriculum leader to influence the perceptions of individuals and groups that make up the organization. In terms of leadership theory, the use of climate building can represent a method of transacting and connecting with followers.

STAFF DEVELOPMENT

Staff development or in-service education represents a direct link between curriculum development and classroom delivery. Without a knowledgeable and committed teacher who holds skills needed to implement the curriculum, all planning is an academic exercise.

Traditionally, staff development was tied to certification and certificate renewal and represented a sort of deficiency model in teacher growth. Experiences were formulated to produce a minimally able teacher or to correct deficiencies in the teacher's repertoire of behaviors. Beginning in the 1960s and continuing to date, a major role of teachers is to implement new curricula. With this "development" emphasis, staff development has become more closely tied to curriculum development. New programs demand new skills!

The move toward greater involvement of teachers in school operations, under labels such as school-based management and decentralized decision making, have changed the face of staff development. The traditional top–down or external approach has been replaced by a participatory model in which teachers often self-select their training.

From the curriculum design perspective, in-service experiences should be tied to program needs and should be offered after the rationale, conceptual base, and developmental process are underway. In other words, in-service should be a natural extension of a chain of events, as illustrated in Figure 4.23.

An important consideration in designing in-service experiences for teachers today is to note their maturity. Increasingly, teachers today are career practitioners, some with more than thirty years of experience. This experience must be noted, and in-service designed to accommodate the needs and styles of these teachers. Because teachers are given full responsibility from the first day on the job, they quickly become proficient. Using Erikson's adult development model (see Chapter 2), teachers may reach an identity stage before age thirty. Traditional stages of adult learning preferences (Figure 4.24) show an increasingly "individualized" format as the teacher becomes intrinsically motivated. In Figure 4.25, some basic principles for adult learning are suggested. Models of in-service are plentiful and include the following:

1. Microteaching. Directed toward highly specific skill acquisition, this technique may use video clips (Stanford University B-2 modules), interaction observation instruments (Flanders), or simply an in-the-classroom show and tell to increase a teacher's skill.

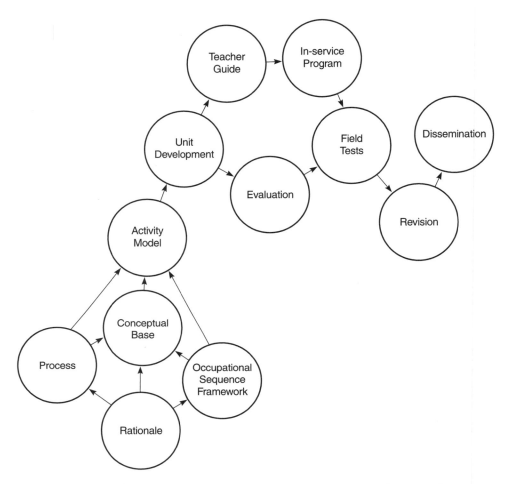

FIGURE 4.23   Staff Development as an Extension of Curriculum Work

2. Clinical Observations.   Modeled on the medical model, the leader helps the teacher to view himself or herself and self-prescribe changes. In curriculum work, certain teaching behaviors may be more appropriate for certain outcomes and students (such as direct instructional techniques for students who are disadvantaged in basic skill areas).

3. Competency-Based.   Here a profile of the teacher needed to guide a program successfully is constructed and the standards or competencies extracted. Teachers, individually or with help, assess their own performances and participate in staff development to become more like the projected profile.

4. Faculty Designed In-Service.   Where schools have adopted a decentralized decision-making model, teachers may be given the power to design school wide in-service. This development may prove very helpful to the curriculum designer

FIGURE 4.24   Teacher Development and Appropriate Strategies

Age 20–30	Because the teacher has been a student for most of his or her life, a "formal school" format, with lecture and grades, is appropriate. This teacher has limited skills and requires additional credentialing. There is little fear of a computer-delivered training program. Motivation is to "get going."
Age 30–40	This teacher is secure, having mastered the "survival stage" of becoming a teacher and gaining a continuing contract. A less formal format is called for, with greater opportunity to socialize and learn from other teachers. Text, discussion, contracts, or pass/fail grading are suitable. Teachers in this range are interested in self-expansion.
Age 40–50	Teachers in this age range are secure, many having taught for twenty years. Most will do what is necessary, but feel that "they've seen this before." Many will be recreational or social learners, and short attention spans are not uncommon. The instruction is best if by peers, and time is important to this learner. Materials should be classroom relevant with larger print sizes if possible.
Age 50–60	This teacher has a rich life history to call on and is generally very positive about training. Learning occurs most readily in a tutorial or small-group format with no formal evaluation.

FIGURE 4.25   Basic Learning Principles for Adults

1. Base learning on previous knowledge and experience.
2. Use adult-to-adult communication rather than teacher-to-student communication.
3. Allow more time for processing of information.
4. Allow participation and sharing whenever possible.
5. Be aware that many events compete for their time.
6. Emphasize the "utility" of the information at all times.
7. Acknowledge the strengths and weaknesses of all individuals.
8. Realize all adult learners possess learning handicaps and methods of compensation.
9. Realize all adult learners are anxiety prone and need reassurance.
10. Realize all adult learners fear failure and loss of self-esteem.

given that research is continually supportive of the school site as the most effective unit for true change. There also is research to support the idea that school-based change is more likely to affect attitude formation (than college instruction) and may allow differentiated training experiences for more mature teachers.

5. Coaching and Mentoring.   The use of teacher experience in coaching and mentoring in-service models is relatively rare. The historic model of the teacher as a "solitary artisan" has meant that teachers do not often share experiences. The construction of school buildings as minilecture halls under one roof has further contributed to this isolation. Coaching models may mean sharing of practices, learning specific skills for individual curriculum components, or pairing teachers across school lines for dissemination of curriculum practices.

6. Teacher Education Centers.   Very promising as a model to further curriculum work is the teacher education center, a place where teachers can gather and construct meaningful materials and learn new methods. Pennsylvania and Texas have built networks of such centers on a state wide basis, while many such centers exist in the individual districts. The physical structure of a teacher center suggests that the curriculum organizes staff development training.

7. Teachers-Training-Teachers.   In highly unionized districts, teachers may have negotiated control of staff development, but this is not necessarily a bad thing from the curriculum development perspective. If teachers can identify practices and train one another through this method, it is likely that highly professional communication will occur about the curriculum and instructional design of any program.

As a final note, it is important that curriculum persons engaged in staff development efforts work to create a "systems thinking" on the part of teachers and staff. In reality, the only rationale for staff development programs is the curriculum being supported.

EVALUATION

Since the early 1980s, the cost of education has driven an accountability movement in America. What originally started as a funding crisis as a result of postwar inflation has now become a perspective—education should have a measurable outcome. Measurable standards and the testing movement have dominated public education since the early 1990s. Curriculum professionals should acknowledge this condition and see it as an asset rather than a hindrance. As such, evaluation can be a tool for curriculum work.

Following on the previous section, it is important for curriculum persons to promote evaluation as a systems concern or from a comprehensive perspective. In too many districts, evaluation is a proof of performance, rather than a tool for fine-tuning a program. In Figure 4.26, evaluation at the school level is seen as something that incorporates many areas of school operation. Some organizing questions are provided to guide discussion of evaluation efforts.

Evaluation has a number of general functions that interface with curriculum work:

1. To make explicit the philosophy and the rationale of the instructional design
2. To collect data for making judgments about the effectiveness of programs
3. For use as a decision-making tool
4. To rationalize changes proposed and implemented

FIGURE 4.26   Evaluation as a Comprehensive Organizer

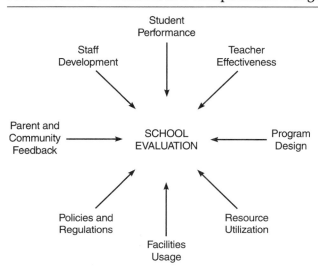

Program Design

1. Is the program concept consistent with the overall philosophy of the district and its leaders?
2. Does the program articulate (fit) with preceding elementary, middle, or secondary programs? Is there a consistent follow-through in other programs?
3. Are resources dedicated to this program commensurate with other programs found in the curriculum?
4. Is there an internal consistency to this program such as a set of objectives that provides structure?

Facilities Usage

1. Does the physical location and allocation of space reflect this program's priority in the curriculum?
2. Are learning areas within the space consistent with the instructional intent in delivering this program to students?

Policies and Regulations

1. Are some policies and regulations essential in allowing this program to function fully?
2. Are there rules or policies that, in fact, contradict the spirit of this program?
3. Is there a better way to handle policy formation and enforcement in operating this program?

Resource Utilization

1. Is there a clear relationship between the allocation of resources and funds and the curricular objectives of this program?
2. Are resources available to support innovative instructional approaches or to promote desired changes?
3. Is there an established procedure for assessing future resource needs and planning for their acquisition?

Continued

FIGURE 4.26   *Continued*

Student Performance

1. Is student evaluation in this program both systematic and continuous?
2. Is student evaluation perceived by teachers as a measure of the program's success?
3. Are parents involved in the evaluation of the student and program?
4. Is student evaluation directional, indicating where improvement is needed?

Teacher Effectiveness

1. Is program improvement based on input by the instructional staff?
2. Is teacher evaluation tied directly to program improvement?
3. Have the talents and abilities of teachers been fully explored in terms of contributing to this program?
4. Are there any unplanned organizational or administrative constraints on teaching styles in this program?

Staff Development

1. Are monies budgeted for staff development tied to the needs and goals of this specific program?
2. Do teachers have the opportunity to critique current staff development efforts?
3. Can it be shown, through evaluation, where staff development in the past has improved this program?

Parent–Community Feedback

1. Are members of the community involved in the formation and maintenance of this program?
2. Are members of the community kept informed about any major changes contemplated or implemented in this program?
3. Does a communication vehicle exist that effectively shares the accomplishments of this program with parents and community?

Source: Jon Wiles, *Planning Guidelines for Middle School Education* (Dubuque, IA: Kendall/Hunt, 1976), pp. 72–73.

Evaluation designs, models determining the scope of inquiry, can have multiple focal points. In Figure 4.27 four such purposes are identified, along with questions to be answered from evaluation efforts. In Figure 4.28, Stufflebeam proposes an evaluation structure that is general to all types of evaluation and one that might be utilized to guide various studies.

For Tyler, evaluation was the final step in a four-step development process leading to program improvement. Looking at each of these steps independently, however, reveals why programs fail and may suggest a specific focus for evaluation efforts in curriculum development:

Analysis Stage

1. The program evaluated has no design and cannot be assessed as a whole.
2. Leaders fear evaluation will reveal weakness and block assessment.
3. The analysis is only verbal, and actual data is not collected.
4. Leaders enhance the assessment because they feel performance is expected.

FIGURE 4.27　Four Purposes of Evaluation with Questions

Approach	Focus	Procedure	Questions
Program Design	Conceptual/ structure	Validation of goals/purposes	Do we have the kind of program intended?
Program Process	Operational/ technique	Program analysis/checklists	Is the program we have efficient in delivering services?
Program Product	Structured feedback	Testing and survey	Does the program work? Are there desired outcomes?
Program Personnel	Observation/ analysis	Review/redesign	Are personnel making a direct contribution to the planned program?

FIGURE 4.28　A Generic Evaluation Design

1. Structure the evaluation.	Identify decision points, define the criteria for making the decisions.
2. Collect data.	Identify the sources, find or construct instruments, define the sample, conditions, and schedule for collection.
3. Organize the data.	Specify a format; construct a storage and retrieval system.
4. Analyze the data.	Specify the procedure and limitations used, and schedule and fund an analysis procedure.
5. Report the data.	Define the dissemination audience, specify an appropriate reporting format (visual and live), indicate actions to be taken.
6. Activate the data.	Define resource requirements for activation, schedule anticipated activities, schedule next evaluation round.

Source: Adapted from a procedure developed by Daniel Stufflebeam, as reported in *Educational Technology,* July 1968.

Design Stage

1. The design is "blue-sky" (unreal) and is following a "bandwagon" (everyone else is doing this).
2. Existing conditions make the design unachievable (financial, academic).
3. The design challenges bedrock values shared by community or district leaders.
4. The design is couched in vague or wordy terms.

Implementation Stage

1. The primary authorities supporting the project leave.
2. The change proves to be too complex for completion.
3. The time line is unrealistic, and the project is abandoned before completion.
4. Training is insufficient for successful transition.

Evaluation

1. No baseline data is present for comparison.
2. Evaluation data is not trusted by those affected by the change.

Evaluation of curriculum efforts is often too narrow and therefore fails to assess the true impact of the program on the student. In Figure 4.29, measures available to someone designing an evaluation effort are shown. Knowledge of valid and reliable instruments (see Burroughs Mental Measurement Yearbook) to measure these outcomes is an important knowledge base for curriculum planners.

Finally, the design of evaluation efforts in curriculum work must acknowledge the realities of the practice environment. The word "research" in schools elicits a negative reaction from many practitioners who have heard the phrase "research says" at too many workshops and who are convinced that research can be manipulated to prove anything. The following suggestions are made by the author:

1. Involve teachers directly in any data gathering and interpretation.
2. Help teachers to understand the different kinds of research evidence (controlled, surveys, meta-syntheses, ethnographic, expert opinion, models).
3. Where possible, use action research at the school level to create a climate of objective analysis of practices.

FIGURE 4.29   Various Measures of Evaluation

Measures of Evaluation
Academic aptitude tests
Reading tests (comprehension and vocabulary)
Achievement tests in subjects
Emotional and social adjustment measures
Health assessments
Home conditions
Pupil questionnaires
Behavior ratings
Interest indexes
Writing sample inventories
Work habit measures
Teacher classroom behavior assessments

Measures of Growth
Aspects of thinking
Work habits and skills
Reading
Development of social attitudes
Development of wider interests
Development of appreciations
Development of social sensitivity
Ability to make social adjustments
Creativeness
Development of personal philosophy
Physical health
Mental health

USING TECHNOLOGY

In the nine short years since the Internet became available for public use, learning has experienced a revolution. Literally millions of sites have been created on the Internet for many purposes. All of these sites represent an access to knowledge.

Schools, traditionally, have held a monopoly on "official learning." As such, school personnel in roles such as curriculum development have been timid in defining the meaning of new interactive technologies in schools. Instead of focusing on substantive issues, such as the organization of these massive knowledge fields, school leaders have opted to concern themselves with equipment purchases and blocking unwanted information.

The dilemma for curriculum leaders is how to move forward with caution. Not only has technology proven very expensive for schools but also public opinion about the use of technologies in school are as varied as the American society. However, to not engage the Internet in schools is to allow an "end run" by business and pressure groups. The 1.7 million home schoolers who have abandoned the public schools represent only the tip of a massive population that might leave schools for more modern venues. Electronic learning (e-learning) and new and interactive "learning portals" have already revolutionized business learning in our society. Surely, the attractiveness of $8,000 per pupil expenditures in public schools will attract further attention.

To their credit, classroom teachers have kept up with the rapid technological change, albeit at home on their own equipment. School leaders must begin to think in nonconventional ways about how these savvy teachers can be utilized within the system. Following are some of the more obvious moves that are currently underway in schools:

- Allow teachers to develop Internet-assisted lessons and place them on rewritable CD-ROMs for quick updating.
- Begin to "web-up" teachers across school and district lines (even worldwide) so that the power of "many" can be realized.
- Pull away quickly from the standardized labs of the 1980s and 1990s, recognizing that the Internet is a tool to individualize rather than standardize education.
- Begin to use the power of persons beyond school in curriculum development: parents, community persons, and students.
- Break out of the lockstep grade promotion (circa 1910) and allow for continuous progress curriculums.
- Challenge "blanket" expenditures and use available funds to explore classroom enrichment using technology.

SUMMARY

Successful curriculum development includes both design and implementation. Many curriculum improvement efforts are unsuccessful because planners fail to use strategies and tools to ensure success in the field.

Leadership in curriculum requires a skillful individual who focuses on the task—the improvement of learning experiences for students. The open nature of the system of education in the United States makes change difficult and often unpredictable. Leaders in curriculum must master the use of time-tested practices to ensure the success of their development efforts.

This chapter has featured some of the major ideas, techniques, and practices used by curriculum developers in the field to be successful. The reader is encouraged to learn more about change in school settings by pursuing the suggested readings in Appendix A.

SUGGESTED READINGS

Anderson, L., *The Change Leader's Roadmap* (San Francisco: Jossey-Bass, 2001).

Harris, Judith, *Design Tools for Internet-Supported Classrooms* (Columbus, OH: Merrill, 1999).

Jonassen, David, *Computers as Mindtools for Schools,* 2nd ed. (Columbus, OH: Merrill, 1999).

Morrison, Gary, *Integrating Computer Technology in the Classroom,* 2nd ed. (New York: Wiley, 2000).

Wiles, Jon, *Leaving School: Finding Education* (St. Augustine, FL: Matanzas Press, 2004).

ENDNOTES

1. Kimball Wiles and John Lovell, *Supervision for Better Schools,* 4th ed., (Englewood Cliffs, NJ: Prentice-Hall, 1975), pp. 65–67.

2. Ralph M. Stogdill, *Handbook of Leadership: A Survey of Theory and Research* (New York: Free Press, 1974).

3. Orin Klapp, *Heros, Villains and Fools* (Englewood Cliffs, NJ: Prentice-Hall, 1962).

4. Peter Drucker, *The Effective Executive* (New York: Harper & Row, 1967), p. 83.

5. Bruce Joyce, "The Curriculum Worker of the Future," in National Society for the Study of Education Seventy-First Yearbook, *The Curriculum: Retrospect and Prospect* (Chicago: University of Chicago Press, 1971), p. 64.

6. Kathryn Feyereisen, *Supervision and Curriculum Renewal: A Systems Approach* (New York: Appleton-Century-Croft, 1970), p. 204.

7. A. Haverstein, *Curriculum Planning for Behavioral Development* (Worthington, OH: Charles Jones Publishing, 1975), p. 6.

5

APPLICATIONS

OVERVIEW

It has been the goal of this book to provide the reader with the essential knowledge needed to practice in the field of curriculum. This professional knowledge, things learned through study, must be applied or activated in order to contribute to better educational programs for students. Withholding such professional knowledge, in a school setting, may constitute an abrogation of professional leadership. Leading, without such basic knowledge, may constitute sheer incompetence.

This chapter presents the reader with eight types of students found in schools at the beginning of the twenty-first century. The task for the curriculum developer is to pull together all that is known to create an improved curriculum experience in these and other such areas. A special case in a pressing area, inclusion, is also presented for the reader's consideration.

Using the many variables introduced in this book, philosophy, history, research, existing programs, social science links, evaluation, and more, this chapter assists the reader in "pulling together" the right stuff. Once assembled, the task of designing a curriculum will unfold as a designing process.

YOUNG LEARNERS

Programs for young children, both preschool and primary programs, are vitally important for both students and society. Knowledge gathered during the past fifty years has demonstrated new understandings of children's capacities to learn and develop. At the same time, the support system for young children (the family) has deteriorated at an alarming rate. Increasingly, curriculum developers will be called on to design meaningful programs of compensation and enrichment at this level.

It is clear that the order of development and the tasks of development in young children are predictable. Our models of how children grow (Piaget, Gessell, Havighurst) are reasonable guides for curriculum development. Not so clear is the effect of environment (including family) on the development of young children. Also not defined is a set of targets that would guide us in the selection of growth experiences. In 1994 the U.S. Department of Education initiated a Chicago-based study of 23,000 kindergarten students (Childhood Longitudinal Study Kindergarten Cohort) to help answer some of these "nature and nurture" questions.

Without clearly defined outcomes, programs for young children have followed several design paths including support programs, nurturing, skill readiness, and enrichment. All programs for young children involve some blend of these factors.

Support programs or subsidies operate from the assumption that a hierarchy of conditions must be present in order for healthy growth to occur. Directed mainly at children without sufficient support, these programs ensure food and housing, clothing, school supplies, transportation, medical assistance, and other support to enable the student to participate. Taken to its full development, the "full service school" concept would house such agencies and support areas under one roof and be coordinated by educators.

Programs that nurture are often designed for younger (preschool) students who are immature or simply not prepared for a formal and academic schooling experience. Many centers provide such service for fees without government subsidy and do not expend energies on skill readiness. Socialization skills and interest development, as well as general maturation, are goals of such programs.

Skill readiness programs are designed to aid in later schooling and represent the largest number of programs for young children. In private preschools, such as the Montessori model schools, children are "trained" to identify and manipulate shapes, numbers, letters, and other learning symbols, as well as learning order, obedience, sharing, and prerequisite social skills. In government-sponsored programs, such as Head Start, and later Title One, students are given "compensatory" practice in readiness skills thought to be learned by other children at home. For more than thirty years such skill programs have been beamed into the homes of American children (*Sesame Street, Electric Company*), free to anyone who wishes to receive them.

Finally, in most primary programs in public schools there is an enrichment component in the curriculum. These experiences (such as visits to the fire station or participation in the second-grade band) are provided with the understanding that a child's background or schemata will determine what can be learned. Like language, experience is a prerequisite to associative learning.

Our commitment to programs for young children in America is significant. Chapter One (Title One), for example, costs the U.S. taxpayers $5 billion each year and has affected more than five million students in forty-five states. Billions more are spent each year on preschool programs by parents. The tasks of such programs, such as attention, memory, language, visual/spatial reasoning, sequencing, and motor skill development, are essential to school success. Although other nations in the world provide various educational services to students as young as age three, the United States is slow to move to provide such programs.

The future of such programming for young children, whether in the public or private sector, looks bright. Research continues to estimate that nearly one-half of all learning by the human being occurs during the first six years of life. Opportunities and avenues for individual student development continue to expand. And the statistics reflecting the changing nature of child rearing (decline of the family) are a constant reminder that we must respond to this area of critical need. Early intervention programs, with developmentally appropriate activities, promoting physical, cognitive, social, emotional, and creative growth, will be an important focal point of education in the twenty-first century.

DISADVANTAGED LEARNERS

More than half a century ago, Robert Havighurst conducted the now-classic Growing Up in River City Study in which he documented socioeconomic status as a predictor of school success.[1] Stated simply, the higher the student's socioeconomic status, the greater his or her chance of academic success. A more contemporary observation might be that the school "free lunch" roster represents the best predictor of the school dropout!

Social components that can detract from, or contribute to, school success include social status (economic lifestyle), language abilities, level of parental education (attitudes toward schooling), and parental involvement in a child's education. Without appropriate support and preparation, a student can enter school without the necessary skills and never catch up. A lack of readiness translates into lower self-esteem, lower peer acceptance, lower motivation, poor attribution for academic effort, and, of course, poor performance. In the United States, nearly 30 percent of all students are noncompleters (dropouts).

In the Havighurst study, students from unstable families and low-income families were four to five times more likely to be tardy and absent. Their grades were poor. They evidenced poor learning ability, a lack of motivation, were often withdrawn or shy, and eventually aggressive and hostile toward their fellow students. Unfortunately, these descriptors sound hauntingly like those emerging from research on children from single-parent headed families (often below the poverty line) that now include fifteen million children in America. These children are found by research to evidence low self-esteem, low achievement motivation, poor peer relations, high anxiety, and are more likely to become juvenile delinquents, use drugs and alcohol, and drop out.[2]

With this larger portrait of "disadvantaged" emerging, curriculum developers will have to scramble to suggest meaningful responses. It seems obvious that the parent or parents of such children will be significant players in any effort given that research correlates the parent with academic achievement, better attendance, reduced dropouts, reduced delinquency, and reduced pregnancy among teens. It also seems logical that we must move to "front load" the massive amounts of money spent on disadvantaged students (dropout prevention, summer school, tech prep) after it is too late to alter their pattern.

Without meaningful connection to the various preschool programs, often funded privately or by federal dollars, school systems have focused on the use of compensatory programs to assist the disadvantaged student. Studies have shown that the "platform" of readiness created by preschool programs quickly evaporates if such programs are not reinforced in the public schools.[3]

The "grandaddy" of such programs in the United States is Title One (or Chapter One depending on the funding cycle) which, until recently, was a program providing extra educational services to low-income and low-achieving students. This program has recently become a "low-income" and school wide funding program thus lowering its educational profile. Title One uses a number of educational and organizational designs up through grade eight, including in-class, pull-out, add-on, replacement, and school wide. The most common pattern in the 1990s has been the "pull-out" and research has shown this to be the most effective way to raise achievement for these disadvantaged students. Unfortunately, the pull-out design is also the most disruptive pattern for regular students in school.[4]

The trend in educational programs for the disadvantaged student is to view development comprehensively and longitudinally. For this reason, the students are now often referred to as "at risk," implying that the problems are more comprehensive than simply being born into a low-income family with poor personal support for education. Curriculum designers can web up these various levels (preschool readiness, basic skill mastery, self-esteem and attribution, juvenile delinquency, and drop out) into a more comprehensive system of education. Record keeping, using a tracking computer program similar to that already used in migrant education programs, seems promising. Parent education materials and training may also hold promise.

PREADOLESCENT LEARNERS

Our knowledge of preadolescence as a stage of human development is relatively new. Although studies can be traced to the beginning of the twentieth century, serious inquiry did not begin until the late 1960s. What was quickly discovered by researchers was that this time in life is one of immense change; more change occurs during the preadolescent period than in any other stage except infancy.

Traditionally, educators have had difficulty designing standard programs for these students because of the diversity of this group of learners. Once viewed from a human development perspective (Figure 5.1), it can be seen that the change

FIGURE 5.1   Preadolescence—Implications for Curriculum Development

Characteristics of Emerging Adolescents	Implications for the Middle School
Physical Development	

Accelerated physical development begins in transescence, marked by increase in weight, height, heart size, lung capacity, and muscular strength. Boys and girls are growing at varying rates. Girls tend to be taller for the first two years and tend to be more physically advanced. Bone growth is faster than muscle development, and the uneven muscle/bone development results in lack of coordination and awkwardness. Bones may lack protection of covering muscles and supporting tendons.	Provide a health and science curriculum that emphasizes self-understanding about body changes. Guidance counselors and community resource persons (e.g., pediatricians) can help students understand what is happening to their bodies. Schedule adaptive physical education classes to build physical coordination. Equipment design should help students develop small and large muscles.
In pubescent girls, secondary sex characteristics continue to develop, with breasts enlarging and menstruation beginning.	Intense sports competition; avoid contact sports. Schedule sex education classes; health and hygiene seminars.
A wide range of individual differences among students begins to appear. Although the sequential order of development is relatively consistent in each sex, boys tend to lag a year or two behind girls. There are marked individual differences in physical development for boys and girls. The age of greatest variability in physiological development and physical size is about age 13.	Provide opportunities for interaction among students of different ages, but avoid situations where physical development can be compared (e.g., communal showers). Emphasize intramural programs rather than interscholastic athletics so that each student may participate regardless of physical development. Where interscholastic sports programs exist, number of games should be limited, with games played in afternoon rather than evening.
Glandular imbalances occur, resulting in acne, allergies, dental and eye defects—some health disturbances are real, and some are imaginary.	Provide regular physical examinations for all middle school students.
Boys and girls display changes in body contour—large nose, protruding ears, long arms, have posture problems, and are self-conscious about their bodies.	Health classes should emphasize exercises for good posture. Students should understand through self-analysis that growth is an individual process and occurs unevenly.
A girdle of fat often appears around the hips and thighs of boys in early puberty. Slight development of tissue under the skin around the nipples occurs briefly, causing anxiety in boys who fear they are developing "the wrong way."	Films and talks by doctors and counselors can help students understand the changes the body goes through during this period. A carefully planned program of sex education developed in collaboration with parents, medical doctors, and community agencies should be developed.
Students are likely to be disturbed by body changes. Girls especially are likely to be disturbed by the physical changes that accompany sexual maturation.	
Receding chins, cowlicks, dimples, and changes in voice result in possible embarrassment to boys.	Teacher and parental reassurance and understanding are necessary to help students understand that many body changes are temporary in nature.
Boys and girls tend to tire easily but won't admit it.	Advise parents to insist that students got proper rest; overexertion should be discouraged.

Continued

FIGURE 5.1   *Continued*

Physical Development (continued)	
Fluctuations in basal metabolism may cause students to be extremely restless at times and listless at others.	Provide an opportunity for daily exercise and a place where students can be children by playing and being noisy for short periods.
	Encourage activities such as special-interest classes and "hands on" exercises. Students should be allowed to move around physically in classes and avoid long periods of passive work.
Boys and girls show ravenous appetites and peculiar tastes; may overtax digestive system with large quantities of improper foods.	Provide snacks to satisfy between-meal hunger as well as nutritional guidance specific to this age group.

Social Development	
Affiliation base broadens from family to peer group. Conflict sometimes results due to splitting of allegiance between peer group and family.	Teachers should work closely with the family to help adults realize that peer pressure is a normal part of the maturation process. Parents should be encouraged to continue to provide love and comfort even though they may feel rejected.
	Teachers should be counselors. Teacher–adviser house plan arrangements should be encouraged.
Peers become sources for standards and models of behavior. Child's occasional rebellion does not diminish importance of parents for development of values. Emerging adolescents want to make their own choices, but authority still remains primarily with family.	Sponsor school activities that permit students to interact socially with many school personnel. Family studies can help ease parental conflicts. Parental involvement at school should be encouraged, but parents should not be too conspicuous by their presence.
	Encourage co-curriculum activities. For example, an active student government will help students develop guidelines for interpersonal relations and standards of behavior.
Society's mobility has broken ties to peer groups and created anxieties in emerging adolescents.	Promote "family" grouping of students and teachers to provide stability for new students. Interdisciplinary units can be structured to provide interaction among various groups of students. Clubs and special-interest classes should be an integral part of the school day.
Students are confused and frightened by new school settings.	Orientation programs and "buddy systems" can reduce the trauma of moving from an elementary school to a middle school. Family teams can encourage a sense of belonging.
Students show unusual or drastic behavior at times—aggressive, daring, boisterous, argumentative.	Schedule debates, plays, playdays, and other activities to allow students to "show off" in a productive way.
"Puppy love" years emerge, with a show of extreme devotion to a particular boy or girl. However, allegiance may be transferred to a new friend overnight.	Role-playing and guidance exercises can provide the opportunity to act out feelings. Provide opportunities for social interaction between the sexes— parties and games, but not dances in the early grades of the middle school.

FIGURE 5.1   *Continued*

Social Development (continued)

Youths feel that the will of the group must prevail and sometimes can be almost cruel to those not in their group. They copy and display fads of extremes in clothes, speech, mannerisms, and handwriting; very susceptible to media advertising.	Set up an active student government so students can develop their own guidelines for dress and behavior. Adults should be encouraged not to react with outrage when extreme dress or mannerisms are displayed.
Boys and girls show strong concern for what is "right" and for social justice; also show concern for those less fortunate.	Foster plans that allow students to engage in service activities, for example, peer teaching, which allow students to help other students. Community projects (e.g., assisting in a senior citizens' club or helping in a childcare center) can be planned by students and teachers.
They are influenced by adults—attempt to identify with adults other than their parents.	Flexible teaching patterns should prevail so students can interact with a variety of adults with whom they can identify.
Despite a trend toward heterosexual interests, same-sex affiliation tends to dominate.	Plan large group activities rather than boy–girl events. Intramurals can be scheduled so students can interact with friends of the same or opposite sex.
Students desire direction and regulation but reserve the right to question or reject suggestions of adults.	Provide opportunities for students to accept more responsibility in setting standards for behavior. Students should be helped to establish realistic goals and be assisted in helping realize those goals.

Emotional Development

Erratic and inconsistent behavior is prevalent. Anxiety and fear contrast with reassuring bravado. Feelings tend to shift between superiority and inferiority. Coping with physical changes, striving for independence from family, becoming a person in his/her own right, and learning a new mode of intellectual functioning are all emotion-laden problems for emerging adolescents. Students have many fears, real and imagined. At no other time in development is he or she likely to encounter such a diverse number of problems simultaneously.	Encourage self-evaluation among students. Design activities that help students play out their emotions. Activity programs should provide opportunities for shy students to be drawn out and loud students to engage in calming activities. Counseling must operate as a part of, rather than an adjunct to, the learning program. Students should be helped to interpret superiority and inferiority feelings. Mature value systems should be encouraged by allowing students to examine options of behavior and to study consequences of various actions.
	Encourage students to assume leadership in group discussions and experience frequent success and recognition for personal efforts and achievements. A general atmosphere of friendliness, relaxation, concern, and group cohesiveness should guide the program.
Chemical and hormone imbalances often trigger emotions that are little understood by the transescent. Students sometimes regress to childlike behavior.	Adults in the middle school should not pressure students to explain their emotions (e.g., crying for no apparent reason). Occasional childlike behavior should not be ridiculed.
	Provide numerous possibilities for releasing emotional stress.

Continued

FIGURE 5.1   *Continued*

Emotional Development (continued)

Too-rapid or too-slow physical development is often a source of irritation and concern. Development of secondary sex characteristics may create additional tensions about rate of development.	Provide appropriate sex education and encourage participation of parents and community agencies. Pediatricians, psychologists, and counselors should be called on to assist students in understanding developmental changes.
This age group is easily offended and sensitive to criticism of personal shortcomings.	Sarcasm by adults should be avoided. Students should be helped to develop values when solving their problems.
Students tend to exaggerate simple occurrences and believe their problems are unique.	Use sociodrama to enable students to see themselves as others see them. Readings dealing with problems similar to their own can help them see that many problems are not unique.

Intellectual Development

Students display a wide range of skills and abilities unique to their developmental patterns.	Use a variety of approaches and materials in the teaching–learning process.
Students will range in development from the concrete–manipulatory stage to the ability to deal with abstract concepts. The transescent is intensely curious and growing in mental ability.	Treat students at their own intellectual levels, providing immediate rather than remote goals. All subjects should be individualized. Skill grouping should be flexible.
Middle school learners prefer active over passive learning activities and prefer interaction with peers during learning activities.	Encourage physical movement, with small group discussions, learning centers, and creative dramatics suggested as good activity projects. Provide a program of learning that is exciting and meaningful.
Students are usually very curious and exhibit a strong willingness to learn things they consider useful. They enjoy using skills to solve real-life problems.	Organize curricula around real-life concepts (e.g., conflict, competition, poor group influence). Provide activities in formal and informal situations to improve reasoning powers. Studies of the community and the environment are particularly relevant to the age group.
Students often display heightened egocentrism and will argue to convince others or to clarify their own thinking. Independent, critical thinking emerges.	Organized discussions of ideas and feelings in peer groups can facilitate self-understanding. Provide experiences for individuals to express themselves by writing and participating in dramatic productions.
Studies show that brain growth in transescents slows between the ages of 12 and 14.	Learners' cognitive skills should be refined; continued cognitive growth during ages 12 to 14 may not be expected.
	Provide opportunities for enjoyable studies in the arts. Encourage self-expression in all subjects.

Source: From Jon Wiles and Joseph Bondi, *The Essential Middle School*, 2nd ed., pp. 29–34. Copyright © 1993 by Macmillan Publishing Company. Reprinted by permission.

experienced by the student is massive and the implications for curriculum design are many. Only during the past thirty years, under the label of "middle school," have curriculum designers tried to create a learning situation appropriate for the preadolescent. Essentially, the rule has been "if the student is the most diverse at any level of schooling, then the curriculum must evidence flexibility to accommodate these differences."

Unlike other levels of education, the American middle school has evolved into a pattern of flexible organizational arrangements that better serves the student. Included in the typical program is a schedule (blocks of time) that allows flexible units of classroom instruction; use of teacher teams with common planning to facilitate individualization of instruction, a subject matter delivery using interdisciplinary organization to provide for the vast range of achievement, and an "exploratory wheel" of nonmastery minicourses to stimulate student interest and allow wise choices in the high school; a beefed-up guidance component to account for the social and emotional volatility of preadolescents (advisory guidance), and intramurals to encourage participation, deemphasize unfair competition, and address physical development.

The Achilles' heel of the middle school design has been an inability to use such organizational structures to overcome a traditional school focus on content mastery. Many middle schools confuse means and ends and, without both a true philosophy and structuring goals, have stopped short of full program development. To simply possess the schedule, teams, interdisciplinary units, guidance program, and so on is not enough. Highly focused student outcomes, behavioral in their definition, allow middle school programs to be evaluated (validated). Unfortunately, the research record for middle schools is very poor.

Middle schools can overcome the "fog" of words by establishing program standards and by using curriculum management plans to lead action toward the development of a complete program. A continuing weakness in all such efforts has been the absence of appropriate (broad) evaluative criteria for measuring success. Life skills, defined by behaviors of students, show promise as a criterion for promoting better middle schools in the twenty-first century.

EXCEPTIONAL LEARNERS

Most educators are all too familiar with Public Law 94-142 (The Education of All Handicapped Children Act) that provides definition for children with special learning needs. Like all children in school, these students are generally protected by the U.S. Constitution:

> *Article 1, Section 8: The General Welfare clause. . . . "The congress shall have the power to provide for the general welfare of the United States . . ."*
> *Amendment VIII: "Nor cruel and unusual punishment inflicted . . ."*
> *Amendment XIV: "Nor shall any State deprive any person of life, liberty, or property without due process of law . . ."*
> *Equal Protection Clause: "Nor deny any person within its jurisdiction the equal protection of the laws. . . ."*

Although it is true that all students are protected "as citizens" by these and other sections of the U.S. Constitution, exceptional children are further protected by the most lengthy set of education regulations ever placed into law. Public Law 94-142 (94th Congress, 142nd law passed) replaced Public Law 93-380 and provided mandatory structures for any curriculum work serving the identified students. (Figure 5.2 defines these populations.)

Any program for exceptional students must rest on six basic principles as defined by law:

1. Zero Reject—All handicapped children must be provided a free, appropriate public education beginning at age three and continuing to age twenty-one.

2. Nondiscriminatory Evaluation—The student must receive a full and individual evaluation prior to placement in any program. This placement must be made by a group (study team) knowledgeable of the student and his or her needs.

3. Individualized Education Program (IEP)—The IEP must be updated annually and show an assessment, yearly goals, evaluation procedures, and time to be spent with a specialist.

4. Least Restrictive Environment—To the maximum extent possible, handicapped students should be educated with children who are not handicapped. Most recently, this section has been interpreted to mean that all handicapped students possible should be included (inclusionary model) in the regular classroom.

5. Due Process—Decisions regarding identification, provision of services, or evaluation may be challenged by any party as to the fairness of decisions and the accountability of the school program in serving the student.

6. Parent Participation—Parents are allowed to review any and all records used for the development of an IEP within forty-five days of a formal request. Parents may also serve as members of the study team and, when deemed to be appropriate by the parent, refuse placement in a designated program.

In public schools, 95 percent of all exceptional children are placed in programs in only four categories: learning disabled, speech and language impaired, mentally handicapped, and emotionally disturbed. The "special" population in American public schools is now about 14 percent of all students, and in some districts this population is consuming up to 50 percent of all educational resources. Obviously, this is an area fertile for further curriculum work.

Three major organizational patterns currently exist to serve special students. In some cases, students are segregated in special program areas (profoundly handicapped) for most of the school day. A second pattern finds students out of regular classrooms for services during part of the day (pull-out) but mainstreamed into regular classes when possible. This model can be further broken down into "like" groups of students or groups of varying exceptionalities (VE). A third pattern, inclusion, finds the exceptional teacher coming to the regular classroom to service students with exceptional needs. Although the inclusion model seems to most fully respond to the intent of Public Law 94-142, in many districts the pattern is selected as a response to the very large exceptional classes and the unavailability of trained exceptional education teachers. In these cases, a trade-off is made between program

FIGURE 5.2   Defining Exceptional Populations Using Public Law 94-142

Trainable mentally handicapped.   A moderately mentally handicapped person is one who is impaired in intellectual and adaptive behavior and whose development reflects his or her reduced rate of learning. The measured intelligence of a moderately handicapped person falls approximately between three and four standard deviations below the mean (51–36 on the Stanford Binet, and 54–40 on the Wechsler), and the assessed adaptive behavior falls below age and cultural expectations.

Severely mentally handicapped.   A severely mentally handicapped person is one who is impaired in intellectual and adaptive behavior and whose development reflects his or her reduced rate of learning. The measured intelligence of a severely handicapped person falls approximately between four and five standard deviations below the mean (35–20 on the Stanford Binet, and 39–25 on the Wechsler), and the assessed adaptive behavior falls below age and cultural expectations.

Profoundly mentally handicapped.   A profoundly mentally handicapped person is one who is impaired in intellectual and adaptive behaviors and whose development reflects his or her reduced rate of learning. The measured intelligence of a profoundly handicapped person falls approximately five standard deviations below the mean (below 25 on the Stanford Binet) and there is limited or no adaptive behavior.

Educable mentally handicapped.   An educable mentally handicapped student is one who is mildly impaired in intellectual and adaptive behavior and whose development reflects a reduced rate of learning. A student's performance on an individual psychological evaluation indicates an approximate intellectual ability between two and three standard deviations below the mean (68–52 on the Stanford Binet, and 69–55 on the Wechsler, plus or minus five).

Students with communicative disorders.   Students with communicative disorders may have trouble speaking, understanding others, or hearing the sounds of their world. They may have difficulty saying specific sounds or words, using words correctly, using the voice correctly, or speaking clearly and smoothly. Some students are unable to make muscles needed for speech work adequately. Other students may have hearing problems that prevent them from understanding the teacher and others around them. Some students need help in learning words and in understanding how to put them together into sentences. To be considered for speech, language, or hearing therapy services, the student should be referred to the speech, language, and hearing clinician for testing, with written permission from a parent or guardian. After all testing (speech, hearing, language, and any other, as appropriate), a staffing committee meets to discuss the student's problem and to decide how best to help the student.

Hearing-impaired students.   Students who are born with a severe hearing loss (70 dB or greater in better ear in speech frequencies), or who acquire a loss before learning language and speech, are considered deaf by state Department of Education definition. These students will be unable to use normal language and speech unless they receive special education instruction. To be considered for enrollment in a hearing impaired program, the student must have a medical evaluation, which would include a general physical examination, an evaluation by an ear specialist (otologist), and a complete hearing evaluation by an audiologist. After all testing is completed, a staffing committee meets to discuss the student's problem and to decide how best to help the student.

Specific learning disabilities.   A student with specific learning disabilities has disorder in one or more of the basic psychological processes involved in understanding or in spoken and written language. These may be manifested in disorders of listening, thinking, reading, talking, writing, spelling, or arithmetic. They include conditions that have been referred to as perceptual handicaps, brain injury, minimal brain dysfunction, dyslexia, developmental aphasia, etc. They *do not* include learning problems that are primarily a result of visual, hearing, or motor handicaps; mental retardation; emotional disturbance; or an environmental disadvantage.

Continued

FIGURE 5.2   *Continued*

To be considered for placement in a specific learning disabilities program, the student must have average to near average mental abilities, normal visual and hearing acuity, and no evidence of a primary physical handicap. Standardized achievement test scores would indicate difficulty in the basic academic areas of reading, writing, arithmetic, and/or spelling. Specialized test scores would show student difficulty in handling information received by sight and/or by hearing, in language usage and/or in fine motor skills.

Emotionally handicapped.   An emotionally handicapped student is one who exhibits consistent and persistent signs of disturbed behaviors, such as withdrawal, distractibility, hyperactivity, or hypersensitivity, which disrupt the learning process.

Emotionally handicapped students show the following behaviors to the extent that they may not be served in the regular school program without at least part-time special placement or consultative services: learning problems that are not primarily a result of mental retardation; severe behavior disorders that cannot be controlled or eliminated by medical intervention; and inability to build or maintain satisfactory interpersonal relationships with adults and peers.

Physically handicapped.   A student who has a crippling condition or other health impairment that requires an adaptation to the student's school environment or curriculum is considered physically handicapped. The student may have an impairment that interferes with the normal functions of the bones, joints, or muscles to such an extent that special arrangements must be made to provide an educational program.

The student may have a special health problem such as cardiac disorders, diabetes, epilepsy, cystic fibrosis, hemophilia, asthma, leukemia, or nephritis, that would require special arrangements to provide an educational program.

Multihandicapped students whose primary or most severe disability is a crippling condition or other health impairment may be included in this program.

Gifted.   A gifted student is one who has superior intellectual development and is capable of high performance. The mental development of a gifted student is defined by the state Department of Education as greater than two standard deviations above the mean in most tests.

A gifted student usually shows the following behaviors: often he/she will finish assigned work more quickly than the other students, will be searchingly inquisitive, and will spend much time reading.

appropriateness and program funding with the major point of contention being the kind of students a "regular" teacher can service with professional competence.

Curriculum designers will experience more restriction in developing programs for this student than any other covered in this chapter. In this category, the funding is categorical and uses of funding highly defined, the system (parent participation) is totally open, and the categories of exceptionality too numerous to allow for careful distinction among learner needs. Dangers in this area include misclassification to increase revenue streams and assigning certain types of students (minority) such as the emotionally handicapped, to ill-defined and overpopulated programs.

Curriculum developers should remember that all students have special capacities and limitations, and they too must be serviced if the program philosophy acknowledges their uniqueness. Figure 5.3 identifies the characteristics of students who may need special attention beyond Public Law 94-142.

FIGURE 5.3   Special Needs of Students beyond Current Legislation

1. Gross Motor and Motor Flexibility
    Incoordination and poor balance
    Difficulty with jumping, skipping, hopping (below age nine)
    Confusion in games requiring imitation of movements
    Poor sense of directionality
    Inept in drawing and writing at chalkboard
    Inaccuracies in copying at chalkboard
    Eyes do not work together
    Eyes lose or overshoot target

2. Physical Fitness
    Tires easily
    Lacks strength

3. Auditory Acuity, Perception, Memory—Speech
    Confuses similar phonetic and phonic elements
    Inconsistent pronunciation of words usually pronounced correctly by peers
    Repeats, but does not comprehend
    Forgets oral directions, if more than one or two

4. Visual Acuity, Perception, Memory
    Complains that he/she cannot see blackboard
    Says that words move or jump
    Facial expression strained
    Holds head to one side while reading

5. Hand–Eye Coordination
    Difficulty in tracing, copying, cutting, folding, pasting, coloring at desk
    Lack of success with puzzles—yo-yos—toys involving targets, and so on

6. Language
    Has difficulty understanding others
    Has difficulty associating and remembering
    Has difficulty expressing himself/herself

7. Intellectual Functioning
    Unevenness of intellectual development
    Learns markedly better through one combination of sensory avenues than another

8. Personality
    Overreacts to school failures
    Does not seem to know he/she has a problem
    Will not admit he/she has a problem

9. Academic Problems
    Cannot tolerate having routine disturbed
    Knows it one time and doesn't the next
    Writing neat, but slow
    Writing fast, but sloppy
    Passes the spelling test, but cannot spell functionally
    Math accurate, but slow
    Math fast, but inaccurate
    Reads well orally, but has poor comprehension
    Does poor oral reading, but comprehends better than would be expected
    Lacks work attack skills
    Has conceptual (study skill) organizational problems in content

10. Parents
    Seemingly uninformed about nature of learning problem
    Seemingly unrealistic toward student's problems

GIFTED OR TALENTED LEARNERS

One of the more difficult student groups for curriculum planners is the gifted and talented population. It has been estimated that about 6 percent of the total school population (2.5 million students) are gifted and another 6 percent display some talent (artistic, musical, social, academic) that makes them distinctive from their peers. Another group of children who are dissimilar but also distinctive are those who are creative. Together, these groups comprise a significant minority of the school population that demands a better program.

The U.S. Office of Education, Gifted and Talented Division, has adopted the following national definition that can serve to guide curriculum planners:

> *Gifted and talented children are those identified by professionally qualified persons who, by virtue of outstanding abilities, are capable of high performance. These are children who require differentiated educational programs in order to realize their contribution to self and society.*

The office goes on to identify six specific abilities that contribute to giftedness: general intellectual ability, specific academic aptitude, creative or productive thinking, leadership ability, ability in the visual or performing arts, or psychomotor ability.

Curriculum planners will have mixed opinions about this kind of definition that seemingly seeks to define education from a psychometric philosophy. If we believe that students have measurable abilities, and we can use assessment by measurement to compare students, then creating six such boxes makes sense. If, however, we take a developmental philosophy, then we might believe that all students possess distinctive traits, many hidden, and that education should seek to facilitate development of these traits in all children. At the least, a developmentalist such as David Elkind would argue, acknowledge the differences between children who are academically gifted, display an unusual talent, or display creative thinking.[5]

There are many issues connected to the identification of a gifted or talented population besides the definition of such traits. First, such a categorization seems to violate an unspoken law of American schooling that "no one will be allowed to perform beyond the norm." Parents and the public seem unconcerned about the special treatment accorded other exceptionalities identified in Public Law 94-142 (gifted is also identified by the law) but become very vocal if gifted children are given extra anything. Perhaps those parents believe that the gifted child is already advantaged and that "fairness" should be the principle of the day.

The concern becomes more active around organizational issues, such as ability grouping. Although this organizational practice is philosophically consistent with the psychometric orientation of conservative philosophies, it directly attacks the fairness issue because being special means being treated as such. Further, the research literature verifies the fears of those not gifted by documenting the negative effects of ability grouping and the impact of ability labeling on teacher expectation and pedagogy in general.

Curriculum planners will find that gifted or talented programs raise even more fundamental issues about responsibilities of the school (program scope) and the nature of the general program that houses nongifted students. Grouping, testing, selection, and evaluation issues will come in tandem with any gifted program. Gender bias and "equity versus excellence" may round out the concerns in developing such a program.

On the other side of educational concerns are the need of the United States to benefit from such students and to lessen our reliance on "importing" gifted and talented peoples to our nation. Forcing such children and their parents to seek a private educational experience so that their child can be adequately serviced is a real concern in the twenty-first century. Increasingly, with Internet and home schooling opportunities, children will not have to come to a building sponsored by the taxpayers to become educated; they have new options.

Needed immediately in our schools is a model of instruction for gifted and talented children that breaks out of the acceleration or performance orientation. Too many school programs consist of "extra work" and "mind-bending" activities without clearly identifying what is intended. Certainly, basic hierarchies or understandable models are needed to help structure these programs.

BILINGUAL LEARNERS

A group demanding very special assistance from curriculum designers in the new century are the non-English-speaking and bilingual students in our schools. There are eighty or so foreign languages spoken daily in American public schools; the vast majority of non-English-speaking students are newly arrived Hispanics, who speak a variety of Spanish tongues. As can be seen in Figure 5.4, it is difficult to clearly identify these English as a second language (ESL) students. Figure 5.5, taken from the 1994 Census data, indicates the scale of our most recent wave of immigration in the United States.

For curriculum planners, so many non-English-speaking students presents a problem larger than simple communication. The very core of American heritage, including history, values, and language, may be challenged. In many Sunbelt states, for example, the 1992 celebration of Columbus' discovery of the Americas became a controversy because the explorer was seen as an oppressor of native peoples.

Service for these students, guaranteed by the U.S. Supreme Court in *Lau v. Nichols*, is not a question. For curriculum planners, such students raise issues like, "Should instruction be delivered in the students' primary language?" If not, then

FIGURE 5.4   Identifying ESL Students

In order to better understand ESL students, here's a list of what they're *not*.

1. ESL students, even in the same classroom, are not a homogeneous group. They may differ in languages, cultural backgrounds, previous education, levels of English proficiency, exposure to English outside of school, and amount of time in the United States.

2. ESL students are not remedial students any more than English-speaking students are remedial in Spanish, French, or German classes. They need a different approach from students who understand and speak English but lack skills in reading or writing, for example.

3. They are not students of English in the sense that native English speakers are. The latter may need to correct minor errors in usage, refining skills, and learn to appreciate literature on a higher level. ESL students, however, may still be struggling with some of the basic features that their English-speaking counterparts internalized as preschoolers—plural forms, use of the negative, word order in questions, and so on.

4. ESL students are not foreign-language students, though this is a much closer definition. The main difference is that they don't have the luxury of continuing to learn and socialize in their most comfortable language while they master a new one. They are forced to communicate through the medium of an unfamiliar language, often before they feel confident in doing so.

And finally, ESL students are students who acquired another language before they were exposed to English; they need to develop both communicative skills and cognitive academic language proficiency in English in order to survive and achieve academically.

---

we must question the very purpose of basic cultural transmission (knowledge) and live with some very ugly statistics concerning Hispanic achievement and drop-out rates.

Even the research findings concerning language programs for non-English-speaking populations or English for speakers of other languages (ESOL) are disturbing. First, all language specialists would concur that learning a language is much easier when you are young. Yet many of the newly arrived students are not children, but are preadolescent or adolescent. Second, the research base finds that the "immersion" model (put them in the regular room) is the worst pattern for achievement in language development, and extended instruction in the native language through grade six shows the most achievement.[6] Finally, as in previous periods in our history, language-deficient immigrants "collect" in certain places and create enclaves of subcultures. Instruction in a native language can simply reinforce such cultural isolation and program students for a restricted adult life.

By the year 2020, 46 percent of all Americans will be a minority, many with language deficiency. In some populated states, such as California, New York,

FIGURE 5.5   **The Scale of Minority Populations in Fifty U.S. Cities**

In fifty of the United States' largest cites (population at least 100,000), Blacks, Hispanics, Asians, and Native Americans collectively are more than half the population:

City	Minority	City	Minority
East Los Angeles, CA	97.2%	Baltimore, MD	61.4
Laredo, TX	94.4	Salinas, CA	61.3
Inglewood, CA	91.5	Elizabeth, NJ	60.3
Hialeah, FL	89.1	Houston, TX	59.6
Miami, FL	87.8	Richmond, VA	57.1
Gary, IN	85.9	New York, NY	56.8
El Monte, CA	84.8	Jackson, MS	56.6
Newark, NJ	83.5	Stockton, CA	56.4
Detroit, MI	79.3	Memphis, TN	56.4
Santa Ana, CA	76.9	Corpus Christi, TX	56.2
Paterson, NJ	75.6	San Bernardino, CA	54.5
Honolulu, HI	74.5	Bridgeport, CT	54.4
El Paso, TX	73.6	Vallejo, CA	53.8
Washington, DC	72.6	San Francisco, CA	53.4
Pomona, CA	71.8	Pasadena, CA	53.4
Oakland, CA	71.7	Macon, GA	53.2
Atlanta, GA	69.7	Ontario, CA	53.0
Hartford, CT	69.5	Dallas, TX	52.3
Oxnard, CA	67.7	Cleveland, OH	52.2
New Orleans, LA	66.9	Flint, MI	51.7
Birmingham, AL	64.2	New Haven, CT	51.0
San Antonio, TX	63.8	Fresno, CA	50.6
Jersey City, NJ	63.4	Long Beach, CA	50.5
Los Angeles, CA	62.7	San Jose, CA	50.4
Chicago, IL	62.1	Chula Vista, CA	50.2

Source: Minorities in Majority, U.S. Bureau of the Census, 1994.

Florida, and Texas, a minority majority will arrive sooner. Curriculum designers will have to address this condition with creativity (using technology), and soon. Philosophies, goals, learning objectives, instructional strategies, learning materials, pedagogy, and evaluative techniques are all in need of development.

ADOLESCENT LEARNERS

In the twenty-first century, the adolescent population of America is increasing. As in previous times, high schools in the United States are working to accommodate a growing and diverse population of students.

No other level of education has historically been tied to a structured knowledge base and tradition. Unlike the elementary and middle level programs, the American high school has been virtually untouched by human development studies. It has been observed that if Rip Van Winkle were to sleep one hundred years and wake up in America, he would recognize the high school immediately!

Traditionally, the high school served as a springboard to higher education. Whereas the first- through eighth-grade programs addressed general literacy and citizenship, the high school "locked onto" college entrance requirements in 1892 (Committee of Ten) and has only rarely meandered from that path in the ensuing 110 years. Despite subsequent broad goals for the secondary school (e.g., the Seven Cardinal Principles), the primary purpose of the institution has been knowledge acquisition and college entrance.

Just as the curriculum planners of the 1900 to 1920 era had to broaden and enrich the secondary curriculum because of the change in adolescent populations, it seems that the twenty-first century begs for adjustments. These design changes would evolve from the following:

1. A population unlikely to achieve universal literacy using secondary standards.
2. A drop-out population (30 percent) that exits without destination.
3. Severe unhappiness by business leaders with worker preparation.
4. A nagging level of illiteracy in America noted by Goals 2000.
5. An increased need for basic life skills curriculum.
6. The advent of computer technology and access to knowledge bases.
7. The certainty of further change in a society already experienced in "future shock."
8. Changes and decline in other major social institutions (church and family).

Exactly what curriculum planners can do about these many concerns is not completely clear, but it is certain that the cycle of curriculum development can serve to focus, select, develop, and assess potential changes in programs for adolescents. Needed are processes that allow the school at the secondary level to change and adapt to the new society around it.

Several major concerns for curriculum development at this level are worthy of mention. First, it has become increasingly difficult to balance "social equality and economic competition." The school, and the high school in particular, is where this "battle of values" is being fought. To the winner goes the American society of the twenty-first century. John Goodlad has observed that a schism has already formed in this most stable of all educational institutions:

What begins to emerge is a picture not of two kinds of instructional activities in each class appealing to alternative modes of learning, but two divisions in the secondary school. On one side are the more prestigious academic subjects, largely shunning manual activity as a mode of learning. On the other side are the nonacademics, generally characterized by trappings of academic teaching but providing more opportunities to cultivate handedness and often featuring aesthetic qualities.[7]

The concern of many educators is that a two-class system may emerge in our secondary schools (accelerated by technological access to knowledge), and that this development is incompatible with democratic principles.

A second concern, and more pressing, is that the public secondary school as we have known it for a century will simply fade away. Recent trends in the flight to private schools, political pressures for schools-within-schools (charter, magnet, or alternatives), and the home-schooling phenomenon all point to a dissatisfied public voting with their feet. Needed, immediately, is a reaffirmation of the purpose of public secondary schools in the United States and new methods of reaching and teaching the new population of adolescents. Drug abuse, lawlessness, even teen smoking present challenges to be met through basic old-fashioned curriculum work.

VIRTUAL AND HOME-SCHOOLED LEARNERS

A great deal has changed in education since the emergence of the Internet in May 1995. Today, the availability of millions of Web sites leading to rich information sources, and the mass availability of personal computers to access this information, means that the monopoly of the school in learning is ending. Increasingly, school curriculum persons will have to accommodate these changes in school settings.

One early trend of the Internet age is virtual learning. At home schoolchildren today can receive a variety of computer-mediated communication (CMC) from school and beyond using all sorts of receiving devices. The rise of computer software and distance learning apparatus allows the duplication of public school curricula by private industries seeking profit. Companies, such as Sylvan Learning Systems and Bill Bennett's K12, are vitally interested in starting what amounts to an "end-run" on public schools.

Accelerating this movement is a home-schooling population that has swelled to an estimated 1.7 million students. Paralleling the growth and use of the Internet by the public, this interest group can be expected to pressure public schools for more access to resources through vouchers and alternative schools (magnet and charter). E-commerce (electronic commerce) companies such as BigChalk, Click2learn, Syberworks, and CyberU, can be expected to view this $389 billion market (education) as a new frontier of commerce.

Curriculum leaders must understand what has happened during the past decade in the world of learning and react quickly to incorporate these changes. This will mean servicing virtual and home-school populations or losing them to the marketplace. Eight changes that have been identified in the new learning age are as follows:

- Simple linear learning has become hypermedia learning.
- Instruction has become construction and discovery.
- Teacher-centeredness has given way to student-centeredness.
- Absorbing knowledge is replaced by navigating knowledge.
- Learning at school is replaced by learning anywhere, anytime.
- General learning (standardized) becomes individualized learning.
- Learning ceases to be work and becomes fun or entertainment.
- Teachers cease being transmitters and become facilitators.

In order to make such a transition to the new Internet assisted learning world, schools will have to experience massive changes. Curriculum leaders will serve as the designers of change in such areas as the following:

- Creating new structures for learning and communicating.
- Designing new facilities and learning systems.
- Assessing the efficacy of expenditures for change.
- Wisely spending the required resources for teacher training.
- Helping to deemphasize any standardized curriculum.
- Refocusing knowledge acquisition to knowledge application.
- Finding and rewarding a new kind of teaching force.
- Facilitating the networking of teachers and students.
- Acknowledging the uniqueness of students.
- Finding large sums of start-up capital to finance such change.

There are important questions to be answered in serving this new and growing population of students. What, for example, are the rights of such students in terms of access to school resources? Are there legal cases that might define work in this area? Have some schools been successful in making transitions to electronic learning? Are there possibilities for enlarged cooperation with business in such areas?

Curriculum leaders have no choice but to explore the concept of "learning portals" where schools set up information and learning experiences for students who access these "new curricula." The challenge for curriculum persons in the early twenty-first century is to meet this paradigm shift head on before forces beyond the schools take away the many options presently available to all of us.

Conclusion

The eight populations reviewed in this section are representative of other populations not mentioned but needing to be served by school leaders. These eight program areas demonstrate the need to redefine and refine school programs. Leaders are needed who understand these conditions and deliver programs to clients whose needs will then be satisfied. Needed, too, are educators who possess a vision of what a school is, and how important curriculum questions are to the form and substance of that institution.

THE SPECIAL CASE OF INCLUSION

One of the most challenging tasks for curriculum developers in this century has been to redesign educational experiences in regular classrooms to meet the requirements of full inclusion. This concept holds that all students will experience greater success in academics and social development if special education students are not separated from their peers based on identified disabilities.

Federal guidelines for inclusion are derived from the least restricted environment (LRE) clause of Public Law 94-142. As early as 1971, Lilly proposed that special education "abandon its present child-centered service function in favor of a teacher-centered program upgrading teacher skills. . . . Special education programs would be discontinued and all special service personnel would be assigned." This recommendation was based on a meta-analysis of fifty "efficacy studies" ($N = 27,000$) that showed "no tangible benefits for special class placements."[8] In 1984 researchers Stainback and Stainback proposed the merger of special and regular education for the same reasons.[9]

In the early 1990s the policy of inclusion led to many new curriculum development efforts. Three models that have received attention are the following:

Collaboration.   A style of direct interaction between at least two co-equal parties voluntarily engaging in shared decision making as they work toward a common goal.

Collaborative Consultation.   A special education teacher provides only strategies and consultation with several regular education teachers.

Co-teaching.   A regular teacher and a special education teacher share equally on a full-time basis the responsibilities of teaching both regular and special education students in the same classroom.

Although studies of these approaches are still being conducted, a review by Gersten found that the pattern was not as important as the teacher. Further, and a bit disturbing, "the most effective teachers had the lowest tolerance for deviant behavior."[10] This finding is somewhat confusing to curriculum developers because early proposals for inclusion hypothesized that the most effective classes would be dependent on tolerant, reflective, and flexible personalities of regular classroom teachers.

In inclusion, curriculum developers are confronted with a value dilemma in which the twin concepts of "equity" and "excellence" are vying for policy. Both the

National Education Association and the American Federation of Teachers have publicly called for a moratorium on inclusion, feeling it "places an undue strain on classroom teachers." Yet, the law states:

> *Children with disabilities will be educated with children without disabilities and that no separate channels should be supported except under the direst circumstances. . . . this model complies most closely with the federal 1990 Individuals With Disabilities Education Act (IDEA)." (20 U.S. Code, 1412 [5] [b])*

In the long run, teacher education programs in universities' elementary and special education preparation programs try to produce a new form of teacher who can service all students. In the present, however, the curriculum staffs in 13,000 American school districts are busy trying to translate these competing values into a program that can be all things to all people.

SUMMARY

In this chapter the reader has reviewed eight areas of curriculum programming, and the additional concern of implementing inclusion. In each case, development work begins with the definition of purpose. Curriculum work is always value laden and is a process of choosing from among alternatives.

In the nineteenth century, curriculum workers focused on the definition and arrangement of knowledge. In the twentieth century, the concern of curriculum has been the delivery of such knowledge to learners who are different and a society that is rapidly changing. The twenty-first century brings curriculum planners a bewildering array of choices and the possibility of using technology to serve an individualized curriculum to each learner according to his or her needs. The theaters of action will, indeed, be many.

SUGGESTED READINGS

Bauer, Ann, *Inclusion 101: How to Teach All Learners* (Baltimore: Paul H. Brookes, 1999).

Crockett, Jean, *The Least Restrictive Environment* (Mahwah, NJ: Erlbaum Associates, 1999).

Sewell, E., *Curriculum: An Integrated Instruction*, 2nd ed. (Columbus, OH: Merrill, 2000).

Smith, Tom, *Teaching Students with Special Needs in Inclusive Settings* (Columbus, OH: Merrill, 2000).

ENDNOTES

1. Robert Havighurst, *Growing Up in River City* (New York: Wiley, 1962).

2. C. Roy and D. Fuqua, "Social Support Systems and Academic Achievement of Single Parent Students," *School Counselor*, 30, No. 3 (1983), 183–192.

3. T. Toch, "How to Help Kids Succeed in School," *U.S. News & World Report* (Oct. 1990), p. 63.

4. T. Fagan and C. Held, "Chapter I Program Improvement," *Phi Delta Kappan*, 72 (1991), 562–564.

5. David Elkind, "Developmentally Appropriate Practice: Philosophy and Practical Implications," *Phi Delta Kappan* (October 1989), 113–116.

6. D. Larsen-Freeman, "Second Language Acquisition Research: Staking Out the Territory," *TESOL Quarterly,* 25, No. 2 (1991), 215–260.

7. John Goodlad, *A Place Called School* (New York: McGraw-Hill, 1984), p. 143.

8. M. S. Lilly, "Teacher Consultation: Present, Past, Future," *Behavioral Disorders,* 2 (1981), 73–77.

9. W. Stainback and S. Stainback, "A Rationale for the Merger of Special and Regular Education," *Exceptional Children,* 2 (1984), 102–111.

10. R. Gersten et al., *Relationship between Teacher Effectiveness and Their Tolerance for Handicapped Children* (New York: Macmillan, 1990), pp. 52–89.

POSTSCRIPT

In the first decade of the twenty-first century, it appears that schools, and education in general, are facing momentous change. Curriculum planning, as presented in this small book, will have to change as well. The author sees an "artistic" future for curriculum development on the horizon.

In his 1916 book, *Democracy and Education,* John Dewey observed that education is the glue that holds the social fabric of society together. As we begin the twenty-first century, such glue is increasingly difficult to find. We seem to know our differences better than our likenesses. Although the theoretical and philosophical concerns of curriculum will certainly continue to search for America's common denominators, it appears that "servicing" the many unique elements of our society will preoccupy the practical or applied side of this field. Persons entering curriculum in the new millennium will be artists, rather than mechanics, as our options unfold.

Two forces in the early twenty-first century capture the author's attention in defining the destination of this field. One is postmodernism as a philosophy. The other is the potential of technology to shape learning. In tandem, these forces suggest that in a period of rapidly accelerating social change, education will become a tool for both meeting and promoting change. Not only will planners be faced with a bewildering series of options but they also will have the technical wherewithal to make them happen. As George Counts dreamed in 1932 (*Dare the Schools Create a New Social Order?*) of education being at the forefront of social change, curriculum planners in the year 2000 and beyond will be able to "program change" in our society.

In their book *Postmodern Education,* Aronowitz and Giroux make the following observation:

> *Postmodernism is certainly a rejection of grand narratives and any form of totalizing thought. It embraces diversity and locality. It creates a world where individuals*

must make their own way, where knowledge is constantly changing, and where meaning can no longer be anchored in history.*

Such an observation shakes the very roots of existing curriculum development procedures and curriculum theory itself. Have we arrived at the point in our society where there is no connection between the past and the future? As a nation populated by a new "minority majority," can we still find a reason for educating all youth? What will serve as "the glue that holds the social fabric of society together"?

Political, social, and economic forces will bring new pressures on schools to do their bidding. Public schools are this nation's largest institution and, therefore, the largest economic market as well. Schools "program" children with values selected by leaders, and this fact is no longer a backstage issue in curriculum work. Various social groups with their histories, language, and cultures demand to be included in the messages of the compulsory school.

A second force, arriving in time to dovetail with such demand, is the technical capacity to meet such needs. Whereas the twentieth-century school was characterized by a single teacher trying to individualize a fixed curriculum for too many pupils, technology in the twenty-first century will allow the simultaneous delivery of tailored curriculums to each of the 5.7 million students in school each day. Whether the existing public school is flexible enough to make this transition remains to be seen. But as students slip away to the Internet, to home schooling, or to special curriculum schools (magnets, charters, alternatives) it is clear that the demand for service will be made. The public will demand that their values be delivered to their children in a form of their liking.

These two forces will place extraordinary stress on the field of curriculum—a field preoccupied with the mechanical reinforcement of the status quo. Like the former Soviet state, the system will likely evolve through a series of stages: deviant behaviors, rebellion, challenge to the system, disintegration, and reconfiguration. How will curriculum leaders react? Will there be denial and an aging, resistant leadership? Will there be entrepreneurship? Will education be privatized? Will there be a philosophical breakdown and reorientation to a training model? Is it possible that the system will simply stagger ahead, continuing to program the young people of this nation for a time past?

Regardless of the future, mastery of the essential elements of curriculum presented in this book are a prerequisite to thinking about such change. Whatever the eventual outcome of the coming years, the field of curriculum will be dynamic and full of ethical concerns. It will be an exciting area in which to practice true leadership.

---

*S. Aronowitz and H. Giroux, *Postmodern Education* (South Hadley, MA: Bergin & Garvey, 1991), p. 60.

Appendix A

THE SELF-TAUGHT READER BIBLIOGRAPHY

For readers educating themselves, or for practitioners updating their knowledge of curriculum, a quick reading list in fifteen areas follows. In each of these categories the author has suggested priority by an asterisk placed after the works thought most useful to someone new to the area of curriculum. These suggestions represent the bias of the author, and the reader may want to replace or enlarge these selections based on personal experiences and needs. In many cases, a brief description of the resource appears in the "Essential Books for Curriculum Study" section of Chapter One.

Philosophy

Bayles, Ernest	*Democratic Educational Theory* (1960)
Broudy, Harry	*Building a Philosophy of Education* (1962)*
Hansen, Kenneth	*Philosophy for American Education* (1960)
Heilbroner, Robert	*The Worldly Philosophers* (1952)
Kneller, George	*Existentialism and Education* (1958)
Scheffler, Israel	*The Language of Education* (1960)
Stanley, W. B.	*Curriculum for Utopia* (1992)

Learning Theory

Ausubel, David	*Educational Psychology: A Cognitive View* (1968)
Bruner, Jerome	*Toward a Theory of Instruction* (1967)*
Combs, Arthur (ed)	*Perceiving, Behaving, Becoming* (ASCD) (1962)
Dewey, John	*The Child and the Curriculum* (1902)
Eisner, Elliot	*Cognition and Curriculum* (1982)
Gagne, Robert	*Learning and Individual Difference* (1967)
Gordon, Ira	*Criteria for a Theory of Instruction* (1968)*
Piaget, Jean	*The Language and Thought of a Child* (1959)
Shedroff, Nathan	*Experience Design* (2001)
Vygotsky, Lev	*Thought and Language* (1934)

Human Development

Combs, Arthur	*Individual Behavior* (1949)
Elkind, David	*A Sympathetic Understanding of the Child* (1971)*
Gardner, Howard	*Multiple Intelligences: The Theory in Practice* (1993)
Gessell, A.	*The Child from Five to Ten* (1946)
	The Years from Ten to Sixteen (1956)
Havighurst, Robert	*Growing Up in River City* (1962)*
Hollingshead, A.	*Elmstown Youth* (1949)
Mead, Margaret	*Culture and Commitment: The Generation Gap* (1970)
Ogbu, J.	*Minority Education and Caste* (1978)
Sternberg, Robert	*The Triarchic Theory of Human Intelligence* (1989)
Stoddard, George	*The Meaning of Intelligence* (1943)
Thorndike, E. L.	*The Measurement of Intelligence* (1926)

Curriculum Theory

Beauchamp, George	*Curriculum Theory* (1968)
Bobbitt, Franklin	*The Curriculum* (1918)
Bruner, Jerome	*The Process of Education* (1960)
Caswell, Hollis	*Curriculum Development* (1935)
Charters, W. W.	*Curriculum Construction* (1923)
Dewey, John	*Democracy and Education* (1916)
Doll, William	*A Postmodern Perspective on Curriculum* (1993)
Goodlad, John	*The Changing School Curriculum* (1966)
Herbart, Johann	*Outlines of Educational Doctrine* (1904)
Hutchins, Robert	*On Education* (1962)
Kilpatrick, William	*Education for a Changing Civilization* (1926)
McMurry, Charles	*How to Organize the Curriculum* (1923)
Smith, B. O. et al.	*Fundamentals of Curriculum Development* (1950)
Stratemeyer, Florence	*Developing a Curriculum for Modern Living* (1957)
Taba, Hilda	*Curriculum Development: Theory into Practice* (1962)*
Tyler, Ralph	*Basic Principles of Curriculum and Instruction* (1949)

Education History

Aikens, M.	*The Story of the Eight Year Study* (1942)
Boulding, Kenneth	*The Meaning of the Twentieth Century* (1964)
Bremeld, Theodore	*Cultural Foundations of Education* (1957)
Callahan, Raymond	*Education and the Cult of Efficiency* (1962)
Cremin, Lawrence	*The Transformation of the School* (1961)
Kliebard, Herbert	*The Struggle for the American Curriculum* (1986)*
Mead, Margaret	*The School in American Culture* (1959)
NSSE Yearbook	*The Curriculum: Retrospect and Prospect* (1971)*
Rice, Joseph	*The Public School System of the United States* (1893)
Tanner, Daniel	*The History of School Curriculum* (1990)*
Whipple, G. (ed)	*The Foundations of Curriculum Making* (NSSE) (1926)

Knowledge

Adler, Mortimer	*The Paideia Proposal* (1982)
Bagley, W. C.	*The Educative Process* (1905)
Bestor, Arthur	*The Restoration of Learning* (1955)
Bloom, Benjamin	*Taxonomy I: The Cognitive Domain* (1956)
Booth, W.	*The Knowledge Worth Having* (1967)
Bruner, Jerome	*On Knowing* (1962)*
Cassirer, Ernst	*The Problem of Knowledge* (1950)
Hirsch, E. D.	*Cultural Literacy* (1987)
Hutchins, Robert	*On Education* (1962)*
Martin, W.	*The Order and Integration of Knowledge* (1957)
Phenix, P.	*Realms of Meaning* (1964)
Rickover, Hyman	*Education and Freedom* (1959)
Rugg, Harold	*Foundations of American Education* (1947)

Pedagogy

Bruner, Jerome	*Toward a Theory of Instruction* (1966)
Gagne, Robert	*Learning and Individual Difference* (1967)*
Gordon, Ira	*Criteria for a Theory of Instruction* (1968)
Kilpatrick, William	*Foundations of Methods* (1926)
Macdonald, James	*Theories of Instruction* (1971)
Maslow, Abraham	*Motivation and Personality* (1954)*
McLuhan, Marshall	*The Medium Is the Message* (1967)
McNeil, John	*The Essentials of Teaching* (1990)
Rogers, Carl	*Freedom to Learn* (1969)
Skinner, B. F.	*The Technology of Teaching* (1968)
Toffler, Alvin	*Learning for Tomorrow* (1974)*

Politics

Apple, Michael	*Ideology and Curriculum* (1990)
Aronowitz, Stanley	*Postmodern Education* (1991)
Bowles, Samual et al.	*Schooling in Capitalist America* (1976)*
Counts, George	*Dare the Schools Create a New Social Order?* (1932)*
Dow, Peter	*Schoolhouse Politics: Lessons from the Sputnik Era* (1991)
Friere, Paolo	*The Politics of Education* (1985)*
Kimbrough, Ralph	*Political Power and Educational Decision Making* (1971)
Kincheloe, Joe	*Thirteen Questions: Reframing Education's Conversation* (1992)
Sarason, Seymour	*The Predictable Failure of Educational Reform* (1990)
Spring, Joel	*American Education: Social and Political Aspects* (1989)
Wildavsky, Aaron	*The Politics of the Budgetary Process* (1979)
Wiles, David	*Practical Politics for School Administrators* (1981)

Human Relations

Allport, Gordon   *Becoming* (1955)
Berman, Louise   *New Priorities in the Curriculum* (1968)
Bruner, J. S.   *Personal and Social Factors in Perception* (1950)
Cartwright, D.   *Group Dynamics: Research and Theory* (1960)
Homans, George   *The Human Group* (1950)*
Katz, D. and Kahn, R.   *The Social Psychology of Groups* (1966)
Lewin, Kurt   *A Dynamic Theory of Personality* (1935)
Likert, R.   *The Human Organization* (1967)
Rogers, Carl   *On Becoming a Person* (1961)
Sherif, M. and Sherif C. *Reference Groups* (1964)*

Leadership

Bennis, Warren   *Why Leaders Can't Succeed* (1989)
Covey, Stephen   *The Seven Habits of Highly Effective People* (1990)
Elmore, R. (ASCD)   *The Governance of the Curriculum* (1994)
Fiedler, Fred   *A Theory of Leadership Effectiveness* (1967)*
Jacobs, T.   *Leadership and Exchange in Formal Organizations* (1970)
Lippitt, Gordon   *Leadership in Action* (1961)
Schein, E.   *Organizational Culture and Leadership* (1985)
Stoghill, Ralph   *Handbook of Leadership* (1974)*

Change Theory

Bacharach, S.   *Education Reform: Making Sense of It All* (1990)
Bennis, Warren   *The Planning of Change* (1985)
Kotter, John   *Leading Change* (1996)
Lionberger, Herbert   *Adoption of New Ideas and Practice* (1960)*
Lippitt, R.   *The Dynamics of Planned Change* (1958)
Miles, Matthew   *Innovation in Education* (1964)
Rogers, Everett   *Diffusion of Innovation* (1995)*
Sarason, Seymour   *The Culture of the School and the Problem of Change* (1971)
Watson, Goodwin   *Change in School Systems* (1967)
Wiles, Jon   *Promoting Planned Change in Schools* (1993)*

Management and Systems Theory

Bernard, Chester   *The Function of the Executive* (1938)
Drucker, Peter   *The Effective Executive* (1967)*
Fayol, Henri   *General and Industrial Management* (1929)
Feyereisen, K.   *Supervision and Curriculum Renewal: Systems* (1970)*
Hersey, Paul   *Management and Organizational Behavior* (1996)
Owens, R.   *Organizational Behavior in Schools* (1998)
Taylor, Frederick   *Principles of Scientific Management* (1947)
Toffler, Alvin   *Powershift: Knowledge, Wealth, and Violence* (1990)

Research

Frisbie, D.	*Essentials of Educational Measurement* (1990)
Hall, Bruce	*Competency-Based Education* (1975)
Hittleman, D.	*Interpreting Educational Research* (1992)
Joyce, B.	*The Self-Reviewing School* (1993)
Mager, Robert	*Goal Analysis* (1962)
Popham, James	*Educational Evaluation* (1975)*
Travers, Robert	*Introduction to Educational Research* (1969)*
Tucker, Bruce	*Conducting Educational Research* (1984)
Tyler, Ralph	*Educational Evaluation* (1969)
Worthen, Blaine	*Evaluating Educational and Social Programs* (1987)

Technology

Bennett, Frederick	*Computers as Tutors: Solving the Education Crisis* (1996)
Boschman, E.	*The Electronic Classroom* (1996)
Gagne, Robert	*Instructional Technology Foundations* (1987)*
Hawkins, J.	*Teaching and Telecommunications* (1995)
Heinich, R.	*Instructional Media and New Technology* (1996)
McLuhan, Marshall	*The Medium Is the Message* (1967)*
U.S. Government Office of Technological Assistance, Department of Education	*Teachers and Technology: Making the Connections* (1995)

Futurism

Boulding, Kenneth	*The Meaning of the 20th Century* (1964)
Centrum, M.	*Educational Renaissance: Twenty-First Century* (1991)
Corn, Joseph	*Yesterday's Tomorrow* (1996)
Fogg, B. J.	*Persuasion Technology* (2002)
Papert, Seymour	*The Children's Machine* (1994)
Perelman, L. J.	*School's Out* (1992)
Tachi, Kluchi	*What We Learned in the Rainforest* (2002)
Toffler, Alvin	*The Politics of Creating a New Civilization* (1995)
Wiles, J.	*Leaving School: Finding Education* (2004)

Appendix **B**

GLOSSARY OF COMMON TERMS

Ability group   Organizing students into homogeneous groups (alike) according to intellectual ability for instruction.

Accountability   Refers to outcome orientation or return on investment. In the classroom, holding teachers responsible for student learning.

Affective   Describes behavior or objectives of an attitudinal, emotional, or interest nature.

Articulation   The vertical coordination of curriculum; from grade to grade.

Balanced curriculum   Incorporates all areas of the curriculum in parity.

Behavioral objective   A precise statement of what the learner must do to demonstrate mastery after a prescribed learning task.

Cognition   The process of thought; logical thinking.

Core curriculum   Integration of two or more subjects around common themes.

Course of study   A prescriptive guide to teaching a subject.

Curriculum   A structured series of intended learning experiences.

Curriculum alignment   Matching what is taught with what is tested; activities are designed to promote predetermined outcomes.

Curriculum mapping   Outlining the content, skills, and concepts of a curriculum into a "framework" or design for instruction.

Developmental task   Social, physical, or emotional experiences encountered as one progresses from childhood to adulthood.

Heterogeneous groups   Student grouping that combines unlikes without regard to artificial categories such as "by intelligence."

Hidden curriculum   Those things experienced by students that are not planned or anticipated.

Individualized   Instruction that accomodates differences of students or focuses on needs and interests of students.

Innovation   A new way of approaching a problem that anticipates an improved condition.

In-service education   Training for teachers to improve skills; also called staff development.

Interdisciplinary   Combining two or more subjects into a new and single organizational construct.

Learning   A change in behavior as a result of an experience.

Lesson plan   A teaching outline noting important points, objectives, evaluation criteria, and resources needed by the teacher.

Needs assessment   A review of conditions under which a program will operate including student background, resources, previous performance, and other relevant items.

Nongraded school   A program in which the progress of students is monitored on a basis other than time in school; often called a continuous progress curriculum.

Norm-referenced   A student's performance is compared to a group of peers or like students.

Paraprofessional   A person hired to assist a certified teacher in a classroom setting.

Portfolio assessment   A sampling of student work in a collection form; used to individualize evaluation of student progress.

Readiness   Refers to a student exhibiting a particular behavior thought a prerequisite for learning.

Regular Education Initiative   Also known as inclusion; proposes a union of general education and special education into one system.

Restructuring   Changing the total school approach to learning as opposed to simple tinkering with the curriculum.

Rubric   A model or design for planning instruction or evaluation.

Scope   The boundaries of the curriculum; what is included and defining what is excluded.

Sequence   The order in which the content or objectives are arranged in the curriculum.

Syllabus   A condensed outline or statement of the major points or topics of the curriculum.

Appendix C

CURRICULUM DEVELOPMENT RESOURCES

Organizations and Associations

American Association for the Education of Severely and Profoundly Handicapped, 1600 West Armory Way, Garden View Suite, Seattle, WA 98119

American Association of Gifted Children, 16 Gramercy Park, New York, NY 10003

American Association of School Administrators, 1800 N. Moore St., Arlington, VA 22209

American Congress of Parents and Teachers, 1715 25th Street, Rock Island, IL 61201

American Educational Research Association, 1126 16th Street NW, Washington, DC 20036

Association for Supervision and Curriculum Development, 1250 N. Pitt Street, Alexandria, VA 22314

Council for Basic Education, 725 15th Street NW, Washington, DC 20005

Council for Exceptional Children, 1920 Association Drive, Reston, VA 22091

Council of Chief State School Officers, 1201 16th Street NW, Washington, DC 20036

International Reading Association, 800 Barksdale Road, Newark, DE 19711

National Art Education Association, 1916 Association Drive, Reston, VA 22091

National Association for the Education of Young Children, 1834 Connecticut Avenue, Washington, DC 20009

National Association of Elementary School Principals, 1801 North Moore St., Arlington, VA 22209

National Association of Secondary School Principals, 1904 Association Drive, Reston, VA 22091

National Association of Social Workers, 759 First Street NW, Washington, DC 20010

National Council of Teachers of English, 1111 Kenyon Road, Urbana, IL 61801

National Council of Teachers of Mathematics, 1906 Association Drive, Reston, VA 22091

National Education Association, 1201 16th Street NW, Washington, DC 20208

National Institute of Education, 555 New Jersey Avenue NW, Washington, DC 20208

National Middle School Association, PO Box 968, Fairborn, OH 45324

National School Boards Association, 800 State National Bank Plaza, Evanston, IL 60204

National Science Teachers Association, 1742 Connecticut Avenue, Washington, DC 20009

Primary Professional Journals

Educational Leadership Journal of Curriculum and Supervision (Association for Supervision and Curriculum Development)

Educational Researcher (American Educational Research Association)

Middle School Journal (National Middle School Association)

NASSP Bulletin (National Secondary School Principals Association)

Phi Delta Kappan (Phi Delta Kappa)

The Principal (National Elementary Principals Association)

Encyclopedias

Encyclopedia of American Education (bibliographies of American educators)

Encyclopedia of Educational Research (researched areas arranged by topic)

International Encyclopedia of Education (overviews of systems in other nations)

Philosophy of Education: An Encyclopedia (covers subjects from Greece to the present)

Handbooks

Handbook of Research on Curriculum (Association for Supervision and Curriculum Development)

Handbook of Research in Educational Administration (Association for Supervision and Curriculum Development)

Handbook of Research on Supervision (Association for Supervision and Curriculum Development)

Handbook of Research on Teaching (summary and analysis of research in all major areas of teaching)

Yearbooks

Yearbook of the Association for Supervision and Curriculum Development
Yearbook of the National Society for the Study of Education

Basic References

Digest of Education Statistics, U.S. Government Printing Office, Washington, DC 20402

Phi Delta Kappa "FastBack Series" (topical booklets)

Electronic Resources

Brown's Directory of Instructional Resources 1997–98 edition (listing of commercial products available) (ASCD CD-ROM)

Content Knowledge: A Compendium of Standards and Benchmarks for K–12 Education, 2nd edition, ASCD 1998 (CD-ROM)

Directory of Electronic Journals, Newsletters, and Academic Discussion Lists

Educator's World Wide Tour Guide (more than 200 leads to classroom use)

NetFirst (bibliographic citations for a wide variety of Internet resources)

School Improvement Research Series (www.nwrel.org) up-to-date research reviews in teacher education

The Research on Technology for Learning, 1998, developed by NCREL on CD-ROM (ASCD)

Appendix D

TEACHING OUTLINES

I. Topical Outline

    A. History and definitions

        See dates of historical significance (Chapter 1)
        See names to know (Chapter 1)
        See definitions of curriculum (Chapter 1)
        See glossary (Appendix)
        See resources (Appendix)
        See historic documents (Chapter 2)
        Readings (Aiken 1942, Callahan 1962, Cremin 1961, 1965, Dow 1975, EPC 1944, Franklin 1749, Katz 1987, Kliebard 1995, Krug, 1972, 1964, NEA 1918, Parker 1894, Rice 1893, Whipple 1926)

    B. Philosophy in planning

        See philosophy and curriculum (Chapter 1)
        See philosophy in a school setting (Chapter 1)
        Readings (Adler 1982, Aronowitz 1991, Bagley 1905, Bestor 1955, Counts 1932, Dewey 1916, Illich 1971, Phenix 1964, Rogers 1969, Stanley 1992)

    C. Foundations of planning

        See ideas and theories (Chapter 1)
        See school models (Chapter 2)
        See research bases (Chapter 2)
        See use of research (Chapter 2)
        Readings (Social Forces: Spring 1989, Toffler 1970, 1990; Human Development: Combs 1959, Elkind 1974, Gessell 1956, Hall 1904, Havighurst 1962; Knowledge: Bruner 1960, King 1966; Learning: Bruner 1966, Gagne 1967, Skinner 1968)

D. Curriculum management	See curriculum as system (Chapter 4) See staging (Chapter 4) See CMP (Chapter 4) See tasks (Chapter 4) See levers (Chapter 4) Readings (Feyereisen 1970, Wiles 1993)
E. Instruction	See models of in-service (Chapter 4) See adult learning section (Chapter 4) Readings (Bruner 1967, Gordon 1966, Maslow 1954, Smith 1962, Vygotsky 1934)
F. Leadership and change	See leadership (Chapter 4) See change (Chapter 4) Readings (Bennis 1989, Jacobs 1970, Sarason 1971, Stogdill 1974)
G. Programs and practices	See program designs (Chapter 5) Readings (Adler 1982, Kaufman 1965, Neill 1960, Whipple 1926)
H. Evaluation of programs	See evaluation (Chapter 4) Readings (Popham 1975, Worthen 1987)

II. Problems and Solutions Outline

An investigation of contemporary problems and issues in curriculum using the efficacy of school programs as a lens. Sample areas and resources follow:

A. The American high school

Resources   M. Aiken   *The Story of the Eight Year Study* (1942)
A. Bestor   *The Restoration of Learning* (1955)
J. Conant   *The Comprehensive High School* (1967)
P. Dow   *Schoolhouse Politics* (1975)
Education Policy Commission   *Education for ALL American Youth* (1944)
Harvard   *General Education in a Free Society* (1945)
E. Krug   *The Shaping of the American High School* (1964, 1972)
M. Mead   *Culture and Commitment: The Generation Gap* (1970)
National Education Association   *Cardinal Principles of Secondary Education* (1918)
J. Rice   *The Public School System of the United States* (1893)
H. Rickover   *Education and Freedom* (1959)
A. Toffler   *Powershift* (1990)

Organizing Questions for Discussion

1. What is the purpose of the American secondary school?
2. How do conceptions of the Committee of Ten differ from the conception of the Commission on the Reorganization of Secondary Education?
3. Why is the American high school so unchanging?
4. What alternative models offer promise for reform in the twenty-first century?
5. How might new technology impact the curriculum of the high school?
6. What is the meaning of the Eight Year Study?

B. Social class, culture, and education

Resources M. Apple   *Ideology and Curriculum* (1990)
S. Aronowitz   *Postmodern Education* (1991)
J. Banks   *Teaching Strategies for Ethnic Studies* (1976)
S. Bowles   *Schooling in Capitalist America* (1976)
P. Freire   *Education for Critical Consciousness* (1973)
P. Freire   *Pedagogy of the Oppressed* (1973)
H. Gardner   *The Unschooled Mind* (1991)
H. Giroux   *Schooling and the Struggle for Public Life* (1988)
R. Havighurst   *Growing Up in River City* (1962)
I. Illich   *Deschooling Society* (1971)
M. Mead   *The School in the American Culture* (1959)
J. Peddiwell   *The Sabre-Tooth Curriculum* (1939)
J. Spring   *American Education: Intro to Social and Political Aspects* (1989)

Organizing Questions for Discussion

1. How does the school balance the goals of social equality and economic competition in the American society?
2. If social class is a predictor of school failure, what steps can be taken to ensure fairness?
3. How should governance of the schools be organized to guarantee decision-making access for all segments of the American public?
4. What reforms in curriculum might take place to acknowledge the cultural heritage of the new Americans and the coming "minority majority" of the twenty-first century?
5. What signs of reform can be identified at the elementary, middle, and secondary levels to address questions of class and culture in public schools?
6. How might technology be used to address the problems in inequality in our public schools?
7. Should the American public school use a multilingual delivery system for classroom instruction?

INDEX